THE THORNY PATH

THE THORNY PATH

Pornography in Early Twentieth-Century Britain

Jamie Stoops

McGill-Queen's University Press
Montreal & Kingston | London | Chicago

ISBN 978-0-7735-5468-9 (cloth)
ISBN 978-0-7735-5516-7 (ePDF)
ISBN 978-0-7735-5517-4 (ePUB)

Legal deposit third quarter 2018
Bibliothèque nationale du Québec

Printed in Canada on acid-free paper that is 100% ancient forest free (100% post-consumer recycled), processed chlorine free

Funded by the Government of Canada | Financé par le gouvernement du Canada | Canada | Canada Council for the Arts | Conseil des arts du Canada

We acknowledge the support of the Canada Council for the Arts, which last year invested $153 million to bring the arts to Canadians throughout the country.

Nous remercions le Conseil des arts du Canada de son soutien. L'an dernier, le Conseil a investi 153 millions de dollars pour mettre de l'art dans la vie des Canadiennes et des Canadiens de tout le pays.

LIBRARY AND ARCHIVES CANADA CATALOGUING IN PUBLICATION

Stoops, Jamie, 1986–, author
The thorny path : pornography in early twentieth-century Britain / Jamie Stoops.

Includes bibliographical references and index.
Issued in print and electronic formats.
ISBN 978-0-7735-5468-9 (hardcover). – ISBN 978-0-7735-5516-7 (ePDF). – ISBN 978-0-7735-5517-4 (ePUB)

1. Pornography – Great Britain – History – 20th century.
2. Pornography – Social aspects – Great Britain. I. Title.

HQ472.G7S76 2018 306.77'10941 C2018-901624-8
C2018-901625-6

Set in 10/14 Baskerville 10 Pr with Uniform
Book design and typesetting by Garet Markvoort, zijn digital

FOR MY FAVOURITE DOCTOR

Contents

Illustrations

Every effort has been made to identify, credit, and obtain publication rights from copyright holders of illustrations in this book. Notice of any errors or omissions in this regard will be gratefully received and corrections will be made in any subsequent editions.

Acknowledgments

Many people have my gratitude for their advice, support, and companionship during the process of conducting this research. Laura Tabili, David Ortiz Jr, and Eithne Luibhéid were patient and courteous from this project's earliest stages as a doctoral dissertation to its completion as a manuscript. Numerous librarians and archivists in both the US and Britain guided me through the research materials; I would especially like to thank Catherine Johnson-Roehr of the Kinsey Institute, who went above and beyond by talking through the project with me at great length and pointing me to sources that I would otherwise have missed entirely. Many colleagues also provided help and friendship during the last several years. Sofia Zepeda made countless writing sessions and research trips infinitely more fun than they otherwise would have been. Friends who deserve special recognition for keeping my sanity intact during the research and writing process include Brooke Hundtoft, Aalok Shah, Rosanne Carlo, Rachael Wendler-Shah, Kati Wint, Matt Coleman, Kammy Dorman, Jessica Shumake, Ryan Cresawn, and Michelle Huang. My parents, Tom and Shauna Stoops, deserve extra-special recognition for taking it so well when I decided to abandon law school to research the history of porn. My godmother, Carol "Tata" Smith, has been a source of unwavering love and support for my entire life. I received crucial monetary backing for my research from several sources, including the Richard A. Cosgrove Graduate

Fellowship, the William H. Hesketh Scholarship, the Barbara Payne Robinson Fellowship, the Heldrich-Dvorak Travel Fellowship, and grants from the Pacific Coast and Midwest chapters of the North American Conference on British Studies. Finally, I'd like to thank the man called the Doctor. He knows why.

THE THORNY PATH

Introduction

In December 1943, British intelligence operatives from the Special Operations Executive (SOE) developed a plan to distribute pornographic leaflets over territories occupied by the Japanese military. These leaflets would depict a Japanese "profiteer" drinking and fornicating with several women, while the accompanying text would urge Japanese soldiers to surrender rather than die for such an unworthy superior. Such a leaflet might seem simple enough to produce, but intelligence operatives laboured for over six months before developing a satisfactory prototype. They struggled to locate a photographer, a model, and other personnel necessary for production. Details such as the typical background and setting of Japanese pornographic photographs created confusion and delays. In addition, the agents involved in the project hesitated to photograph scenes of genuine sexual intercourse, instead pursuing the far more difficult strategy of cutting and pasting heads onto existing scenes. As an unnamed operative stated in a progress report: "The pornographer's path is thorny and there may yet be some unforeseen hitch, but as you will see we have not been idle."[1]

During the same year that the SOE embarked on the seemingly Herculean task of producing a single pornographic leaflet, two retired adagio dancers named Irene England and Charles Domec-Carre began producing and selling pornography out of their London flat, a practice they carried on for the next fifteen years.[2] In the four decades leading up to these events, numerous other British pornographers, all of whom had considerably fewer resources at their disposal than those available to the SOE, produced and sold pornography out of their shops or homes. Others smuggled foreign pornography into the country through the use of mail-order services. Still others produced and consumed pornography in an entirely non-commercial setting, using pen pal services to find companions with whom to exchange explicit photographs and letters.

The question of why the pornographer's thorny path proved daunting for the SOE but navigable to others leads us to a series of larger questions regarding who participated in the trade, what they thought about it, and how they related to aspects of sexual culture considered normative or "mainstream." The fact that the SOE apparently did not consider consulting with people active in the pornography trade suggests that its operatives conceptualized pornography as a self-evident and easily reproducible object rather than as a complex genre requiring the insights of experts familiar with its standards and tropes. Given the SOE's fumbling progress toward producing the leaflet, however, this clearly was not the case. If pornography simply acted as a reflection of heteronormative sexuality, its methods and meanings should have been perfectly legible to representatives of the British state. The fact that these elements proved baffling to SOE operatives shows instead that these pornographic works occupied an underground or subversive position in British sexual culture, a position not equally accessible or understandable to all actors in British society. By exploring who did and did not become involved in the pornography trade and why, this book reassesses the relationship between pornography and other aspects of culture and sexuality in a specific historical context.

The methods by which I seek to address these questions of the relationship between culture, sexuality, and pornography in the early twentieth century might appear obvious, yet are exceedingly rare in existing historical studies of pornography. To put it simply, this book builds its analysis by beginning with basic questions about the conditions under which pornography was produced, bought, sold, and used. In its focus on the business operations and daily workings of the pornography trade, this study views pornography simultaneously as a commodity and as a practice rooted in historically specific material conditions. Pornography is a commodity, but producing and consuming it are also sexual acts. People made pornography, paid for it, held it, looked at it, masturbated to it, thought about it during sex. Thinking of pornography as both object and practice requires us to move past sweeping generalizations and decontextualized analysis to look closely at the quotidian details of how pornography was made, bought, sold, consumed, and incorporated into other aspects of sexual life in early twentieth-century Britain. Analysis of these simple details reveals that participants operated within complex transnational networks as well as smaller, localized clusters of pornographers and customers.

Pornography did not exist in isolation. Its production and distribution responded to changes in other areas of society and culture, including medicine, the judicial system, imperial politics, and technological change. Analyzing both the pornography trade itself and the socio-cultural forces surrounding it, I explore the early twentieth-century emergence of social networks and clandestine communities centred on the production and consumption of pornography. In both their social interactions and cultural productions, these networks frequently subverted normative sexuality by creating spaces for queer or non-normative models of sexual interaction.[3] The networks and groups I refer to as the British pornography trade largely remained confined to the British Isles, but they were connected to transnational networks anchored by localized nodes in large population centres like London, Paris, and New York, as well as in smaller towns and cities. Their business strategies and personal choices were shaped not only by the restrictions imposed by state and civil authorities, but also by the larger transnational systems that connected buyers, sellers, and pornographic materials across the globe. While the term "pornography trade" implies a monolithic industry, the early twentieth-century British trade was far more complex, operating as a nebulous and fluid cluster of shifting networks and participants. As will be discussed throughout the book, the flexible nature of these networks is only one of numerous features that sets this trade apart from conventional understandings of pornography production. Later chapters will explore the complicated reasons people chose to become involved in these networks, as well as the ways these interactions shaped the resulting pornographic products.

CONTEXT AND SIGNIFICANCE

Why study pornography in early twentieth-century Britain? Beyond the obvious comparative utility of a historical study that differs significantly from contemporary cases, the specific example of pornography in Britain during the early twentieth century deserves scholarly attention for several reasons. First, the period between 1900 and 1945 saw the emergence of technologies that fundamentally altered the nature of pornography production and distribution, including the birth of film and the development of more accessible photography than had been available in the nineteenth century. This represented a dramatic shift from previous eras in which most pornography was costly, difficult to distribute, and accessible only to educated elites.[4] Regardless of location, therefore, the early twentieth century is a crucial period in the history of pornography and sexuality.

Britain was also the site of significant political and social turmoil during the early twentieth century. Between 1900 and 1945, the British Empire experienced unprecedented upheaval and social change. The dual traumas of the First and Second World Wars and other disasters like the global Great Depression created widespread fear and anxiety surrounding the future. At the same time, shifts in existing social hierarchies benefited some social groups while challenging the superiority of others. Women's suffrage, immigration from the colonies, and the increasing relevance of working-class politics all worked to challenge power structures long perceived as natural or even sacred. The empire peaked in size, yet also began to fragment as colonized peoples agitated for independence or dominion status. In short, the pornographers and consumers I discuss in this project occupied a world of uncertainty and flux. This offers opportunities to demonstrate how the position of pornography in society shifts in response to international crises and domestic tension.

Finally, Britain's position as centre of the world's largest and most powerful empire means that it was uniquely connected to the rest of the globe during the early twentieth century. No other nation between 1900 and 1945 could claim as much political and economic influence or as much cross-cultural interaction. No other country was as thoroughly connected to the commerce, politics, and culture of the rest of the world. We tend to think of imperialism and international trade in terms of the formal economy, but the shipping lanes, transportation infrastructure, and systems of imperial control connecting British political and business interests to the rest of the world were not restricted to officially sanctioned actors. Rather, as I discuss throughout this book, they were also employed by people involved in illegal and clandestine activities like pornography distribution. To study early twentieth-century British pornography is not, therefore, to restrict our gaze to pornography that circulated on one small island nation. Instead, it provides the ideal vantage point from which to explore pornography in a transnational global context.

DEFINING PORNOGRAPHY

Daunting difficulties and contradictions emerge in any attempt to define pornography. Some scholars make a clear distinction between pornography and erotica, two categories whose difference lies in perceived quality or presence of emotions like anger or affection.[5] Other definitions either implicitly or explicitly define pornography according to medium. In contemporary analyses in particular, pornography is often assumed to be a visual rather than written medium.[6] Definitions also conflict on the basis of acts depicted. Some definitions require an unambiguous depiction of a sexual act, while others would include images like artists' nude models. The problem becomes even more pronounced with regard to historical examples. Until well into the postwar period, the British government used "obscenity" as a blanket legal term that covered examples that contemporary viewers would categorize as pornography, as well as materials viewed as crude, violent, or politically subversive but not sexually explicit.[7] One cannot, therefore, simply adopt the official definition used at the time, as the legal category of obscenity did not necessarily correspond to the social and cultural distinction between sexually explicit materials and other obscene items.[8]

In an attempt to resolve these tensions, I employ the broadest possible definition of pornography: as used throughout this project, pornography can be understood as any material intended to sexually arouse, regardless of artistic quality, medium, or act depicted. This approach has a number of strengths. First, it avoids placing either a positive or negative value judgment on pornography as an artistic production or social phenomenon. Second, it focuses on virtually the only agreed-upon element found in otherwise inconsistent definitions of pornography: sexual arousal. Finally, excluding reference to specific media or sexual acts avoids imposing contemporary concepts of pornography onto historical populations. Using this broad definition allows for a highly detailed analysis that compares different media and avoids the problem of delineating the unstable boundary between high-quality erotica and low-quality pornography, a boundary that would have meant little to pre-1945 legal authorities. While I believe this usage serves as the best available option, I acknowledge that it does not fully account for the ambiguities inherent in any discussion of sexualized content. Some producers from the period, for instance, argued vociferously against the conflation of pornography and erotica; erotic writer Anaïs Nin famously railed against what she perceived as the repetitive and dull pornography favoured by most collectors.[9] Nin's perspective, however, collides with the many works that blur the line between these categories, as well as the many less elite pornography producers who defended the artistic value of their work. While my broad usage of the term pornography does not offer a definitive solution to these long-standing tensions, it does offer a more complete and inclusive body of sources than is often employed in studies of sexual content.

HISTORIOGRAPHY OF BRITISH PORNOGRAPHY

Despite pornography's central position in feminist theory and its frequent appearance in popular media, historians have produced few studies of pornography and its circulation. Even fewer studies focus on pornography in Britain or the period from 1900 to 1945. Instead, the Victorian period serves as the cornerstone of the modern history of pornography. Notably, the work of literary criticism that first opened the door for historical academic studies of pornography, Steven Marcus's *The Other Victorians*, focused on the mid-Victorian period.[10] Since then, historians like Lisa Z. Sigel, Julie Peakman, and Iain McCalman have made significant contributions exploring the history of pornography in eighteenth- and nineteenth-century Britain.[11] The methods and conclusions employed by these scholars, while utterly persuasive in their discussion of eighteenth- and nineteenth-century pornography's position relative to mainstream sexual culture, cannot be easily transplanted to the later time period of this study. A number of social factors including a changing judicial culture, the shifting sexual mores between the wars, and technological advancements all suggest an early twentieth-century shift toward an entirely different relationship between pornography and normative sexual culture than existed in the nineteenth century.[12] This changing context and the increasingly transnational state of the pornography trade have been explored by Colette Colligan, but her work focuses primarily on those expatriate pornographers operating out of Paris. By contrast, those who continued to live and exchange pornography within Britain and its empire have remained largely unexplored.[13] In addition, this body of work, while making critical advances in the field, generally approaches pornography either with a focus on cultural histories of pornographic representation or as a legal, institutional history, with much less attention to social history elements such as distribution or conditions of production.[14]

Outside of history, a much larger body of theoretical work addresses pornography in contemporary contexts. Much of this theoretical work originates with feminist scholars. Given the academic and cultural significance of these theories and the impossibility of analyzing pornography without referring to them, they warrant brief discussion here. Feminist debates surrounding the question of pornography have been famously heated and divisive, inviting comparisons to warfare and pitched battle. From the late 1970s, feminist theorists divided into camps that can be broadly categorized as "anti-pornography" and "anti-censorship."[15] Led by Andrea Dworkin and Catharine MacKinnon, the anti-pornography school of thought argues that patriarchy is produced through sex. Pornography therefore constitutes the ultimate manifestation of male domination and female oppression.[16] While Mackinnon and Dworkin produced important observations regarding the need to assess sexuality as intertwined with larger social inequalities and power relations, their view of power as breaking down along strictly gendered lines works to erase intersecting factors like race, class, and nationality.[17] On the other side of the debate, anti-censorship feminists have also been criticized for oversimplifying inequalities and social hierarchies.[18] Both sets of theorists also focused on the contemporary film and magazine industries, leaving open major questions about pornography produced in a very different economic and technological context.

In the late 1980s, some feminist and queer scholars began to break away from the pro-/anti- approach that had dominated the debate for years. Drawing upon queer and Foucauldian frameworks, these scholars have produced a new body of scholarship known as porn studies. Beginning with the work of Linda Williams in 1989, these scholars have aimed to move away from polarizing debates and toward a critical analysis of pornography's changing role across different times and cultural contexts.[19] This effort has, among other achievements, led to the creation of the academic journal *Porn Studies,* a development that illustrates the growing prominence of the field.[20] The growth of porn studies as a field has created a crucial set of theoretical advances that allow for the kinds of critical approaches to pornographic materials that have long been applied to other genres and forms of cultural production.[21] Moreover, porn studies scholars have forged links to other queer scholarship that illuminates the shifting and constructed nature of sexualities.[22] While porn studies scholars have made much-needed calls for historicizing pornography, the field as a whole remains heavily focused on contemporary pornography in general and film in particular; moreover, as previously mentioned, historical work within porn studies generally aligns with cultural history approaches.[23] As a result, major questions regarding the social history of pornography production, circulation, and regulation in specific historical contexts remain largely unanswered.

THE NATURE OF PORNOGRAPHY IN EARLY TWENTIETH-CENTURY BRITAIN

This brings us back to the methods employed in this book. By grounding the critical approaches of porn studies scholars in a social history framework and emphasizing the context in which pornography was produced, circulated, consumed, and regulated, we arrive at a more complete picture of pornography's place in society. In the case of early twentieth-century Britain, analyzing pornography from the ground up reveals some surprising characteristics. First, pornography circulated within well-established networks of people who often developed ongoing business and personal relationships through their involvement in the trade. Second, the trade occurred on a transnational scale, connecting these local British networks to a much larger global context. Finally, the pornography trade produced queer spaces and practices that often served as a site of contestation and opposition to the heteronormative order.

Given the fact that all of these characteristics deviate significantly from the terminology and theoretical frameworks employed in most historical analysis of pornography, it is worth pausing to clarify certain terms and concepts. First: "transnational." As a general rule, "transnationalism" calls attention to processes and networks that span or transcend the borders of nation-states.[24] As a way of describing systems of pornography distribution in pre-1945 Britain, the term "transnational" operates on several levels. As a major imperial power, Britain itself had a transnational presence in the world. For the purposes of this project, however, other transnational processes prove more important. The transnational cultural flows of the pornography trade involved both the physical movement of bodies and the circulation of cultural materials and ideas across borders. Pornographers often migrated, crossing borders while maintaining business and cultural connections with their home countries. British pornographers settled in Paris, opening bookshops and selling their wares to customers back in London.[25] Others moved to Britain from Portugal and Germany, importing goods from their countries of origin.[26] Pornographic materials circulated within the British Empire, where both Britons and colonized peoples participated in the trade.[27] Given the nature of these transnational networks, it is important to avoid juxtaposing the local and the transnational as opposites. Rather, transnational processes manifested on the local level, and the local exerted influence or pressure on transnational forces.[28] Thus, this project focuses heavily on people and products within Britain but analyzes these subjects as part of a smaller node in a transnational network.

Lastly, as the primary theoretical lens through which this material is analyzed, the relationship between queerness and heteronormativity warrants discussion. Heteronormativity is an unstable cluster of norms and practices rather than a term with a fixed definition. Those acts and practices considered heteronormative today differ from those of the early twentieth century. Regardless of specific context, however, heteronormativity is produced when the hegemonic social order embraces a particular model of gender and sexuality that becomes the unquestioned norm against which all other identities, gender presentations, and sexual practices are defined.[29] To paraphrase E.P. Thompson, heteronormativity is a relationship, not a thing.[30] "Heteronormativity" as used in this project should not, therefore, be construed as a static and transhistorical standard but as a shifting and unstable cluster of gender roles and sexual norms promoted as "normal" or mainstream during the period from 1900 to 1945. Chapter 1 will offer a brief overview of what sexual practices and norms were considered "good" or "healthy" in early twentieth-century Britain, but one should remain aware that heteronormative sexuality is a constantly shifting set of practices and categories rather than a single, easily defined trait or characteristic.

"Queer," similarly, is a positional term that shifts in tension with heteronormativity.[31] Queer, rather than operating as a synonym for homosexuality, refers more broadly to views or practices that destabilize and critique heteronormative structures and categories.[32] The broadness and flexibility of queerness and queer theory have been the subject of much discussion and debate since their emergence in the 1990s. While originally operating largely in connection with LGBT identities and groups, it has since expanded to encompass everything from Native American studies to cultural representations of South Asian women to political discourses of terrorism and Islam.[33] Moreover, "queer" has expanded from solely an identity category to a critical framework for studying social relationships and power dynamics, often involving groups that would in no way self-identify as queer subjects.[34] One could make (and, indeed, many have made) the argument that a framework so elastic as to encompass seemingly everything may ultimately become meaningless.[35] This project offers a group of subjects vulnerable to the same critique; if many of the pornographers, consumers, and distributors involved in the British pornography trade were heterosexual, middle-class, male, and otherwise seemingly normative or privileged in British society, how can the pornography trade be viewed as fostering the growth of queer spaces?

While concerns over the elasticity of queerness are valid, I would argue that there are several reasons why queerness represents the best way of understanding the groups and processes discussed in this project. First, as argued by Michael Warner, queerness emerges through a process by which regimes of power construct specific sexualities, practices, and gender presentations as normative and others as deviant, a process that exposes those deviant sexualities and persons to multiple forms of marginalization.[36] As queer historians like Nayan Shah have illustrated in work on non-LGBTQ queer spaces like San Francisco's Chinatown, possible alternative terms like "non-normative" not only lack queerness's theoretical background and history, but also fail to call attention to the role of power and violence in creating these categories.[37] In addition, queerness, while not always referring to a clear identity category like LGBT, has a long history of association with active resistance through underground socialization and community formation. Simply describing a sexual practice or group as "deviant" in its sexuality fails to acknowledge the ways in which queer groups and spaces turn marginalization into spaces of resistance.[38] Finally, queer studies, along with the closely related field of porn studies, necessarily focuses on interactions between normative and deviant sexualities, rather than simply comparing the two categories side by side; as queer theorists and historians like Matt Houlbrook have shown, the state and powerful civil actors often simultaneously create spaces in which deviant sexualities can flourish while exposing those same sexualities to violence and marginalization.[39]

To return this discussion to the early twentieth-century British pornography trade, only by thinking in terms of queerness can we fully appreciate the complex interplay of the pornography trade and the heteronormative forces of state and civil society that worked to construct it as a deviant practice or community. As shown in this book's last three chapters, the construction of pornography as a manifestation of deviant sexuality occurred across multiple fields, including law, philanthropy, international affairs, and mainstream media and entertainment. Rather than being entirely imposed from above, however, queerness emerged through the practices and materials produced within the trade's clandestine spaces and networks. While this may sound like a juxtaposition of the stifled, oppressive sexuality of the British mainstream on the one hand and the liberated, free sexuality of the pornography trade on the other, it is important to avoid such oversimplifications. To describe a space or practice as queer does not imply a lack of problematic internal power dynamics or inequalities.[40] Indeed, as the following chapters illustrate, the pornography trade was far from an egalitarian sexual paradise. It was, however, a queer community or space in the sense that it was constructed as sexually deviant by heteronormative state and civil society and that those active within the trade often engaged in deliberate or implicit resistance to those normative standards. My approach to pornography and queer sexuality in this book therefore relies less on celebrating the queerness of the pornography trade and more on focusing on the ways in which power and resistance produced specific conditions within pornography networks, and, conversely, how the day-to-day practices and material conditions of these networks illuminated overarching tensions between normativity and deviance in British society.

PORNOGRAPHY IN THE ARCHIVE

Any historical study of pornography must contend with a deeply flawed and fragmented archive. Pornographic materials proved vulnerable to loss or destruction at various points; they might be discarded after use, hidden away and forgotten, or destroyed after legal proceedings.[41] Even those items that avoided deliberate destruction often lacked the archival care and preservation efforts afforded to other kinds of art and printed materials. In other words, we cannot assume that even such rich repositories as the Kinsey Institute provide anything close to a representative sample of the pornography that would have circulated in a particular time and place.

The flaws in archival samples of pornographic ephemera, however, pale in comparison to the problems encountered in the quest for legal documents, personal accounts, business records, and other sources related to production, distribution, and the day-to-day lives of those involved in pornography. Beyond the clues gleaned from pornographic materials, the only available information about most of those involved in the pornography trade came into existence when these people intersected with legal authorities. Some of the problems and gaps resulting from this legal reality should be obvious; such a collection of records excludes the luckiest and most discreet, those who never suffered legal penalties for their activities. More importantly, however, this archival reality excludes entire categories of people involved in the trade whose specific roles did not expose them to legal intervention. Pornographic modelling and performance, for instance, violated no British laws, leaving models almost entirely absent from the record.[42] Only specific forms of consumption (such as those involving transmission through the post) violated British obscenity law, leaving some aspects of consumption practices unclear. As a result of these archival limitations, this book's attempt to map the contours of the early twentieth-century

British pornography trade leaves major areas like modelling largely unexplored. I want to be clear, however, that these gaps do not reflect these roles' lack of importance; on the contrary, one would be hard-pressed to find a more essential participant in the pornography trade than the model. Instead, these absences in the book should be read as a reflection of their corresponding absence in available archival materials. Every effort, however, has been made to reconstruct the experiences of these silent actors from remaining traces relating to other roles in the trade such as that of distributor and producer.

CHAPTER OUTLINE

This book's methodology centres on balancing social and cultural analysis of the pornography trade and its materials with the broader forces surrounding it, with close attention to moments of interaction or conflict. The first three chapters analyze the inner workings of the pornography trade itself, emphasizing everyday practices and interactions. This begins in chapter 1 with an analysis of the localized social organization of networks within Britain. Chapter 2 expands in scope, exploring the broader transnational systems that shaped these local interactions. Chapter 3 conducts a close reading of pornographic content through the lens of the trade described in the previous two chapters. As a whole, the first three chapters survey the terrain of the pornography trade in Britain and around the globe during the early twentieth century.

The book's last three chapters shift perspective to the British state and mainstream civil society, focusing on policy choices and moral positions that worked to create the environment in which the pornography trade could flourish. Chapter 4 discusses the British press's role in promoting or minimizing certain public discourses concerning pornography. Chapter 5 analyzes the diminished position of elite moral hygiene pressure groups like the National Vigilance Association (NVA), which had in previous periods led efforts to limit or eradicate the trade. Chapter 6 focuses on state entities ranging from Parliament to the Home Office, illustrating that various political and economic interests produced specific forms of anti-pornography policy. Together, these three chapters argue that a variety of competing political and social interests limited incentive to actively pursue pornography in early twentieth-century Britain, resulting in the development of social and cultural spaces within which the trade could operate.

The conclusion assesses the implications of this historical study for the contemporary politics of pornography. I do not argue that the model of transnational networks and queer spaces employed in this particular case study can or should be simplistically applied to other contexts. Rather, I contend that studying pornography cultures requires reading pornographic materials with close attention to specific material and historical conditions of production, consumption, and regulation. Only with this awareness of changing historical conditions can we develop a complete picture of the role played by pornography in specific cultural and social contexts.

CHAPTER ONE

"Discreet and Careful"

Pornography Producers, Distributors, and Consumers in Britain, 1900–1945

On 8 May 1923, officers from the London Metropolitan Police arrested pornography distributors Cyril Benbow and Mervyn Hyde. The copious amounts of seized materials used in the subsequent trial included sex toys, evidence of Hyde's cross-dressing habits, and pornographic materials produced in a variety of media. The trial's most intriguing exhibit was not, however, a box of shocking pornographic photographs or Hyde's collection of leather fetish gear. The most damning and, for our purposes, informative piece of evidence police discovered consisted of a simple list of names, addresses, and brief comments regarding each person's temperament and relationship to Mervyn Hyde. This list included men and women, British citizens and overseas foreigners, a retired captain of the Royal Automobile Club, and a sex worker specializing in clients who "like[d] corporal punishment."[1]

The list, provided to Benbow by Hyde as a source of potential customers for pornographic products, revealed a network of individuals connected by their shared interest in pornography and, to a lesser extent, sexual practices like bondage, domination, and sadomasochism (BDSM). Documents from the case file confirm that some of these individuals met in person.[2] Others may have limited their involvement to mailed correspondence. Hyde's notation clearly shows, however, that their knowledge of each other went well beyond anonymous purchases. By writing "It might help you to mention my name so do so" beside the entry for Major C.A. Hope, Hyde indicated that the two men enjoyed a relatively friendly relationship. The entry for Madame Dennis Le Conte, in contrast, offered the following cryptic warning: "*Don't* mention my name and be very *discreet* in your first letter – discreet and careful."[3] While the people on Mervyn Hyde's list differed in terms of race, class, gender, and occupation, they did share important characteristics: their sexual proclivities, their desire to purchase pornography, and their cross-gender and cross-class interactions with other people in the network placed all of them well outside of early twentieth-century Britain's normative sexual order.

The Benbow and Hyde network stands out as an unusually well-documented element of the early twentieth-century British pornography trade. In terms of its organization and activities, however, the group was far from unique. Rather, it serves as an example of how the pornography trade operated and how its members interacted within queer spaces such as long-distance pornographic correspondence networks. This book is not the first to view the Benbow and Hyde case through a queer lens. Lisa Z. Sigel, for example, has focused on the corset and cross-dressing items traded by the defendants, presenting a persuasive case that this constituted queer kink.[4] The sub-genre of pornography and fetish items sold by Benbow and Hyde is not, however, the only reason their network should be considered a queer space. In fact, not all of Benbow and Hyde's customers shared the same preferences in pornography. One client, for example, included in his order form specific descriptions such as images of "two corpulent women" and "young pregnant ladies."[5] Another client requested only highly popular flagellation titles like *Flossie: A Venus of Fifteen*.[6] Nevertheless, these different customers operated within the same network using a common vocabulary and forms of interaction that differed significantly from heteronormative standards of proper conduct.

The most significant point at which this book departs from existing research on pornography is in its focus on the material and social context in which the trade operated, and the ways in which this focus illuminates tensions between heteronormative and queer elements within British society.[7] Material conditions and practices are essential for illuminating these power dynamics and relationships:

how pornography was made, where it was sold, how much it cost, how distributors and customers spoke to each other, and other seemingly quotidian details surrounding the creation and transmission of pornography reveal far greater insights into the people involved in pornography and their position relative to other groups and actors. This chapter thus explores the ways in which pornography networks operated and organized; it then moves on to a discussion of how viewing these practices through a queer lens offers insights into pornography's place in British society.

Before delving into the operations of the pornography trade, it is worth pausing to discuss the terminology employed in this chapter and throughout the book. While terms like "subculture" and, to a lesser extent, "industry" imply a well-organized group with clearly delineated boundaries, the examples discussed through this chapter reveal the early twentieth-century British pornography trade as a far messier and less cohesive entity. Evidence discussed below clearly shows organization and long-term interaction between participants, as in the case of the Benbow-Hyde network, but this does not imply consistent membership or homogeneous practices common to all members. Instead, I describe the organization of the pornography trade in terms of "networks" in order to signal the importance of continuing relationships while also acknowledging the fluid boundaries and changing membership of these groups.[8] It is important to note, however, that surviving archival sources often provide information for only certain elements or members of these networks. For example, criminal cases often exposed distributors but not models or consumers to the public eye. The specific cases and elements discussed here must necessarily serve as incomplete, limited glimpses rather than precise maps of entire networks. With these limitations in mind, we turn to the question of what can be known about pornography and the people involved with it in the early twentieth century.

GENDER, SEXUALITY, AND CULTURE IN EARLY TWENTIETH-CENTURY BRITAIN

Between 1900 and 1945, Britons grappled with dramatic changes to their gender systems and sexual social order. These changes emerged from a variety of causes and touched all areas of daily life. Among other changes, the women's suffrage movement achieved peak visibility in the first decade of the twentieth century, with partial suffrage granted in 1918 and full suffrage in 1928. Alongside formal political participation, women sought increased physical and social mobility and pushed to improve their employment prospects.[9] This apparent breakdown of gendered hierarchies was also evident in popular culture and entertainment. Female fashion became less restrictive, while younger generations embraced activities like dancing and attending jazz clubs. Conservative commentators looked with alarm upon the short hair and raised hemlines of the New Woman and the Modern Girl, who continued to have an active presence in cosmopolitan cities and artistic circles.[10] The mobilization of female labour and the devastating injuries suffered by men during the First World War contributed to a general sense of crisis in the relationship between the genders.[11] Gender norms were further challenged by changing labour requirements and social upheaval at the onset of the Second World War.[12] Men and masculinity in particular seemed to teeter on the brink of crisis. In response, images of ideal British masculinity sought a precarious balance between strong and gentle: a middle-class, masculine sensibility that allegedly stood in contrast to both aristocratic foppishness and the brutish violence of working-class men, but which was also vulnerable to accusations of weakness.[13]

Changes in British sexuality were subtler but in some ways more profound than these gendered changes. Edwardians and interwar Britons prided themselves on moving away from the hypocrisy of the Victorian years, yet these shifts were reflected more in a general loosening of cultural norms than in concrete legal or practical change. Homosexuality and prostitution remained demonized and heavily policed, marriage became more rather than less important as a marker of adulthood, and divorce remained scandalous and difficult to achieve.[14] On the other hand, the work of Margaret Sanger in the United States and Marie Stopes in Britain made birth control a publicly contested possibility for the first time.[15] In intellectual circles, the hysterical rhetoric surrounding masturbation and active female sexuality began to wane, albeit without a corresponding change in broader cultural views.[16] Any trends toward sexual liberation, however, faced serious obstacles during moments of crisis like the First World War, the global Great Depression, and the Second World War, which carried with them waves of moral panic and heightened policing of deviant sexualities. Sexuality in post-1900 Britain was therefore characterized less by revolutionary change than by signs of possible revolution to come. Whether this revolution would represent a welcome change or a terrifying cultural collapse depended on the position of the observer.

The most contested aspects of sexuality and gender norms were those perceived as central to British identity. While the Victorian period involved a rigidly enforced class system, a clear divide between urban and rural, and little colonial migration to the metropole, all of these boundaries and hierarchies were challenged in the first half of the twentieth century. Much of this contestation centred on questions of sexuality and gender. Those who moved from country to city in search of work, for example, were overwhelmingly female, stimulating dialogue about the urban corruption of innocent young women.[17] Sexual contact between male immigrants from the colonies and white British women served as a cornerstone of anti-immigrant rhetoric.[18] The growth of working-class influence in politics created tension in spaces where working-class and bourgeois moral codes and notions of respectability collided.[19] Sexuality thus served as a field where competing actors and groups fought over diverse and sometimes only tangentially related aspects of the British social order. This contestation, the process by which heteronormative and deviant sexualities were constructed, is the backdrop against which we must explore the experiences of pornography producers, distributors, and consumers.

Given this chapter's focus on the pornography trade's queer spaces and its relationship to normativity, one might well ask what exactly constituted heteronormative sexuality in early twentieth-century Britain. While attempting to precisely delineate the practices and categories that would have been considered "good," "healthy," or "normal" would be an impossible task, historians like Jeffrey Weeks and Angus McLaren have produced extensive scholarship on the boundaries of acceptability and sexual deviance in British societies.[20] Keeping in mind that normativity constantly shifts and differs depending on social location, we can nevertheless use this established literature to identify general points of consensus about what would have fit the definition of normative sexuality. Broadly speaking, healthy sexuality occurred between monogamous, emotionally attached, opposite-sex individuals. Sex for pleasure alone rather than for the purposes of conceiving children or strengthening the marital relationship earned condemnation based on a variety of medical and moral rationales.[21] Gender dimorphism also reigned supreme; while the precise nature of gender roles existed in a state of disagreement and flux, the necessity of distinct roles for men and women rarely came into question.[22]

This is not to suggest that any of these views were uncontested or their boundaries clear. On the contrary, issues like birth control stimulated fierce debate and controversy. In general, however, early twentieth-century Britons were expected to adhere to monogamous heterosexuality and clearly defined, binary gender roles. While it is necessary to keep these overarching norms in mind, I do not find it helpful to attempt a comprehensive list of normative practices and categories against which to compare or define queer opposites. Instead, later chapters will discuss the stated reasons and underlying logics of pornography regulation, which will allow us to map the interplay of deviance and normativity in the British Empire before 1945. In the meantime, however, this chapter will focus on those individuals and categories marginalized as sexually deviant due to their involvement in pornography, thus providing a stronger sense of who fell outside of normative boundaries and why.

PRODUCERS AND DISTRIBUTORS, 1900–1918

As has been well documented by previous historians, the 1890s saw a concerted effort by the British state to purge the country's pornographic book publishers. Measures aimed at high-end presses were largely successful, creating a flourishing Parisian expatriate community that included such notable pornographic publishing figures as Charles Carrington.[23] The long-term effects of these efforts have, however, been overstated. While some observers have gone so far as to argue that "by 1910 there was virtually no production of pornographic materials" in Britain, this assertion not only ignores the many forms of pornography production besides literary printing, but also overlooks the Edwardian abandonment of the draconian measures employed in the 1890s.[24] Moreover, focusing exclusively on printing and other formal types of production in the pornography trade erases the wide array of roles and methods adopted by producers and distributors. As the various cases discussed in this chapter amply demonstrate, the porn trade was alive and well in Edwardian Britain. It did, however, operate under major constraints. While pornographic photography operations and mail-order businesses dealing in typewritten short stories rose from the ashes of the dismantled late-Victorian trade, this system lacked the large presses and professional operations found in Paris and other European cities.[25] Rather than making the British trade irrelevant to the larger context of transnationally circulated pornography, these limitations merely bound British participants into tighter networks characterized by long-term contacts and small-scale but efficient methods.

British policy rendered the country inhospitable for pornography producers through the turn of the century. As late as 1901, prominent British pornographers like Henry Sidney Nichols were still forced to flee to Paris for fear of being sentenced to several years of hard labour.[26] Even pornographers living beyond the official reach of British law had cause for concern during the first year of Edward's reign. Thanks to pressure from the British state, French pornographers were arrested in Cairo and a ring of Continental European pornographers faced trial in Trieste.[27] However, these extraordinary efforts to root out pornographers at home and abroad were suddenly abandoned after 1901. The causes of this abrupt policy shift will be discussed more fully in chapter 6, but this backdrop is necessary for an understanding of the local, tight-knit organization of the trade on British soil in the Edwardian years. The British pornography trade did not immediately rebound with large numbers of new publishing operations or massive studios, but distributors and enthusiasts did continue to participate throughout the entire period under discussion. For example, the social purity publication *The Vigilance Record* reported dozens of British defendants in pornography-related cases between 1904 and 1913, some of which involved the production of as many as 40,000 photographic prints or cards.[28] National and provincial newspapers also reported frequent arrests and investigations of pornographers, most of whom sold small quantities of materials from bookshops or similar establishments.[29] Based solely on the cases that came to the attention of law enforcement officials and the press, then, the Edwardian trade in photographs was significant. The actual size of the trade, which would have included far more participants than those whose names appeared in newspapers and police reports, was far greater.

Cases that came to the attention of legal authorities or journalists during the Edwardian years provide clear examples of how pornographers shaped their operations in the face of crackdowns on high-end publishers. The vast majority of Edwardian sellers and distributors mentioned in newspaper accounts or court records fell into two categories: shopkeepers who sold pornography as a side business, and street hawkers who approached customers on the street and primarily dealt in postcards. Several examples of the first category illustrate the scale of the trade and the types of spaces in which pornographers operated. One 1904 case prosecuted in Newcastle, for instance, involved a collaborative effort between a photographer named Duncan Forbes and a stationer named John White. During an investigation into Forbes, a member of the National Vigilance Association attempted to purchase "foreign cards" from his shop, only to be told that Forbes was out procuring some at that moment. The undercover investigator later returned to purchase the cards, leading the police to seize a total of ninety-one items from both men. This case illustrates several important points. First, pornography was not the primary business of either participant, both of whom ran their own shops. Second, this was a haphazard operation, with Forbes leaving his shop in the middle of the day to resupply rather than having a large amount of stock on hand.[30] As this case demonstrates, typical Edwardian producers and distributors operated at a different level than elite erotic publishers like Charles Carrington. Rather than participating in a vast and well-ordered cartel, Edwardian pornography networks were more likely to consist of collaborations between shopkeepers, photographers, and any regular customers they managed to attract.

Forbes and White were not the only Edwardian pornographers to follow this pattern. Henry James Nicholls, charged with violating the Obscene Publications Act in 1904, worked as a Liverpool hairdresser but also sold postcards out of his shop.[31] Later that year, five men appeared before a Bath magistrate on similar charges; while the relationship between these men was unclear, all were shopkeepers or tradesmen and all sold postcards, indicating a shared supplier or other business links.[32] Gloucester shopkeeper Dorothy Kernahan was brought before the court after 110 postcards and other assorted writings were seized from her shop.[33] In each of these cases, the pornography trade was a side business for shopkeepers or other tradespeople whose main line of work brought them into close and frequent contact with the public. The pornography sold was in the form of postcards, typed stories, and other low-cost materials that did not require a printing press or other expensive equipment. Here, the items sold and the physical spaces in which pornography circulated tell us much about the social context of the Edwardian pornography trade. Lacking the ability to engage in high-end erotic book publishing or to operate shops specializing in pornographic books, as was possible in cities like Paris, British pornographers developed a far smaller and more makeshift distribution system.

Like virtually every other industry, the pornography trade underwent significant changes at the onset of the First World War. British officials, ignoring the realities of the postcard trade by assuming that the war in France had cut off Britain's only major supply of pornography, set aside most anti-pornography efforts.[34] The small number of distribution cases reported by authorities between 1914 and 1918 has been seen as evidence of Britain's minimal role in the pornography trade after 1900.[35] As discussed in chapter 6, however, this may in fact be an illusion resulting from selective enforcement rather than the actual interruption of a unidirectional trade in which French pornography flowed to British consumers. For example, catalogues produced in Great Britain between 1913 and 1914 advertise a variety of pornographic wares, indicating production or at the very least a highly sophisticated distribution apparatus that existed independently of foreign suppliers.[36] Moreover, the domestic distributors of pornographic photographs and cards discussed above were sufficiently well established by 1914 that they certainly would have had the ability to copy existing stocks of photographs even if they lacked the ability or inclination to produce new ones.

Given the significant changes in the trade between 1900 and 1945 and the extremely small scale of production in Britain up to 1918, one might be tempted to write off the early years of the twentieth century as irrelevant to the later interwar trade. To do so, however, would mean ignoring the consistent activity of people like Dorothy Kernahan and Duncan Forbes within Britain prior to 1914. These people did not passively receive naughty books from French publishers. Rather, they developed networks of distribution and exchange that would endure for the next several decades. Charles Carrington and Henry Sidney Nichols might have been driven from British shores, but Britain's culture of pornography did not grind to a halt in their absence. Those who carried on after 1900 developed practices that would be expanded upon by producers and other participants who took advantage of the gradual decline in legal penalties and lack of anti-pornography initiatives characterizing Edwardian and interwar British policy. Photographers and writers who began production operations after 1918 did not revive a dead trade. Rather, they tapped into existing networks of producers and consumers who had adapted the trade in the face of significant legal and economic interference.

PRODUCERS AND DISTRIBUTORS IN THE INTERWAR YEARS

Regardless of these limitations during the Edwardian period and the First World War, Britain's pornography trade was clearly thriving by the interwar years. This increased activity led to more frequent encounters with law enforcement and other state entities, providing a body of evidence from which we can identify major characteristics of the interwar trade. While legal penalties eased significantly after 1901, interwar British pornographers, their distributors, and to a lesser extent their customers faced significant social and legal obstacles. The forms this marginalization took, however, depended greatly on variables such as race, class, citizenship, and other characteristics. As the examples discussed here demonstrate, the pornography trade embodied significant diversity. Some practitioners fit popular conceptions of the impoverished criminal underworld, but others hailed from solidly middle-class or even aristocratic backgrounds. These distributors ran different legal and social risks depending on their class and citizenship status, which directly affected their responses to intervention by legal authorities.

Immigrants, one of the more vulnerable groups involved in the trade, formed a large proportion of the people arrested for pornography-related offences. Immigrants often used their connections to their own or their parents' country of origin to import foreign pornography. They also, however, became involved in domestic production or distribution networks even when it involved no apparent connection to the wider transnational trade outside of Britain. During the 1920s and 1930s, for instance, several shopkeepers from Poland or Russia faced arrest and prosecution for the display or sale of obscene publications. These shopkeepers typically sold pornography as a sideline with the majority of their business consisting of tobacco or non-pornographic books. Kitty Lichtenstein, born in Russia, owned a Greek Street bookshop from which she sold small quantities of flagellation-themed stories and postcards.[37] In another case, a Polish national named Isaac Sugarman faced heavy fines in 1930 for displaying obscene pamphlets in the window of his tobacco shop.[38] While police records seem to show that immigrants were disproportionately involved in the pornography trade, these sources should be interpreted with caution. Police reports contain no clear evidence indicating selective enforcement, but the extensive work done on the deliberate targeting of immigrants by British law enforcement during this period suggests that it is a strong possibility.[39]

While many of the distributors arrested by British authorities belonged to marginal categories like immigrants and the working poor, the interwar pornography trade had its own internal hierarchies, which we can map by exploring their working conditions and the spaces in which they operated. Wealthier book importers and publishers had the ability to take greater measures to avoid detection or to minimize any potential legal penalties. For example, several bookshop owners kept two separate premises next door to each other or located on the same street. William Hamilton, accused of publishing obscene materials in 1933, kept his main bookshop at 15 Phoenix Street, while his supply of pornographic or banned materials resided at 13 Phoenix Street.[40] The practice of keeping pornographic stock in a separate location did not entirely insulate shop owners from police intervention, but it decreased the chances of detection and protected the legal books from seizure.

Once arrested or otherwise publicly exposed as active in the pornography trade, pornographers and consumers adopted a variety of defensive strategies. Shopkeepers like Isaac Sugarman and Kitty Lichtenstein rarely displayed overt defiance, typically apologizing for their transgressions and complying fully with police efforts.[41] At no point did either of them deny that the materials in question qualified as obscene. Lichtenstein, in fact, admitted that she had been worried about police detection for some time.[42] This may have been related to her status as an immigrant; as the Richard Elias case (discussed later in the chapter) demonstrates, the sale of pornography could result in deportation for immigrant offenders. Shopkeepers who sold pornography only as a sideline may have had little personal stake in the pornography trade compared with those more deeply involved in production and large-scale distribution.

Producers and British-born distributors often proved far less co-operative than foreign shopkeepers, and were far more likely to express opposition to legal intervention. Producers like erotic postcard dealer Alexander Bloom denied that their wares were obscene or argued that only "small-minded people" could find them objectionable.[43] When confronted by a police officer who accused him of selling obscene photographs, Eric Sheldon Haynes declared, "I am an artist. These [photographs] are not indecent. There is nothing indecent about the human form."[44] While Haynes may very well have been sincere in believing that his photographs were not indecent, they were clearly intended to be erotic (see figures 1.1 and 1.2). In

Figure 1.1 | Undated female nude photograph from case file of *Rex v. Eric Sheldon Haynes*.

arguing and contradicting the views of the investigating officers, Haynes exercised an option that was clearly not available to his immigrant counterparts within the British trade.

Some defendants bluntly refused to divulge information regarding their business partners or the source of their pornography,

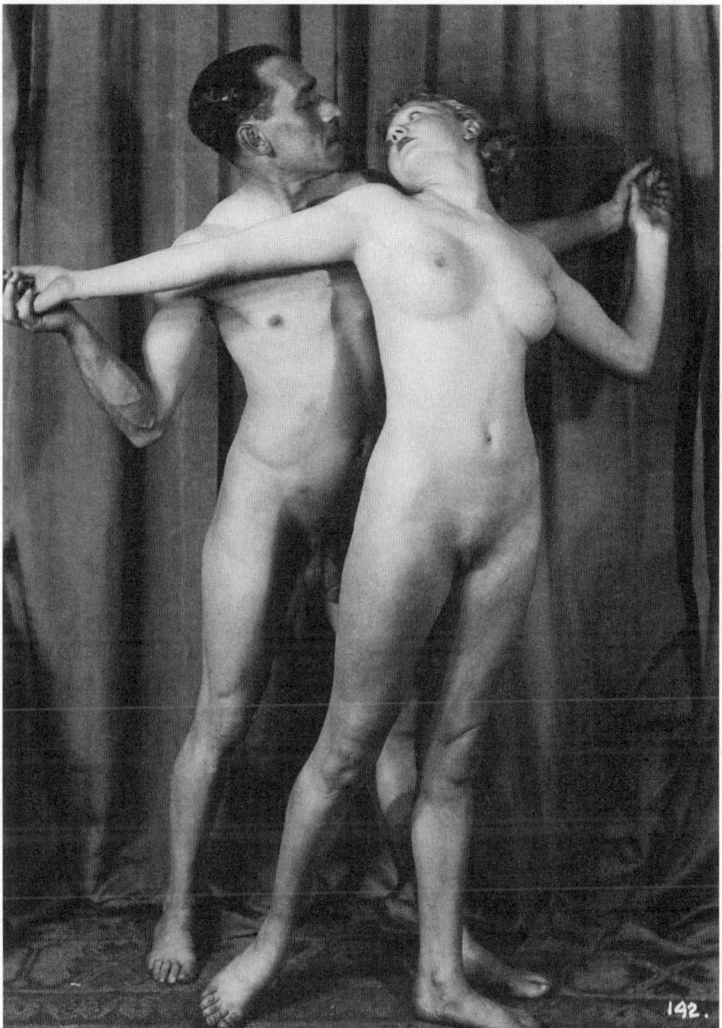

Figure 1.2 | Undated male and female nude photograph from case file of *Rex v. Eric Sheldon Haynes*.

even when it might have reduced their legal penalties or otherwise aided in their defence. Edward Duplex, convicted of violating the Vagrancy Act in Manchester in 1929, refused to tell police where he acquired his obscene prints and as a consequence faced one month's imprisonment.[45] During the same year, Liverpool resident

Mr Shuttleworth also refused to inform on his supplier even when pressured by authorities.[46] While personal loyalties may have been a factor in their refusal to reveal sources, Duplex and Shuttleworth may also have been making practical business decisions. Many pornographers continued their trade despite multiple convictions; recognizing that business relations would probably resume after paying a fine or completing a brief prison sentence, some pornographers were reluctant to implicate their suppliers.[47] Regardless of motive, such actions helped to guard the rest of the network from state intervention.

A handful of pornographers antagonized authorities by using more direct methods. The 1930 investigation into the aforementioned printer of pornographic cards, Alexander Bloom, resulted in the dismissal of the case when the bench found that the police had provided insufficient evidence that Bloom had ever printed such cards. The case's lead detective reported the following exchange after the case had been dismissed: "After the case Mr. Bloom came up to me, beaming with joy and said 'I am not going to print any more of those cards.'"[48] Bloom's impudent comment, which provided a useless confession to a now-powerless police officer, offers a glimpse of overt defiance and contempt for the moral authority of the London Metropolitan Police. Rather than viewing police intervention merely as an occupational hazard, pornographers like Alexander Bloom approached them as forces of opposition to be resisted and mocked. This opposition, however, was far from a united front. Ability and inclination to actively resist hinged on factors ranging from income to citizenship status, all of which contributed to internal variations within the trade.

While interactions between pornographers and the authorities were an important factor in the structure and development of pornography networks, the relationships between different pornographers must also be considered. Rather than acting alone, those active within distribution networks often co-operated and collaborated. As in the case of Cyril Benbow and Mervyn Hyde, distributor Trevor Evans helpfully provided fellow pornographer Charles Barnick with a list of potential customers. Barnick had purchased both a grocery and part of a pornography operation from Richard

Elias, who had also been acquainted with Trevor Evans.[49] Evans not only identified Elias when questioned by police, but also possessed information regarding Elias's marriage, family, and children. When he discovered that the police had initiated an investigation of his operation, Elias quickly hid his supplies with a trusted friend named Lawrence Goldman, who apparently fulfilled this function on a regular basis; police found a friendly, handwritten note from Elias in Goldman's apartment, written on the back of a nude postcard.[50] In short, people involved in the British pornography trade interacted extensively even when not working together as co-owners or partners in the same enterprise. In some cases, such as Lawrence Goldman's role in hiding materials, this co-operation did not even include any financial benefits for those involved.

Relations between different pornography distributors and producers could be hostile rather than co-operative. Evans, upon hearing of a complaint that he dealt in obscene wares, informed the investigating officer that he had many competitors and suspected that they had reported him to the police.[51] Low-level postcard dealer Arthur Sandford also referenced his competitors, telling potential customers that he offered far better prices and higher-quality photographs than could be purchased from other sellers.[52] Such complaints and rumours point to a decentralized trade consisting of competing networks rather than a single monolithic industry; pornographers knew each other and may have collaborated or had friendly relations in many circumstances, but they also sometimes found themselves vying for customers or experiencing other forms of tension. This loose cluster of different actors and groups belies popular ideas of the pornography trade as a rigidly organized criminal enterprise overseen by a Mafia kingpin, an image that would continue to appear in lurid Hollywood renderings of the pornography trade over the course of the twentieth century.[53] Instead, it seems that the localized British pornography trade was a small world, but not one with a single centre.

While the majority of official concern centred on London, these kinds of distribution networks also incorporated other regions of the British Isles. In 1929 and 1930, arrests and prosecutions occurred in numerous locales including Bolton, Bradford, Ipswich,

Liverpool, Glasgow, Nottingham, and Manchester.[54] In all of these locations, pornography distributors followed similar patterns of activity. Like Elias and Barnick, pornographers outside of London owned small operations that depended on informal networks and long-standing business relationships with their customers and suppliers. Leo Locket, for example, resided in Leeds but regularly supplied two distributors in Bolton.[55] It would be far easier for a Bolton distributor to reach Manchester or other cities than the much more distant location of Leeds, demonstrating that connections within the pornography trade did not depend on convenience alone.

Other elements also show that people actively cultivated relationships within the pornography networks and did not effortlessly enter into the trade. In some cases, pornographers sacrificed significant privilege in order to become involved in pornography, indicating that involvement in the trade cannot be reduced to an issue of economic desperation. Fetish photographer John Willie, born John Alexander Scott Coutts, belonged to a privileged family and attended the prestigious Sandhurst Royal Military Academy. Despite his wealthy background and education, however, he chose to move first to Australia and then the United States to work as a photographer and illustrator of bondage pornography.[56] Many of the best-known Continental erotic photographers also enjoyed considerable wealth and privileged social status.[57] For these pornographers, their trade fulfilled some kind of personal or social need, allowing them to encounter like-minded people or a more compatible set of sexual norms.

Despite their crucial role in pornography production, British authors rarely faced direct legal penalties for their work. As a result, information about them remains elusive. Nearly all wrote under pseudonyms. Rene Raymond, for example, wrote some of the books published by his press as James Hadley Chase.[58] Many British pornographic authors chose French pseudonyms such as Pauline St Marcelle and Pierz Devereux, surely in an attempt to exploit France's well-established reputation as the source of all things naughty.[59] In addition to the expensive pornography sold in published novel form, however, a new set of authors began to emerge. In several cases, suspects arrested for distribution of postcards and other goods also traded in handwritten or cheaply typed short stories sold in envelopes or loose sheets. J. Severn, prosecuted in Canterbury in 1929, sold handwritten short stories through the post.[60] Irene England typed stories produced by her partner Charles Domec-Carre, although her statement does not clearly explain whether these stories were Domec-Carre's original creations.[61] Unlike the mainstream publishing industry, which had set roles and duties for publishers, authors, and booksellers, pornographers displayed at least passing familiarity with different elements of the industry and could step into a new role when necessary.

Pornographers involved in film production also have a minimal presence in the archive. Due to difficulties related to transport and screening, far fewer cases of film distribution came to the attention of authorities compared with photographs, books, and magazines. Most cases of seized films involved a package mailed to a private customer. Some involved in pornography, however, found ways to screen films for a larger audience. During the early 1920s, unconfirmed rumours claimed that women frequenting the area around London's Palace Theatre sold tickets to screenings of pornographic films taking place in nearby private residences.[62] While police largely dismissed claims of underground film rings screening pornography for public audiences, several confirmed cases exist. As early as 1921, Worcestershire constables raided a theatre and found at least fifty people viewing a "grossly obscene" film.[63] For the most part, however, during the interwar years film remained a small element of a trade that depended to a large degree on materials that would be easier to transport than large reels of celluloid. In a system that depended on small-scale production, personal connections, and localized ties, film represented too much trouble to appear as a major element of the trade.

PRODUCTION AND DISTRIBUTION SHIFTS DURING THE SECOND WORLD WAR

The activities of pornographers and consumers during the Second World War illustrate the extent to which the industry had developed since the Edwardian and interwar years. As discussed earlier in this chapter, British authorities believed that the First World War had largely eliminated the pornography trade by virtue of cutting off foreign supply. While this was clearly overstated, the pornography trade did have a minimal presence in the British press and in law enforcement documents between 1914 and 1918.[64] Some of this lack of attention almost certainly stemmed from the fact that pornography was simply not a priority, but it also seems that wartime pornography purchases and sales remained on a small enough scale to justify claims that the trade was non-existent.

During the Second World War, however, the loss of the foreign trade with Germany, France, and the rest of Continental Europe had a decidedly less significant impact on the activities of British pornographers. A 1943 report to the League of Nations stated that while the war had cut off all foreign sources of pornography, domestic producers continued to operate and had increased the supply of some forms of pornography such as photographs and cheap books.[65] Many of the pornographers identified in the same report distributed locally produced photographs through mail order, often operating out of a small shop or single room. Moreover, British pornographers and consumers did not merely make do with recycled postcards. On the contrary, film screenings featuring multiple participants in well-populated areas continued as late as 1943.[66] The adaptability of the trade to disruptions in foreign supply, coupled with the fact that several of the pornographers listed in the report had previous convictions, demonstrates the extent to which pornography trade rebounded after the harsh state policies of the 1890s.[67] Local distributors in Britain may have been accustomed to obtaining their stock from French or Spanish suppliers prior to the outbreak of war, but they adapted and found other ways to keep the market for pornography alive until regular trade could be established.

Beyond simply maintaining its activities, however, the British pornography trade actually expanded its reach into new markets during the Second World War by selling to enlisted men. Numerous authorities expressed concern about cases involving pornographic postal packets finding their way into the hands of enlisted men and officers. For example, police involved in a 1941 investigation into a mail-order business paid unusual attention to the participation of a twenty-two-year-old customer, noted in police records as being an enlisted soldier in the army.[68] In another case, the London Metropolitan Police investigated the dissemination of over three thousand indecent leaflets, some of which had been sent to members of the military.[69] With an unprecedented number of British men serving in the military at home and abroad, the trade quickly expanded to incorporate military networks in addition to their older systems of bookshop and domestic postal distribution. Other wartime cases show the speed with which new pornographic materials could appear. In 1940, scarcely a year into the war, London street hawkers sold copies of a pornographic pamphlet called "Mae West's Ultimatum to Hitler."[70] The precise content of this pamphlet remains unclear, but the wartime context provides a strong sense of its likely message. The robust presence of the British pornography trade through the Second World War does more than simply illustrate that pornography production survived through the economic isolation and hardships of the 1940s. It also illustrates the extent to which the trade rebuilt and coalesced into stable networks over the course of the Edwardian and interwar periods.

BRITISH CONSUMERS, 1900–1945

Compared with archival sources on the experiences of producers and distributors, information on the experience of consumers remains far more elusive. As will be discussed at greater length in chapter 3, some conclusions about consumers can be drawn from the types of materials that were popular or that producers thought would appeal to consumers. We cannot, however, assume that different consumers experienced pornography in the same way or that they interpreted the values and messages of a particular piece of pornographic ephemera in the manner we might expect.[71] Moreover, it is often difficult to tell on the basis of one arrest or incident whether the person in question was a habitual pornography consumer deeply familiar and active in pornography networks or if that person might have been only an occasional buyer, a distinction with strong implications for the consumer experience. These daunting limitations notwithstanding, consumption practices and the experiences of consumers are not completely closed off to us. Through a close reading of specific cases involving seized order forms and other materials relevant to the purchase or ordering of pornography, we can uncover patterns in consumption practices that proved consistent across multiple networks and producers. While not providing a comprehensive account of how everyone experienced pornography, such a focus on the processes of finding and ordering pornographic materials still allows for a broad discussion of consumers.

Compared with producers and distributors, consumers experienced continuity from the Edwardian years through the Second World War, consistently relying on local distributors and mail order even as policy shifts altered the landscape for producers and those seeking large-scale supplies of pornography from abroad. Repeat business and steady involvement with a single network was a common aspect of the consumer experience. Several statements made by pornographers and distributors indicate that consumers often became regular customers rather than one-time purchasers. Upon meeting an undercover police officer posing as an interested customer, Richard Elias stated that he hoped the man would "prove to be a good customer and run a nice account with me."[72] Other evidence also provides examples of customers who developed long-standing ties to a particular distributor. Many of the letters intercepted by authorities en route to a pornography distributor contained inquiries regarding the stock available, questions regarding shipping practices, and other forms of communication that went well beyond the ticking of boxes on an order form.[73] Cyril Benbow, for example, wrote one personal letter to a customer in which he recommended a replacement for a book that had recently gone out of stock.[74] Given the transit time for international mail before 1945, these inquiries and responses would have required customers and producers to maintain ties for an extended period.

In some cases, pornographers sought out customers from specific populations. During the interwar period, school authorities intercepted several catalogues and order forms addressed to students at Eton College.[75] Pornographers also made more direct attempts to solicit the business of students and other young people. Proprietors of nude mutoscope shows sometimes solicited the business of girls and boys as young as fourteen years of age.[76] Contrary to the narratives of child corruption promoted by the state and social purity organizations discussed at length in chapter 5, however, the majority of cases involving the sale of indecent materials to young people featured young adults at colleges rather than underage children. In 1903, for example, police investigated several instances of pornographic circulars sent to Cambridge undergraduates.[77] In general, however, pornographers preferred cultivating business relationships with people who could become repeat customers rather than those too young or poor to have disposable income. Given the affordability of materials discussed below, this still meant that consumers came from a broad cross-section of British society, ranging from a twenty-two-year-old soldier to Sir E. Flower, MP for Bradford West.[78]

The long-term relationships between consumers and distributors of pornography sometimes facilitated customers making the transition to production or distribution. In one example, wine salesman Leonard William Steer, arrested in 1937, admitted to distributing "spanking stories" for supplemental income. He first became involved in the pornography trade by purchasing flagellation photographs and stories for personal use from a shop in France. Later, he met with a supplier operating under the pseudonym Mr Brown, who gave him envelopes of spanking stories to sell. Steer had clear financial incentive to become involved in the trade; while his commission for wine sales averaged 4s per week, selling envelopes of spanking stories to shopkeepers earned him 15s during the same period.[79] The financial benefits do not, however, adequately explain his participation in pornography distribution. Only by becoming familiar with pornography networks and distribution practices as a consumer was Steer able to develop the contacts necessary to meet Mr Brown.

Rather than choosing their pornography from a set of limited options, consumers actively shaped the types of pornography produced. Kenneth Sydney Richards, filling out an order form for nude photographs, specified the following details: "One 6/- Set

Unretouched Anatomical Studies preferably assorted male and female, failing this all Female, age of model 20/21 years."[80] The supplier of Richards's photographs, George Cox, was also referred to other customers, who preferred unretouched (ie., featuring visible pubic hair) photographs and who had requested such materials from firms that sold only altered photos.[81] Some consumers demanded more specific materials. An intercepted order request sent by R.D. Thompson to a Trieste pornographer included a sketch showing the poses he wanted depicted in the photographs, including the specific elements of a standing man masturbating in the presence of a second, seated figure.[82] Some photography companies, many of which advertised in American pulp fiction magazines available to British consumers, catered to customers who desired made-to-order pornography. Wisconsin-based pornography outfit Maorman Publishing Co., for example, employed an "acrobatic" female model who did "special requests."[83]

In the few cases that provide specific information regarding consumption, suppliers catered to a variety of interests. For example, the supply ledger seized from Irene England and Charles Domec-Carre contained a lengthy list of abbreviations describing the type of material requested by clients, including the following: "Flag=Flagellation, Vamp=Vampire, Org=Orgy, Les=Lesbian, P=Piss, and Hom=Homosexual."[84] As in the case of the Benbow and Hyde network, these customers did not necessarily share sexual object choice or even a common thematic interest such as flagellation. Despite their differences in sexual interests, these several dozen customers interacted with each other as well as with their suppliers. Police reports from the England/Domec-Carre case described a lending library system in which customers could donate and exchange books and other materials.[85] As these examples demonstrate, relationships between producer, distributor, and purchaser often occurred as a negotiated process of communication through long-standing and established networks. Moreover, cases like Steer's illustrate that the line between consumer and distributor could be a blurry one. This is not to suggest that consumers, distributors, and producers all experienced these networks in the same way or that they shared precisely the same views and interpretations of pornographic materials; consumers, after all, ran far less of a risk and could extricate themselves from the world of pornography far more easily than someone participating in these activities for profit. The repeated and long-term nature of much of this interaction between consumers and pornographers, however, does point to the importance of networks and personal ties for the continuing operations of the British pornography trade.

PORNOGRAPHIC MODELS

No actor involved in the pornography trade played a more visible part yet has left less of a trace in the archive than the model. Modelling was not itself a crime, meaning that models did not generally make their way into police or court records unless they were also involved in other aspects of the trade.[86] As a result, conclusive evidence regarding the working conditions or social status of pornographic models remains elusive. Given the small amount of information available for models working specifically in the British context, this section expands its scope to include models working in the US and Continental Europe. This is, of course, a problematic choice. As will become clear in chapter 2, experiences and material realities of the pornography trade varied significantly according to locale. We cannot, therefore, assume that the experience of a pornographic model in Germany or the US matched that of a British model. Despite these concerns, however, the significance of models to the pornography trade demands consideration. Examples of models' experience outside of Britain provides, if nothing else, a range of possibilities for the roles models might play in the trade.

Newspaper advertisements provide cursory information about pornographic models operating in the British context. Regional and national newspapers included frequent advertisements for "artists' models," a category that encompassed models sitting for painters and other "legitimate" artists as well as for pornographic materials.[87] A survey of artists' model advertisements yields no information about pay or the details of working conditions. Such ads do, however, indicate that models posted their own ads and responded to postings by photographers. For example, one 1941 ad featured in the *Gloucester Echo* read "Artist's and photographic model seeks engagements; moderate fee," while another ad posted two years later in the same paper read, "Attractive girl reqd. as photographer's model."[88] While pornography is often associated with a sprawling metropolis like London, ads posted in British newspapers requested the services of models in a variety of locations; for instance, at least three separate ads involving nude modelling listed a contact address in Cheltenham, while several others advertised in Nottingham or Gloucestershire.[89] These ads provide little information about the class or background of the women involved, but the use of classified advertising to communicate and book appointments does suggest that pornographic models were not necessarily destitute or chosen solely on the basis of easy availability. On the basis of these artists' model ads, therefore, we can conclude that modelling was a relatively selective process that required time to establish contact between model and photographer, rather than being a slapdash or spontaneous activity.

A handful of models came to the attention of the British press for unrelated scandals or criminal activities, offering us glimpses of some women involved in the trade. In 1940, twenty-year-old model Dolores Christina Riszton, a.k.a. Beatrice Christina Whittington, faced charges for the use of a false name. This charge seems to have been a pretense used to intervene on the matter of her frequent fraternization with RAF officers, an activity that may or may not have been sex work.[90] In 1948, one seventeen-year-old model named Catherine Ridout faced armed robbery charges after staging a holdup involving a pepper pot as a "gun."[91] While these two cases indicate that modelling was a sideline to prostitution or criminal activities, other stories point to models of slightly better means. For instance, one story reported on a well-known Hungarian conductor who faced lawsuits for maintenance after fathering children by several women, including an unnamed artists' model.[92] Given that this unnamed model had the wherewithal and capacity to bring suit against a wealthy and relatively famous man, this woman probably did not come from the same economic background as Catherine Ridout.

While pornographic modelling is often framed as a female activity, men appeared in pornographic photographs and films as well. Like their female counterparts, they typically came to the attention of newspapers or law enforcement after committing crimes unrelated to their modelling work. For example, when seventeen-year-old Gerardo Cappuccitto stood trial for murder in 1903, his occupation as an artists' model received little more than a passing mention by a witness. As in the case of several of the female models mentioned above, Cappuccitto does not appear to have been destitute; he lived with several relatives who testified in his defence. One of these relatives, a female cousin, also worked as an artists' model.[93] Four years later, thirty-year-old Joseph Luccioni and his brother Frederick stood trial for theft. While employed as a waiter and involved in various forms of petty crime at the time of his arrest, Joseph was also known as a former artists' model.[94] To be clear, these records contain no evidence regarding the precise nature of either man's modelling activities, and it is entirely possible that neither was involved in anything remotely pornographic. Moreover, two isolated cases hardly constitute a clear pattern or trend. Given the paucity of records concerning models, however, it is worth considering the implications of these rare examples. Both men lived in London's Italian immigrant community, both subsisted on modest incomes based largely on manual labour, and neither man appeared to exist in a state of extreme deprivation or poverty. These factors, as well as the existence of multiple artists' models in a single family, point yet again to the conclusion that modelling served as an economic option for marginalized members of British society, such as Italian immigrants, but that it was not the kind of last resort often associated with other forms of sex work.

One of the few well-documented British arrests involving a male pornographic model concerns Richard Elias, a Polish immigrant and grocer. Elias began producing and distributing pornographic photographs after encountering financial difficulties with his grocery store. In addition to acting as photographer and distributor, Elias performed in many of the photographs. Some of the photographs also featured his live-in partner and another female acquaintance.[95] As this case illustrates, the distinctions between producer, distributor, and performer were often ambiguous. Under the right circumstances, a grocer selling pornographic photographs on the side could quickly become a producer and model. Moreover, the models appearing in the photographs had a personal relationship that preceded their professional one.

The Elias case also offers support for the idea that women posing in pornographic photographs sometimes worked as prostitutes. In response to an inquiry regarding one of the photographs, Elias's female partner interjected that customers could purchase not only the photographs, but "the models as well." Elias went on to explain that he could arrange for customers to get in touch or have a private meeting with any of the women posing in his photographs.[96] While this does not mean that all or even the majority of women posing for pornographic photos could be classified as prostitutes; it does imply that work as a nude model could be linked to other forms of sex work. The fact that Elias's female partner made the initial offer of prostitution, however, casts doubt on the hierarchical female prostitute/male pimp dynamic expected in such scenarios.

Aside from the rare example of Richard Elias, information about male models and performers is as fragmented as the facts surrounding female models. Visual details of pornographic ephemera, however, provide hints of their background. For example, men performing in pornographic films of the 1920s and 1930s often appeared in fake mustaches or other obvious disguises intended to conceal their facial features; female performers, in contrast, rarely if ever adopted such costumes.[97] Male performers may have perceived greater threats to their reputation or legal standing if they were recognized, which suggests that they appeared only in the occasional film or photograph and otherwise operated in mainstream contexts. Another significant detail is the frequent appearance of tattoos on male models and performers, particularly those posing for homoerotic photographs (see figure 1.3).[98] Before the Second World War, less than 10 per cent of the American population had a tattoo, yet as many as 90 per cent of enlisted men in military branches acquired at least one tattoo while in service, indicating that many male models were drawn from the same populations of

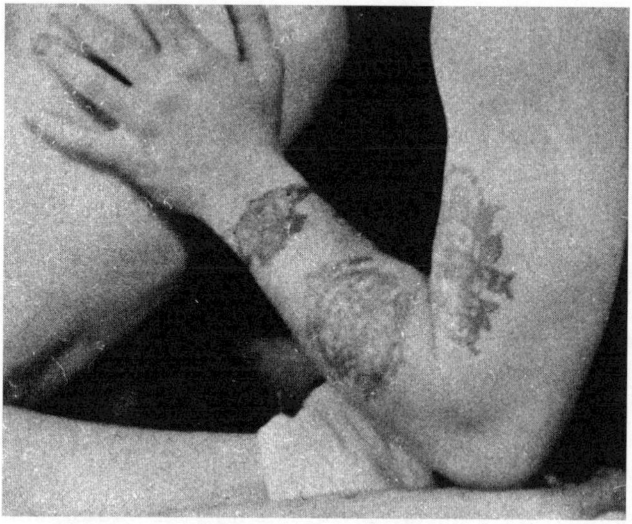

Figure 1.3 | Detail of man's tattooed arm in homoerotic photograph, undated.

working poor that made up enlisted men and sailors.[99] Notably, these tattooed men rarely appeared in disguise or with faces covered, unlike their non-tattooed counterparts. While these scattered pieces of evidence are far from conclusive, they do indicate that both male and female models generally came from working-class backgrounds. Despite this general trend, some middle-class or wealthy people also posed for erotic photographs.

PERSONAL TIES AND NON-COMMERCIAL PORNOGRAPHY, 1900–1945

Examples of middle-class or well-off people appearing in pornographic photos brings us to an important aspect of the early twentieth-century pornography trade: the prevalence of friendships, sexual relationships, and familial ties among people occupying different roles in the trade. Middle-class or wealthier people who posed for pornographic photos, for example, were typically married to or had some other personal relationship with the photographer. As discussed above, Richard Elias and his partner posed together for pornographic photographs. In other cases, only one-half of the couple posed before the camera. After leaving Britain, John Willie married his favourite boot and corset model, Holly Faram.[100] The French company Yva Richard adopted a similar arrangement, the wife modelling for photographs and the husband operating as photographer. This pairing, however, appears to have been a more equitable partnership than that of John Willie and Holly; the company's name, for example, derived from the first names of each (Nativa and Richard).[101] Other husband–wife pairs owned and operated nude photography studios. Studio Manasse, which supplied many of the studio-style nudes used in American pulp fiction magazines, was owned and operated by Olga and Adorjan Wlassics, a Hungarian couple based in Vienna. Olga maintained the studio and its signature style well after Adorjan's death, illustrating that she had significant involvement in the photography apart from modelling.[102] While London-based couple Irene England and Charles Domec-Carre produced pornographic photographs from 1939 until their arrest in 1958, British records contain fewer examples of husband–wife pairs than in Continental Europe.[103]

People connected by other personal relationships also collaborated on the sale of pornographic products. According to the testimony of a former employee, erotic book publisher Henry Sidney Nichols worked alongside his family. Nichols's stepdaughter, Miss Horsefield, not only owned part of the operation but acted as treasurer and handled many of the business's finances.[104] In another London-based pornography operation, Charles Haynes Jr followed in his father's footsteps by selling albums of erotic photos.[105] Outside of Britain, Wilhelm von Gloeden shared both personal and professional connections with at least two other photographers. His cousin, Guglielmo Pluschow, originally taught von Gloeden certain aspects of photography and later began photographing male nudes in the same Arcadian style.[106] Vincenzo Galdi, who worked in Pluschow's Rome studio and may have been either a relative or a lover of the older photographer, also adopted nude photography as a trade.[107] These three men exemplify the intertwined nature of the personal and professional in the early twentieth-century pornography trade. They shared family ties and other social connections, but they also developed similar business practices and visual styles.

The significance of personal relationships goes well beyond connections between models and photographers. Consumers and collectors exchanged graphically sexual letters or nude photographs, sometimes without any profit motive. While some of these people employed pen pal services that charged fees for placing individuals in contact with each other, others found companions with whom to exchange pornographic letters and images through other means.[108] One unnamed man, convicted in 1941 of sending nude photographs through the post, found pen pals through the advertisement section of a nudist periodical. His arrest led to the imprisonment of several of his correspondents, non-commercial pornography writers and enthusiasts who resided in various locations across England.[109] During that same year, London police arrested a grocer and a hotel manager for screening pornographic films in a hotel room, a practice consistent with the interwar custom of private screenings at shifting locations.[110] Significantly, the grocer did not charge admission and had no apparent financial incentive to screen films for a public audience. The film screenings clearly held social rather than economic significance.

The case of Methodist lay minister Harold Hall provides important insights into the ways in which Britons produced and exchanged non-commercial pornography. Hall, charged in 1949 with sending obscene materials through the post, claimed that he had established contact with a man named Delling for the purpose of gathering a dossier of evidence on the pornography trade for the police.[111] Despite numerous letters of support from the Methodist church leadership, several aspects of the story make Hall's claims of pure motives questionable. His letters contained not only requests for erotic photographs of Delling, which arguably should have provided sufficient evidence for his dossier without continuing the correspondence, but also lengthy pornographic scenarios featuring Hall and his wife, Betty. In addition, one of Hall's letters indicated that he had previously sent a graphic pornographic photo of Betty and himself to Delling. While the letters and photographs Delling sent to Hall are not in the case file, Hall's letters contain several interesting features. Rather than going directly into pornographic content, the first letter exchange focused on introductions and a friendly discussion of interests and hobbies. Once the letters became pornographic, they featured Hall and his wife as the central players, using Delling's nude photographs and letters as a major component of the sexual scenario. As a result, the erotic fantasies were highly personalized rather than generic descriptions of sexual acts.[112]

In addition to Harold Hall, other married or partnered couples employed pornographic letter-exchange services. The letter-exchange sections found in American pulp fiction magazines seized by British authorities contained numerous letters claiming to be from married couples who wished to correspond with singles or other couples. These requests for pen pals promised to exchange photographs as well as personal stories of the couple's "experiences."[113] While the use of pseudonyms and long-distance communication renders it impossible to confirm that any given letter was actually produced by a married couple, the repeated appearance of these requests suggests that married couples' participation in erotic correspondence enjoyed acceptance among networks of people who exchanged pornographic materials in a non-commercial setting.

In some cases, non-commercial pornography was used for criminal harassment. In 1923, an unknown adult, whom police determined to be highly educated and an Englishman based on his writing style, sent a graphically pornographic story involving an intergenerational sexual relationship to a male student at Eton.[114] In another incident, a highly publicized 1936 criminal case involved a man named Frederick Holeman, who sent pornographic letters to the parents of several young women. These letters included lengthy descriptions of the girls' fictional sexual misdeeds as well as detailed instructions on the forms of disciplinary canings they should receive.[115] In the case of Anatole James, the use of pornography as a method of harassment expressed clear class-based antipathy. All of the men who received his graphically pornographic poems and letters attended Eton or held aristocratic titles. James had particularly strong feelings toward one target, an Eton don who had received a citation for violating blackout regulations. James, in contrast, trained as an electrician and never attended a university.[116]

In these cases, then, the personal needs met by the pornography trade included not only achieving sexual fulfillment, but also venting other emotional or social frustrations like class-based anger. Regardless of individual motive, however, the documented existence of ongoing non-commercial pornography exchanges requires us to broaden our understanding of the spaces in which pornography circulated and the experiences of those who produced and consumed it. We now turn to the question of the specific ways in which both commercial and non-commercial pornography travelled from place to place and from creator to consumer.

METHODS OF OPERATION

British pornographers and consumers utilized all available methods of communication, ranging from face-to-face contact to anonymous newspaper advertisements. In-person solicitation of customers sufficed as a way of making contact with more casual consumers, while the use of advertising or the postal service had the potential to reach more customers but also required more effort and knowledge of pornography networks. Face-to-face solicitation generally occurred in highly public venues such as markets and streets. Arthur Sandford, for example, came to the attention of police after selling pornographic postcards near bookstalls at the Farringdon Market.[117] In 1929 defendant Edward Duplex sold indecent prints to spectators at a Manchester football match.[118] In these cases, customers would not necessarily have any particular knowledge of the pornography trade, could easily have been one-time buyers, and may not have had consistent involvement in a distribution network.

In contrast to one-time personal transactions, communication through newspapers and the post required a deeper understanding of norms and practices of distribution networks, including specialized slang and jargon. In the pre-1945 British pornography trade, these terms frequently appeared in written communication. While some terms may have been recognizable to a broad customer base, others probably would only be familiar to those acquainted with certain sub-genres of pornography. Advertisements found in British newspapers and foreign pulp fiction magazines employed euphemistic terminology designed to provide a signal to those who understood the vocabularies of pornography distribution without alerting the casual viewer. "Tight lacing," for example, indicated materials specifically designed for corset and bondage enthusiasts.[119] "Action photo" meant depictions of sexual acts rather than an artistic nude pose.[120] "Classical" was understood as code for homoerotic pornography or images of nude men and boys.[121] Numerous pornographic books and magazines, regardless of country of origin, included references to Hollywood, Broadway, or Paris in their titles, thereby exploiting the reputation of France, California, and New York as modern-day Babylons.[122] While the pornography trade was by no means a unified monolith and there was considerable variation between the norms and language of specific networks or producers, the frequent appearance of these terms and themes indicates the existence of a common vocabulary that would have been understood across different parts of the trade.

Disclaimers appeared as a standard element of advertisements and order forms. Customers who purchased photographs through mail-order frequently signed a statement certifying that they attended school as art or biology students, thereby maintaining the fiction that erotic nudes were produced as educational materials. For example, bondage photography distributors Eric Sheldon Haynes and George Harry Cox included a section on their order forms certifying that the purchaser was at least eighteen years old and an art student buying the photographs for legitimate study of the human form.[123] Other publishing companies and distributors included similar requirements on their catalogues, specifying that certain materials could be sold only to students or professionals of medical disciplines. The Esoterika Biblion Society, for example, stated in a catalogue that only medical professionals could purchase copies of William Stekel's *Pamphlet for Sadism and Masochism*.[124] None of these operations had any kind of system to verify claims of art-student or physician status, but the ubiquity of such forms demonstrates the utility of these minimal legal protections. Customers familiar with the language and practices of pornographers would have understood such disclaimers as a formality and not a serious bar to purchasing materials, a reality that may not have been so apparent to the inexperienced eye.

Pornographers and their customers adopted a variety of practices designed to guard against detection and prosecution. Irene England and Charles Domec-Carre kept a ledger in which each private client had an assigned number rather than a name.[125] The use of pseudonyms was a common and expected aspect of interaction with fellow pornographers, seen in examples such as Leonard Steer's assumption that he had not been given his supplier's legal name.[126] The use of pseudonyms, however, clearly did not preclude long-standing business and personal relationships. Calls for letters posted in letter-exchange services, for example, usually used only a first name, and there is no evidence to suggest that those involved would have received greater knowledge of their pen pals' identities, yet these letters referred to ongoing communications between the pseudonymous writers.[127]

Simple measures such as sealed envelopes afforded some dealers a measure of plausible deniability. British authorities recognized different "classes" of sellers depending on whether they opened packages prior to sale. Those who restricted their trade to sealed envelopes could plausibly argue that they did not know the contents (usually typed pornographic short stories or photographs), although this did not entirely insulate them from prosecution.[128] Those who traded solely in sealed envelopes typically dealt in pornography on a small scale through bookstores and tobacco shops. Other sellers took similar precautions to conceal the precise nature of the materials sold. Businessman H.R. Hales, whom police suspected of importing pornographic films from Hamburg, claimed that he ordered a variety of films from his suppliers and did not watch any of them or know their exact contents.[129] Police and customs officers considered these sellers less harmful than the "pernicious" class of sellers who knew the contents of their packages and concealed them from the authorities.[130] While it is unlikely that the trade truly adhered to this strict binary between the ignorant and knowledgeable seller, some casual sellers took steps to limit their involvement in the trade and thus were unlikely to be involved in production or large-scale distribution of pornography.

Lending libraries and subscription services also helped to maintain anonymity and security of participants. The lending library system run by Irene England and Charles Domec-Carre allowed the operation to function as a largely enclosed system of thirty to forty participants. In addition to helping them escape detection, the lending library system reduced costs as it allowed participants to use and return materials rather than requiring new prints or stories to be produced for each transaction.[131] Larger and better-known sellers, such as the Erotika Biblion Society of London and New York, used the lending library system in order to argue that the organization should be classified as a private club rather than a commercial pornography outfit.[132] All of these measures may have had the purely practical purpose of reducing the risk of detection, but they also had the cultural effect of binding participants together into tighter social networks dependent on repeated interaction rather than isolated transactions.

DEMOGRAPHICS OF THE BRITISH PORNOGRAPHY TRADE

As the examples given in the preceding sections indicate, few generalizations can be made regarding the class, gender, national origin, or profession of those active in pornography distribution or consumption. However, some clear trends do emerge. For example, male pornographers outnumbered female pornographers, and immigrants were disproportionately represented among those facing obscenity charges. Lower-middle-class workers such as booksellers, salesmen, and grocers appeared frequently. Many of those arrested had previous convictions and participated in the trade for an extended period of time. Very few producers and distributors performed a single exclusive set of services or dealt only in one product; participation in the pornography industry required a fairly broad skill set, including photography, bookkeeping and record management, and writing short pornographic stories. Additionally, it involved business relationships with other pornographers, both within Britain and abroad.

Customers also came in many varieties. The professional background of those exposed as purchasers of indecent materials ranged from Cambridge student to clerk.[133] More male than female names appeared on seized packages and address lists. Within the Benbow and Hyde network, the ratio of male to female names was thirteen to seven, with four sexually ambiguous names.[134] Professionally published novels and films would have been prohibitively expensive for many (for example, a film discussed by Benbow cost £8), but a set of twenty imported French photographs and postcards sold for 6s during the 1920s.[135] Customers could purchase domestically produced pornography for as little as sixpence for four photographs.[136] Pornography was therefore accessible to a wide range of classes.[137] The sexual proclivities of pornography consumers also appear extremely diverse. Order forms and materials purchased include heterosexual and homoerotic themes, violent BDSM and studio nudes, and relatively unusual scenarios such as bestiality or vampirism.

Women appeared in police files, court records, and newspaper reports as customers, distributors, and producers. These anecdotal examples raise questions about the position of women and the role of gender in these networks. While available evidence does not allow for any quantitative assessments of the number of women in the trade or gendered differences in their participation, known examples of women in the pornography trade illustrate the possibilities and limitations for female participation in production and distribution networks. The frequent use of female names or pseudonyms clearly indicates that pornography networks generally accepted the presence of female producers, writers, and distributors as normal or even desirable. Pornography operations outside of Britain also offer some hints as to the possibilities of female participation. Some foreign women, particularly in France, owned their own bookshops or photography studios and clearly occupied a position of relative strength within pornography networks.[138] Moreover, these overseas female suppliers interacted with local British intermediaries like Leonard William Steer, contributing to a larger environment of female participation within British networks.

A member of Benbow and Hyde's circle, Madame Carmen Corti, provides one of the few detailed examples of a woman involved in the British pornography trade. A customer in the Benbow-Hyde network, Corti sought a variety of materials including books and letters. These materials could have been intended for either personal or professional use. At the time of her arrest in 1923 for violation of the Alien Registration Act, police found pornographic photographs alongside whips, dildos, and other paraphernalia related to her work in prostitution.[139] A woman of colour, Corti alternately claimed that she was an American "mulatto" from New Orleans and that she held British subject status as one born in the West Indies.[140] Authorities could verify neither of these claims and as a result released her after ten weeks of detention.

While pornography may have been incidental to events like Corti's arrest and near-deportation, her story offers a rare look at one participant in the early twentieth-century pornography trade. Pornography clearly featured in her professional life, as police discovered nude photographs of her among prostitution-related materials.[141] As a sex worker, immigrant, and woman of colour, she occupied a marginal social position. She did not, however, live in dire poverty. The inventory of her flat's contents indicated several rooms and expensive items such as mahogany furniture and silk wall hangings.[142] Corti also displayed considerable agency and independence. While in contact with Benbow and Hyde, she actively employed the network to solicit clients.[143] After her release from detention, rather than simply return to her previous activities, she brought suit against the office of the Secretary of State for lost income and the cost of possessions seized during her incarceration.[144] For Carmen Corti, participation in the pornography trade was one of several characteristics that contributed to her social and legal marginalization. Like many others involved in pornography, however, she did not quietly accept this marginalization but actively resisted the intervention of authorities. Police reports and trial records of the Edwardian and interwar periods reveal this striking and consistent pattern. Those active in the pornography trade consistently protested and worked against interference, despite the fact that these protests rarely succeeded. This persistent opposition to official interference and continuing participation in the trade leads us to a series of other questions, particularly since, as shown throughout this chapter, it does not seem that involvement in the pornography trade was highly remunerative. The question of why people would continue to involve themselves in the pornography trade despite limited material or economic benefits brings us to this chapter's final question: what does it mean to view the British pornography trade through the lens of queerness?

PORNOGRAPHY AND QUEERNESS

As discussed in the Introduction, queer history requires us to focus on the ways in which specific identity categories, practices, and behaviours become constructed as normative or deviant, and how normativity confers status and privilege just as deviance leads to various forms of marginalization. Applying this focus to the early twentieth-century British pornography networks discussed in this chapter illustrates several key ways in which pornography's deviant status worked to marginalize and limit options for those involved in the trade. People who bought and sold pornography faced potential arrest, public humiliation, and other social and legal penalties. To avoid such outcomes, participants in pornography networks went to great lengths to establish safer forms of interaction such as long-distance communication, ongoing associations with "safe" or reliable acquaintances, and the operation of discreet, behind-the-counter operations less likely to attract official notice. In other words, the logics underlying the day-to-day practices of the pornography trade come into focus when we consider how pornography and those associated with it were excluded from mainstream sexual norms.

Queerness is not, however, a passive category imposed from above. To queer is, as argued by Nikki Sullivan, "to make strange, to counteract, to delegitimize … heteronormative knowledges and institutions."[145] In other words, to view a social group or category as queer implies either deliberate or implicit resistance or critiques to surrounding heteronormative systems. Pornography, like other queer spaces and practices, served as a site of contestation because it created spaces for a marginalized sexual practice to flourish in the face of mainstream models of correct sexuality. Queering the early twentieth-century pornography trade is not a matter of assigning an identity label to those active in the trade or arguing for a cohesive political consciousness like that of the contemporary Western LGBTQ+ movement; indeed, the people discussed in this chapter certainly did not conceive of themselves in such terms. Viewing early twentieth-century pornography through a queer lens is critical because it calls attention not only to how pornography was constructed as deviant, but also to the ways in which the queer economy of pornography worked to critique and destabilize normative standards.

To view the pornography trade through a queer lens therefore requires attention to relationships and conflicts both within the pornography trade and between the trade and the surrounding heteronormative forces of state and civil society. In other words, we must consider the question of why pornography was not just a commodity like any other, and what its status meant for those involved. In addition, we must ask what threat pornography posed and how it served to challenge overarching systems of heteronormativity. This brings us back to the central topic of this chapter: the material practices and social interactions of pornography producers, distributors, and consumers. As this chapter's analysis has shown, those involved in the porn trade organized themselves into informal networks for the purpose of exchanging either commercial or non-commercial pornography. These networks involved specialized jargon, clandestine communication, strategies to avoid wider public detection, and the development of long-term connections among those making pornography and those wishing to purchase it. In many cases, such as the Benbow-Hyde network, connections formed between participants crossed social boundaries and categories that would have separated those participants in other, more normative contexts. While they did not resemble LGBT communities or other groups more often classified as "queer," this category of people was clearly constructed as deviant by larger systems of heteronormativity. Moreover, since participation in pornography networks required an active effort, attempts to make, sell, and consume pornography constituted at least implicit resistance to normative sexuality. Later chapters will explore the relationship between the pornography trade and heteronormative forces of state and civil society in greater detail. As this chapter has shown, however, queerness exists not just as an abstract quality or as a subset of some massive category labelled "British sexuality," but as a phenomenon whose history can be traced through close attention to material conditions and systems of production. In other words, the quotidian details of what pornographers and consumers did – where they worked, what materials they made, how they made them, and what those materials cost – tells us a great deal about their place in British society and their relationship to sexual normativity.

CONCLUSION

In this chapter, I have attempted to illuminate the common practices and material conditions of the early twentieth-century pornography trade. At its most basic level, this evidence conclusively shows that British pornography producers remained active in the country well after notable publishers like Charles Carrington fled to Paris. Richard Elias still took pornographic photos, Irene England typed stories, Alexander Bloom printed postcards, and untold numbers of Britons created pornographic photographs and letters for exchange through the post. Beyond this evidence, however, analyzing these practices and conditions leads to larger conclusions regarding queerness and its place in the pornography trade. A queer analysis forces us to reassess the relationship between pornography and mainstream culture. Rather than existing as the "dark" or "hidden" side of mainstream sexuality, the pornography trade developed its own social networks, vocabularies, and practices that deviated from British social categories and hierarchies. The trade and those active in it stood in many ways in opposition to mainstream norms; its businesses and social networks cut across boundaries of ethnicity, gender, and class in ways that clearly did not reflect acceptable social interaction in mainstream culture. In addition, members of pornography networks defended their activities, resisted official intervention, and co-operated to avoid prosecution. For men like Mervyn Hyde and women like Carmen Corti, the pornography trade offered sexual and social options unavailable elsewhere.

Despite these frequent displays of oppositional values, it would be incorrect to think of the pornography trade as a criminal underworld or as an isolated group of social outcasts. Participants in the pornography trade negotiated both mainstream and queer venues, moderating their behaviour depending on context. Married couples who exchanged pornographic photographs and letters with pen pals, for example, participated in a heteronormative institution while engaging in a queer practice. British citizens such as teachers or ministers who consumed pornography in their spare time existed both within and outside the boundaries of heteronormative respectability. The pornography trade thus represented a subversive element in early twentieth-century Britain, but it was not an isolated anomaly. The following chapter adopts a wider view, exploring how transnational forces helped to shape the localized trade and how it, in turn, contributed to the increasingly transnational culture of pornography.

CHAPTER TWO

"An Enormous Business to Be Done"

Britain in the Transnational Pornography Trade

On 19 April 1922, sorters at the General Post Office (GPO) discovered two pornographic films in a box addressed to João de Brito, a London resident who had immigrated from Portugal in 1915. The box, which the sorters examined because the highly flammable celluloid reels had not been packed according to regulations, had been mailed from Lisbon by a Manuel de Sousa. The subsequent investigation by the London Metropolitan Police revealed that João de Brito worked as a sales manager for Messrs Salzac Film Company Ltd., a firm specializing in importing films to Britain and exporting others to Spain and the rest of Europe. The police, upon discovering that de Brito had travelled to Calais two months before the film shipment was seized, surmised that he had gone from Calais to Portugal to purchase the pornographic films and arrange for their transport. De Brito denied that he had travelled to Portugal, claiming instead that he had visited Spain to secure non-pornographic film orders for his employers; the pornographic films, he suggested, might have been sent as a prank or a gift. The Home Office, hearing of the case, inquired into Manuel de Sousa and found that he held a position in the Portuguese Colonial Office. While convinced of de Brito's guilt, the lead detective's case failed due to his inability to secure a confession or investigate de Sousa.[1]

As it became clear that the police lacked sufficient evidence to charge de Brito with deliberately importing obscene materials, Home Office officials quietly evaluated the possibility of deporting him without formal charges. They noted that the incident had the dubious distinction of being the first known case of pornographic films being imported onto British soil from abroad and expressed concerns that it represented the beginning of a dangerous trend. As such, their primary concern centred on removing de Brito before he had the opportunity to introduce any additional foreign moral contaminants to the British public. After examining de Brito's correspondence and securing further interviews with him, however, the Office of the Undersecretary of State, the Investigative Unit of the General Post Office, and the London Metropolitan Police all agreed that they could find no legitimate grounds for deportation or other penalties. Deportation efforts were abandoned, with one investigator observing (with, I would argue, a high degree of optimism), "Doubtless the shock [de Brito] has received will not be soon forgotten."[2]

Despite numerous unanswered questions regarding João de Brito's intentions for the films and the extent of his involvement in pornography distribution, his case illustrates several key points about the transnational dimensions of the early twentieth-century British pornography trade. Like many of those involved in pornography distribution, de Brito had extensive contacts outside of Britain. Moreover, his alleged supplier worked in his own country's colonial administration, a position providing de Brito with indirect access to imperial markets and cultural flows. The de Brito case's status as Britain's first recorded instance of an imported pornographic film sheds light on the important position immigrants occupied as intermediaries and agents who introduced new materials and technologies into local networks. Finally, the British government's ultimate failure to prosecute or deport de Brito despite overwhelming circumstantial evidence and a highly implausible defence provides an example of how operating through a transnational distribution network rather than buying and selling on a strictly local level could be a strategy designed to protect against legal penalties.

While chapter 1 explored the complexities of local networks involved in Britain's pornography trade, examples like the de Brito case force us to expand our scope to consider much larger transnational systems. While both world wars temporarily impeded British access to overseas commerce, the Edwardian and interwar pornography trade operated within a system of transnational networks, with people like de Brito forming connections between participants in different locales. This transnational element has important implications for an analysis of Britain's local pornography trade. The local and the transnational did not exist as binary opposites. Rather, transnational cultural flows and economic systems were apparent on the local level. Conversely, local forces affected the movement of products and ideas through transnational networks. British pornography networks thus adopted certain characteristics and forms of interaction due to their position as nodes in a transnational network, as well as in response to cultural and economic forces particular to Britain and its empire. One should remain aware, therefore, that other pornography cultures involved in this same transnational system organized very differently than the British case due to their own specific local pressures.

Despite these differences in how national and local pornography cultures would have formed within larger transnational systems, there are numerous, striking points of similarity in patterns of transnational activity between pornographers and their customers in Britain, the US, and Continental Europe. Men and women like João de Brito had to operate within and across multiple cultural contexts, developing common business practices and forms of communication. By taking a close look at the lives and experiences of these intermediaries and expatriate producers the transnational systems they operated within come into focus. Attention to transnational connections in the pornography trade not only provides an additional layer of complexity to our understanding of the material practices and spaces of the British pornography trade, but also provides important context for understanding the regulatory responses of the state and the concerns of British civil society; as a range of scholars including Matt Houlbrook and Anne McClintock have illustrated, the same processes that labelled groups like British pornography networks as deviant also policed racial, national, and imperial categories, thus promoting concepts of Britishness juxtaposed against the foreign Other.[3] Transnational activities thus facilitated the flow of pornography and provided advantages to some participants in pornography networks, but they also reinforced many of the cultural narratives that ensured that pornography, as a deviant practice, was limited to certain spaces. In order to more fully comprehend narratives of foreign intrusion and cultural pollution and their relationship to early twentieth-century British heteronormativity, we must first delve deeper into the transnational processes that facilitated the pornography trade.

TRANSNATIONAL BRITAIN

Early twentieth-century Britons lived in a world of increasing transnational connectivity. The development of colonial holdings across the globe created infrastructure and trade routes that facilitated the flow of people, goods, and cultural practices between Britain and the rest of the world. Beyond imperial connections, improved transportation capabilities made travel to the Continent and North America safer and more practical than it had been in previous centuries. Within Britain, this transnational connectivity had varied results. In urban centres like London's Soho, many Britons embraced the cosmopolitanism that came with close and frequent contact with immigrants, travellers, and commodities from around the world. Restaurants offered Italian cuisine, jazz clubs employed Afro-Caribbean musicians, and average Britons bought books and magazines imported from other countries and written in a variety of languages.[4]

This transnational connectivity did not, however, result in universal cosmopolitan appreciation of new food and music. Immigration and the white supremacist ideology undergirding the imperial project contributed to a sense of anxiety surrounding race and nationality. Xenophobia increased during the bloody chaos of the First World War, which led many Britons to question the safety of Britain's position in the world.[5] While Asians and West Indians formed a crucial part of the war effort between 1914 and 1918, their presence in British port cities was met with race riots in 1919.[6] Non-colonial migrants such as Spanish and Jewish populations also appeared as a eugenic threat in medico-scientific and popular discourse. In some circles, this anti-immigrant racist anxiety contributed to the development of British fascist sentiments prior to the Second World War.[7] Many of these fears took on a specifically gendered tone, with miscegenation and pronatalist imperial duty featured as central to the rhetoric surrounding anti-immigrant riots and policy.[8] In short, early twentieth-century Britons existed in a state of tension between their desire for the material benefits of transnational connectivity and their fears over the cultural change that would be wrought by those same connections.

Where did pornography fit within this tense and contested transnational context? As historians like Matt Cook have argued in regards to sexology and homosexual communities, frequent travel and socio-economic ties between the world's largest cities could produce transnational or "pan-national" discourses of sexuality.[9] In the pornography trade, however, transnational discourses incorporated a far broader range of participants than sexologists and middle-class male travellers. Much like sexual relationships between colonial migrants and British subjects or between men of different nationalities, pornography forged transnational connections between individuals and communities.[10] Unlike physical sexual encounters, however, pornography could create these connections from a distance. While several cases discussed here involved the formal international migration of suspected or convicted pornographers, the transnational systems of the early twentieth-century pornography trade typically involved networks created through long-distance contact. While the sexual connections made within the pornography trade primarily involved fantasy rather than skin-to-skin contact, these interactions nevertheless created cultural ties and communities that spanned the boundaries of nations and empires. For many of the people discussed in this chapter, both economic prosperity and sexual fulfillment could hinge upon interactions with customers or partners halfway around the world. In the case of the pre-1945 pornography trade, then, the significance of sex in building a transnational community is clear.

The transnational nature of the trade also shaped the content produced. As surviving examples of pornographic ephemera reveal, pornography produced by and for people of extremely diverse backgrounds contained similar themes and stylistic features. While sexual cultures varied from one nation or region to another, pornography was an area in which these different sexual cultures met and interacted. The same pornographic materials may have held different meanings depending on location and cultural milieu, but the similarities in content indicate that at least some tropes and common themes were already recognized and employed by producers and customers around the globe by the beginning of the twentieth century. In the following sections, I identify the different venues and methods in which these patterns emerged and flowed through transnational networks.

TRANSNATIONAL MAIL-ORDER BUSINESSES

Producers and distributors operating within this transnational pornography trade used a variety of methods in order to conduct their business in relative safety. The best-documented and most frequently discussed pornography distributors were those who operated mail-order businesses. As seen in the previous chapter, mail-order businesses also appeared as a feature of localized British pornography enterprises. Those operating on a transnational level, however, were of a larger and more complex scale. During the early twentieth century, numerous Paris-based mail-order businesses carried on the long-established tradition of catering to their allegedly sexually repressed brethren across the Channel. According to popular opinion and the position of the Home Office, the French bore virtually all responsibility for the circulation of pornography in Britain. While French dealers certainly did not have a monopoly on the pornography market, Paris-based publishers and distributors did print and ship large quantities of pornographic materials to British customers.[11]

Placing the blame for pornography imports on French perversion did, however, ignore one small detail: many of these major Parisian producers were actually expatriate British citizens who relocated to France and operated English-language publishing firms and bookshops. This process began in the nineteenth century, and peaked during the severe anti-pornography efforts undertaken by the British state during the 1890s.[12] By 1903, a flourishing community of English-language publishers and booksellers ran highly visible businesses in the centre of Paris, where they could operate with near-impunity. Their customers included large numbers of British tourists and businessmen who visited these shops during their stay in the city.[13] As most of these customers were temporary visitors, we can only speculate as to how much French-produced pornography arrived on British shores stowed in holiday-goers' luggage.

The owners of these Paris shops and publishing houses represented the most elite group of English-language pornographic publishers. Charles Carrington, born Paul Ferdinando to Portuguese parents in London, enjoyed both admiration and infamy throughout Europe and across the Atlantic. Well after his death in 1922, American and French catalogues advertised books as Carrington reprints, often erroneously, in an effort to capitalize on his name.[14] Due to the strong international reputation of Parisian pornographers, producers in other countries described their products as French or gave their publications French titles, thereby contributing to the widespread misconception that the French completely dominated the trade.[15] As will be discussed at length in chapter 6, however, British state officials were all too happy to let this long-standing misconception go unchallenged in order to support the narrative that pornography was a strictly foreign rather than British issue.

While France remained the largest foreign source of pornography in Britain throughout the first half of the twentieth century, the transnational trade in pornographic goods was not a simple matter of materials and images flowing outward from a Parisian centre. Among other factors, the American pornography trade expanded significantly during the interwar years. After the First World War, American publications began appearing on lists of evidence seized from British pornography distributors. By 1934, local

British constabularies began to identify the United States as the principal source of indecent magazines as well as a prominent supplier of books, postcards, and other materials.[16] In a single year, the Home Office issued destruction orders for over fifty American magazine titles, publications originating in cities across the United States, including New York, Philadelphia, and numerous smaller American towns.[17] In all of these cases, American dealers and British customers employed the postal service rather than engaging in the face-to-face business dealings and lending-library systems that characterized the smaller, local elements of the British trade.

While American and French pornographers received the most attention from British officials, other Continental Europeans also played an important part in the creation of transnational pornography networks. Some Continental mail-order pornographers relocated frequently, taking entire businesses from one country to another. Otto Graul (alias Rudolf Heine), Konrad Mayer, Franz Zhiuk, and Julius Pollak, suspected of selling indecent publications to British customers, all faced arrest in Trieste in 1901. Authorities suspected the group of producing pornographic photographs, printing obscene pamphlets, and circulating advertisements for their products. Graul was born in Frankfurt and, prior to his arrival in Trieste, had distributed pornography in Amsterdam, Budapest, Salzburg, Turin, Bologna, and various other cities across Europe. His frequent moves to new cities, sometimes precipitated by an arrest or prosecution in the previous location, were often accompanied by the adoption of a new pseudonym. Konrad Mayer, who operated as the group's photographer, also relocated on numerous occasions. Originally born in Budapest, he at some point formed a business partnership with Graul and accompanied him to Turin and other locations. Zhiuk and Pollak, both natives of Trieste, joined the operation after Graul and Mayer arrived in the city.[18]

As the arrests of these men show, frequent movement could not completely eliminate the possibility of legal penalties. It did, however, provide them with a certain level of protection. For example, none of the men could be prosecuted for offences committed outside of Italy; they served brief prison sentences in Trieste, but enjoyed immunity from prosecution for selling internationally through the post.[19] The factors that hindered cross-border prosecution in this case also applied to countless others during the early twentieth century. These barriers to prosecution across national borders encouraged both the transnational distribution of products and the movement of bodies, which in turn reinforced the reach of transnational cultural networks into localized nodes.

In addition to frequent relocation, transnational mail-order pornographers developed other strategies to minimize risk. As is apparent from the case of Otto Graul and his associates, the use of pseudonyms was as common in transnational contexts as it was in London's street-level distribution operations. In addition, few businesses depended exclusively on pornography sales. The interwar French company Yva Richard, for example, sold lingerie and clothing designed for boot, corset, and bondage fetishists. The other half of the business consisted of bondage-themed photographs of models wearing Yva Richard products. The company could thus claim that their photos merely advertised the company's apparel and were not intended as pornography.[20] Even those who limited their business ventures to publishing often produced clearly non-pornographic texts along with their pornographic products. These might be controversial and possibly banned texts such as *The Well of Loneliness* or the works of Émile Zola, but some booksellers included large quantities of uncontroversial, unequivocally respectable literature in their catalogues.[21] Such publishing strategies protected printers and distributors from having entire inventories seized and destroyed in the event of a legal challenge.

In all of the examples discussed above, pornographers conducted the majority of their business through the postal service. Beginning around 1900, the Home Office kept lists of known Continental dealers. These lists, in some cases consisting only of names and addresses, nevertheless provide insight into the remarkable diversity of the early Continental postal trade. Most known dealers operated out of Paris, but significant operations could also be found in Barcelona, Rotterdam, and Budapest, with smaller numbers in Milan, Brussels, and other European cities. The majority of dealers had male names, but the Home Office issued arrest warrants for several women as well. These lists also reveal that many dealers remained active in the same city for years. Of the fifteen names listed in 1900, seven remained listed as active dealers twelve years later. Many of the known dealers who began with one location before 1900 expanded their businesses by 1912, in some cases operating in three or more countries.[22] This serves as a testament to the British state's limited ability or willingness to act against foreign pornographers after 1901, since even those whose name and location were well known were apparently safe from the reach of British diplomatic pressures.

All of these dealers mailed books and postcards to customers in Britain, packaging them discreetly and using various pseudonyms and secondary addresses in order to avoid seizure by post office sorters. As a result, a kind of arms race developed between British authorities, who sought to develop a list of known addresses from which to confiscate packages, and pornographers, who responded to seized orders by simply renting a new location or shipping goods from new addresses.[23] These customs and postal searches largely ceased in 1914 due to the assumption that the war in France had cut off the international trade. As discussed in the previous chapter, this wartime policy shift initiated a four-year period of minimal attention to pornography-related issues, although the domestic trade quietly continued for the duration and there is no evidence to suggest that the war significantly reduced the larger systems of transnational trade. In fact, many of the Continental dealers known to the British government in 1900 and 1912 quickly resumed trade with British customers during the interwar years, as seen in several cases discussed below. Since the trade existed in fluid transnational networks rather than in static locations, temporary localized disturbances had little lasting impact. Transnational networks thus resulted not only in shared cultural dialogue and exchange, but in overall stability within the system.

LOCAL AGENTS AND INTERMEDIARIES

During the interwar years, an increasing number of dealers selling to British customers from abroad did so through local intermediaries like João de Brito. As discussed in the previous chapter, Britons became more involved in pornography production during the interwar period compared with the Edwardian years, but they still depended heavily on imported foreign pornography. The local agents and intermediaries employed by foreign pornographers became integrated into the distribution networks that had slowly grown in Britain after the government began to abandon the severe legal policies of the 1890s. These intermediaries typically placed advertisements in British papers before passing domestic orders along to foreign dealers. For example, a Norwich resident named Mr Hahn collaborated with a German dealer, placing ads and funnelling British orders to Germany.[24] Another man in Sunderland, named Summers, engaged in similar work with a dealer in the Netherlands.[25] Both of these intermediaries lived primarily in Britain but made trips to the countries where their suppliers resided.[26] In ways that mirror the divide between the wealthier booksellers and working-class or migrant hawkers within British networks, the experiences of these intermediaries reveal the significant inequalities that existed within the transnational pornography trade. Wholesalers with the means to operate across borders remained relatively safe from prosecution, while their less financially secure local agents took far greater risks. To return to the case discussed at the beginning of the previous chapter, Barcelona-based pornography dealer Ricardo Gennert escaped penalties from British authorities while his British agents Cyril Benbow and Mervyn Hyde were arrested. Despite these risks, the rewards proved tempting to many potential intermediaries. Gennert, communicating with Benbow in 1923, wrote the following: "In 1897–1900 I did enormous business in Great Britain by advertising in 'Photo Bits,' 'Illustrated Bits,' 'Pick-me-up,' 'Judy,' and others, but one day all advts were stopped and even these papers are today no more published ... So I *know* there *is* an enormous business to be done."[27] Gennert went on to offer his contact 33 per cent of all profits if he could secure significant orders rather than small, infrequent sales.[28] In exchange for this high percentage, British agents essentially took on all legal risks in the event of discovery by authorities. It is worth noting, however, that the intermediaries employed by Gennert during the 1920s did not merely revive the systems that had been shut down in 1900, as Gennert describes. Rather, these intermediaries now operated within tighter and more cohesive networks in which intimate, albeit frequently anonymous, interactions with local intermediaries replaced the more passive forms of mail ordering from magazine ads employed by Gennert twenty-five years earlier. Intermediaries may have been at greater risk, but they were also in demand due to the legal and economic realities of interwar Britain.

While Cyril Benbow and Gennert's other agents were British, many of those operating in Britain were immigrants or children of immigrants. Charles Barnick, arrested in London in 1931, was born in Britain to German immigrant parents. Under questioning, Barnick admitted that he obtained his pornographic goods from German suppliers.[29] While records contain no definitive explanation for the prevalence of immigrants in the transnational pornography trade, the connections that people like Charles Barnick and João de Brito had with their own or their parents' countries of origin suggest that language skills may have been a factor. Bilingual residents of Britain would have been particularly well placed to forge business connections between foreign producers and English-speaking British customers. It therefore comes as no surprise that so many of the immigrants arrested for violating obscenity laws had personal or familial ties to countries known for their pornography distribution, such as France, Spain, and Germany.

The examples of Charles Barnick and Ricardo Gennert clearly display the practical benefits of employing local intermediaries in the transnational pornography trade. While Barnick and Benbow eventually faced arrest and prosecution, both Gennert and Barnick's unknown German suppliers remained safely beyond the reach of British law. Ricardo Gennert in particular exemplifies both the stability and adaptability of the early twentieth-century trade; while he and other Continental dealers sometimes operated businesses for twenty-five years or more, they altered their methods of locating clients and selling goods. Rather than relying entirely on easily seized catalogues and postal orders as he had prior to 1914, Gennert sought out a London contact to whom he could ship large quantities of pornographic materials for distribution.

Numerous agents and intermediaries worked with French suppliers, as French mail-order businesses often faced strong scrutiny.

This was particularly true in the first year or two of the Edwardian period, before the British state began to abandon its more severe anti-pornography measures. For example, Walter Wilkins, who sold his products on behalf of the Cosmos Library in Paris, was sentenced to two years in prison in 1901 after being arrested for distributing pornography.[30] During that same year, police arrested a London distributor named Edouard Masson, who told police that his pornographic photos came from a firm called Lear and Co., based in Cairo. The owner of Lear and Co., a French citizen named Leon Branch, had worked with Masson in London before relocating to Cairo. In a rare case of the British government successfully securing the arrest of a foreign distributor, Branch's supply of photos was seized and he was prosecuted in the French Consular Court.[31] The arrest of Leon Branch stands out, however, as a relatively isolated case. Intermediaries based in Britain or its colonies frequently faced arrest and prison sentences, but their suppliers rarely suffered legal penalties. Moreover, even these rare victories largely ceased after 1901, with overseas suppliers rarely sought out for illegal products sold on British soil.[32] Their local intermediaries, however, remained vulnerable. Transnational organization, while providing the trade with stability and adaptability in numerous ways, also contained vulnerable actors who served as points of contact between localized nodes and more distant elements of the transnational system. As time passed, however, these vulnerabilities became less severe and few intermediaries faced the kinds of serious prison sentences that pornographers had faced in the nineteenth century, a shift that will be discussed more fully in chapter 6.

BRITISH DEALERS

While it appears likely, based on the stringent nature of their obscenity laws and the harsh measures taken against pornographers in the previous century, that the British acted as net importers of pornographic materials, interwar pornography distributors based in Britain also exploited transnational pornography markets.[33] This serves as one of the most noteworthy changes in transnational pornography flows during the early twentieth century. While few if any cases of British exporters can be found prior to 1911, by the interwar years British pornographers had clearly developed their networks to the point where exporting became a viable option. In 1923, for instance, Ricardo Gennert's London contact Cyril Benbow responded to a customer's request for a pornographic film by informing him: "The last one I obtained was a 520 ft one ... in English money roughly 8 pounds. This film has now gone to Florida."[34]

During the same year, a clerk at a shipping firm reported to the police that his employers had on several occasions collaborated with a film company in order to ship indecent films to a customer in Karachi. An undercover investigation confirmed that prospective customers had received samples of pornographic celluloid images, but the case collapsed after the suspects refused to arrange a second meeting with the informant. Subsequent interviews with film industry experts left the lead detective satisfied that few pornographic films were being produced in Britain, and those few in existence were probably intended for export to South America.[35] Significantly, this shows that films, the most expensive and difficult form of pornography to produce, still existed in significant enough quantities to be exported to other countries rather than simply being sold or shown for high prices in local markets.

In addition to films, dealers exported books and photographs from Britain. In 1925, Irish newspapers publicly blamed England for obscene materials circulating on Irish soil. While conveniently reinforcing images of English moral inferiority in the Free State press, the numerous confirmed cases of British dealers suggests that the tale held at least a hint of truth.[36] In 1911, for example, the London Metropolitan Police received word that convicted pornography distributor Charles Haines had shipped a "grossly obscene" album of photographs to a customer in Greece. While Haines sold comic books and other materials within Britain, police found none of them to be pornographic or obscene on the same level as the contents of the Greek shipment. With no evidence that these photographs had been marketed or sold on British soil, police declined to press charges.[37] The following year, the United States Post Office reported that a package of obscene materials shipped from Loughton, England, had been intercepted on its way to a customer in

Chicago. Shortly thereafter, authorities seized another package on its way from one firm in Britain to another in New York.[38] Just as Ricardo Gennert and other Continental dealers remained legally protected by communicating with British customers through intermediaries and the postal service, British pornographers like Charles Haines found ways to minimize risk by restricting their sales to foreign rather than local markets.

British immigrants to the United States and other countries also participated in transnational distribution systems. Between 1900 and 1939, the New York Society for the Suppression of Vice (NYSSV) recorded dozens of cases in which English and Scottish immigrants faced arrest and prosecution for the distribution of photographs and books. Some of these cases may have involved local producers and customers, but other British distributors clearly remained in contact with European wholesalers after their arrival on American shores. One Scottish immigrant, arrested in possession of over two hundred pornographic photographs, confessed that he imported his goods from a Barcelona wholesaler named Zarubaly.[39] Zarubaly also appeared on the Home Office's list of known Continental dealers, demonstrating that pornographic materials could and did travel along the convoluted path from a Continental European wholesaler to an American customer through a British intermediary.[40] Additional cases uncovered various smuggling operations, such as one in which British couriers brought Italian pornographic materials into the United States.[41] Direct links between Britain and the United States can be seen in the 1914 case of William Sloan, who confessed to importing two thousand photos from his firm in Britain.[42]

Beyond the US and the previously mentioned Parisian expatriate pornographer communities, British migrants also produced and distributed porn in other regions. Stephen Daniel Frances, for example, spent decades writing and distributing pornographic novels from his adoptive home in Spain.[43] Others may have participated in the non-commercial pen pal exchanges discussed in chapter 1. As the cases of immigrants to the United States, France, and Spain indicate, the British cannot be viewed solely as recipients of globally produced pornography. Rather, they actively contributed to the development of transnational distribution networks. The activities of British producers and distributors also point to the fluid movement of products and people within the transnational trade. Instead of occupying a clearly defined economic hierarchy of "producer" and "consumer" countries or a rigid system of production, participants of different nationalities and social locations moved between different roles and positions, sometimes over the course of several decades.

THE COLONIAL MARKET

This relatively egalitarian and easy movement within European and Anglo-American transnational circuits also, however, encountered more rigidly hierarchical economic and social boundaries in the imperial context. Both before and after the First World War, British travellers found ways to obtain pornographic materials either in the colonies or during their journey between colony and metropole. In 1907, for instance, Chaplain S.D. Cuthbert of the troopship *Plassey* reported his discovery that several troops had obtained indecent postcards when the ship stopped in Port Said. Thoroughly scandalized, Cuthbert seized over fifty sets of photographs, throwing most overboard and sending others as samples to the White Cross League (a prominent moral reform society). Upon receiving the report, Admiralty officials noted that a similar incident had occurred on the troopship *Dunera* when it docked in Las Palmas in 1904.[44]

While Chaplain Cuthbert was unable to determine precisely how the postcards came aboard, he cast suspicion on the Arab and Greek vendors who paddled to the side of troopships in small boats in order to sell fruit and other goods. A letter from the Office of the Consulate General of Port Said assured the Admiralty that the problem had largely been taken care of. In a clear display of Orientalist scapegoating, this official blamed Arab vendors, pointing out that the only licensed hawkers were respectable Maltese merchants who would certainly never engage in such activities.[45] Regardless of the ethnic background or nationality of those who sold the postcards, it is clear that by the first decade of the twentieth century there already existed a colonial pornography market of street-level vendors catering to British and European travellers as they passed through major ports. There is no evidence, however, that colonial subjects owned and operated the kind of large-scale pornographic photography and film operations seen in Britain, the US, and Western Europe. Instead, they acted mainly as distributors, securing their wares from European expatriates and selling them to other travellers or local residents.

Despite the Consulate's assurances that the events aboard the *Plassey* and the *Dunera* were isolated incidents, British soldiers and sailors stationed abroad continued to purchase pornography into the 1940s. For example, when a pornographic novel addressed to P.C. Hastings was intercepted in the post of the Bloomsbury Police Station in 1950, he stated that he had first been exposed to pornographic materials when stationed in India a few years before. Books and pictures routinely circulated throughout the soldiers' canteen or living quarters, quite possibly as the only available sexual outlet after colonial authorities enacted policies that officially discouraged visits to local brothels.[46] Few data exist regarding how much pornographic material, if any, these men brought back to Britain from the colonies. Evidently, however, many continued to consume or even produce pornography after their tour of duty ended. While this conveniently fed into narratives of white sexual corruption at the hands of colonial subjects, the flow of pornographic goods operated in a more complex fashion, relying upon the active involvement of British consumers in transnational and imperial distribution networks.

Pornography and other obscene materials did not just move from colony to metropole and vice versa. Rather, external parties like Continental pornographers catered to both British customers and those residing in British imperial settings. For example, in 1928 Australian authorities complained of several cases in which they had discovered unspecified erotic materials hidden inside items shipped by a Viennese bronze and marble firm. Subsequent correspondence revealed that there had been similar cases within Britain of obscene materials being smuggled inside Viennese bronzes.[47] This case illustrates not only the considerable ingenuity and effort of early twentieth-century pornography distributors, but also the common features of pornography distribution in geographically distinct locations connected by imperial and transnational networks.

While the origin of the pornography sold to the troops on the *Plassey* and read by P.C. Hastings is unknown, numerous Europeans living in the colonies produced erotic postcards and photographs. Rudolf Lehnert and Ernst Landrock, born in Bohemia and Switzerland, respectively, started a photography business in Tunisia in 1904. Due to their nationalities, the French government interned both men during the First World War. After their release, they relocated their business to Cairo.[48] Many of their postcards and photographs depicted desert landscapes, images of North African tourist sites, and scenes from Tunisian or Egyptian villages. They also produced numerous images of North African nude models. Like much of the nude photography circulating in the early twentieth century, catalogues listed these images as "anthropological" or "materials for artists." Many of the poses were, however, clearly artificial and erotic in nature.[49] In addition to selling photos in Tunisia and Egypt, Dresden collaborators printed Lehnert and Landrock photos and sold them across Europe.[50] Their catalogues included descriptions in both English and French, indicating a diverse and transnational customer base.[51] Because of Lehnert and Landrock's European connections, it would be entirely possible for a British traveller such as a sailor or soldier to buy Lehnert and Landrock nude photographs in Cairo or Tunis, then continue to purchase their products through catalogues after returning to Britain. Through this type of transaction, pornographers like Lehnert and Landrock added yet another layer of complexity to the pornography trade. Beyond simply contributing to transnational flows of culture and capital, sales to British customers from French Tunisia or Morocco also formed connections between different European empires.

Wilhelm von Gloeden is another example of an expatriate Continental European photographer whose work connected vastly different cultures and economies. Born into the Prussian nobility in 1856, von Gloeden relocated as a young man to Taormina, Sicily, hoping that the warm climate would cure his tuberculosis. There, he took up photography as a hobby. When he lost his family fortune in

1895, photography became his sole means of financial survival. His nude photographs of young Sicilian boys and men in faux-classical Arcadian settings circulated throughout Europe and earned him enormous respect in the European art world. Postcards based on his work, which von Gloeden began printing in 1900, proved particularly popular in Britain.[52] Despite von Gloeden's status in artistic communities, customs officials and post office sorters often targeted his photos for confiscation.[53] After von Gloeden's death, the Mussolini regime seized prints of some of the photographs and unsuccessfully attempted to prosecute his heir and favourite model for pornography distribution.[54] In the life of Wilhelm von Gloeden we see the fine line between art and pornography in the early twentieth century; even nude art studies of indisputable quality could be repurposed and sold for purely erotic purposes.

The work of Lehnert and Landrock and Wilhelm von Gloeden reveals some of the strategies photographers and distributors operating within the transnational market employed to avoid being labelled obscene or pornographic. Terms like "anthropological" and "classical" could operate as code for pornographic works. Collections or photographs classified as anthropology studies had a plausible excuse for nudity. These images, catalogues claimed, simply presented people of various ethnic groups in their natural state. Even a cursory examination of anthropological nudes, however, belies their authenticity as genuine reflections of native (un)dress. Lehnert and Landrock's Egyptian and Tunisian women, for example, sometimes appeared completely nude in an outdoor setting. In other images, the photograph captured the model draped only in a long head covering.[55] As the scholarship of Sarah Graham-Brown has shown, this unrealistic juxtaposition of covered hair and nude body served to reinforce Orientalist notions of Middle Eastern female sexuality.[56] While anyone with a passing familiarity with Egyptian or Tunisian cultures would instantly have identified the inauthentic nature of these photos, these stereotypes allowed distributors to market images of women of colour that would have been unacceptable had the models appeared European.

The use of the "classical" label, similarly, allowed for a level of homoeroticism that would have been considered indisputably obscene in other contexts. By adorning his Sicilian models with laurel wreaths and using Greek amphoras as props, Wilhelm von Gloeden found ways to present his photos as authentic renderings of classical Greek culture rather than simply as images of nude men and boys embracing.[57] Similar uses of the terms "anthropological" and "classical" can be found in numerous early twentieth-century catalogues and advertisements, and referred to books as well as photographs.[58] While pornographers based in Britain and western Europe also had marketing methods designed to reduce the risk of confiscated products and prosecution, the anthropological and classical styles of erotic photography were really only available to those producers based in Africa or the Mediterranean and who employed "exotic" models. As a result, pornographers operating in some regions had a slightly more secure, if still legally risky, position in the trade. This form of pornography production and distribution, rather than simply existing within a transnational context, actually required transnational circuits in order to thrive. Without the combination of privileged photographers and distributors from the metropole, people of colour available to work as models, and a European/Anglo-American customer base who viewed these models through a racialized lens, this strand of the pre-1945 pornography trade would have encountered very different regulatory and cultural obstacles.

Wilhelm von Gloeden's life provides rare insights into the relationship between a photographer, his models, and the local community. While Sicily did not have a colonial relationship with Germany, it existed in a state of significant economic and political disadvantage compared with more developed European nations. The relationship between a wealthy German aristocrat and impoverished Sicilian peasants therefore offers an important case study of power within the transnational pornographer/model relationship. After his death in 1931, the residents of Taormina remembered von Gloeden as a major source of economic growth. Models received a generous fee and a fixed percentage of all profits from photographs. Some used these funds as capital for fishing boats and other small-business equipment, a financial resource that would have been available through few other avenues. In addition, von Gloeden provided dowries for girls whose families were too impoverished to supply one. The good relationship von Gloeden enjoyed with the people of Taormina was clearly demonstrated in their stewardship of his home and studio during the period in which he temporarily fled the country during the First World War.[59] While it is highly unlikely that Wilhelm von Gloeden's equitable relationship with his models and his accepted position in Taormina were standard among expatriate European photographers, it does suggest that relationships between foreign photographers and local models could be negotiated and reciprocal rather than purely exploitative. Here, the transnational culture of pornography translated into the flow of capital from central to southern Europe, while economic and cultural conditions in that same local context directly affected the materials and tropes that would circulate within transnational networks.

While the Home Office dedicated relatively little attention to the flow of pornographic photos from the colonies or the less economically developed parts of Europe, materials sent to colonial customers proved highly alarming. In 1923, the Dominion Division of the Home Office wrote to the Commissioner of Accra, Gold Coast, informing him that letters from his area had been sent to a known French pornography distributor named E. Raveleau. Similar letters, presumably including requests for pornographic materials, were sent from Lagos to three other French distributors.[60] Pornography distributors actively sought the business of colonial customers. Upon discovering that circulars advertising pornographic books had been sent from New York to Zanzibar, Home Office Secretary J.F. Henderson wrote to the United States Solicitor of the Post Office, inquiring as to whether or not the American government could prosecute the offending publishers. Henderson identified one particularly problematic aspect of the case: "Recently we have been informed that copies have been sent to Europeans as well as Natives in East Africa, and no doubt are being sent to other parts of the world."[61]

While colonial subjects had less of an influence and a smaller role in production in western European and North American transnational networks than Europeans or Anglo-Americans (an imbalance discussed further in chapter 3), they had a high degree of access as customers. Their sources for pornography went well beyond unsolicited American catalogues; instead, they were able to take advantage of the latest in pornographic technologies. For example, in 1911, South African authorities seized a shipment of what appeared to be harmless brass rings. Upon closer inspection, however, these brass rings proved to be embedded with a crystal containing a miniaturized pornographic image.[62] This technology, known as a Stanhope, served as one method of shipping large quantities of pornographic photographs in a fairly small package. It is worth noting, however, that viewing a Stanhope required a special lens. In short, South African consumers not only had the contacts and capacities to order Stanhopes, but presumably also had the means to view them as well.

As historians like Ann Laura Stoler have shown, maintaining European prestige in the colonies depended in part on presenting an image of sexual respectability.[63] The prospect of indigenous colonized people purchasing European and American pornography, much of which featured Caucasian women as models, could easily be interpreted as a threat to the moral authority of colonial administrators. On a more concrete level, attempts to regulate indigenous access to transnational pornography networks indicates a more complicated role for colonized peoples than a simple division between European photographers and customers and indigenous models. Moreover, the ability of colonial subjects to access transnational pornography networks complicated the state's attempts to establish clear national or ethnic boundaries between populations. Colonial subjects may have had fewer opportunities to participate in production and more limited access to products, but these limitations were far from complete. The global pornography trade did not have a rigidly defined core and periphery. Rather, cultural flows circulated through complex, decentralized transnational networks that bolstered colonial hierarchies in some contexts but challenged them in others. To return to the question of queerness, we can clearly see the tension between normative societal pressures to maintain clear national and ethnic boundaries on the one hand and the transnational pornography trade's muddying of those boundaries on the other.

As we will see in chapter 3, however, pornographic materials also reinforced racist hierarchies and racialized sexual stereotypes. This follows from the material conditions and interactions of the transnational trade; there was significant economic incentive to court colonial customers and employ people of colour as models, but these participants do not appear among the producers and distributors whose decisions most directly shaped pornographic content.

TRANSNATIONALISM AND CONSUMPTION

While records from police departments and other government agencies provide clear evidence of transnational distribution, information regarding the details of consumption remains elusive. Similarities in products produced in various locations are discussed below, but it is entirely possible that people of different countries displayed very different preferences in the type of pornography they chose to purchase. Evidence indicates, for example, that flagellation-themed pornography originated in numerous countries, but it cannot be proven that people in two countries like Britain and Spain were equally likely to purchase pornography featuring flagellation. Even if one readily accepts the likelihood that consumption patterns differed from one location to another, similar themes appeared in marketing materials and other seized items from numerous countries.

American pulp fiction magazines distributed in Britain served as an important medium for pornography advertising and distribution, one that clearly displayed transnational trends and marketing efforts. Pulp fiction magazines provided mildly racy stories and drawings featuring nudity and implied sexuality, but no graphic sexual content. Advertisements appearing in the back pages of the magazines, however, allowed readers to purchase truly pornographic photos, books, and even films. For example, 1930s issues of seized magazines *Tattle Tales* and *Paris Gayety* contained ads for the American company Gargoyle Press, a producer of highly explicit flagellation literature.[64] Flagellation themes also appeared in 1937 police reports related to the case of Leonard William Steer, who confessed to selling "spanking stories" supplied by a Paris producer named Mademoiselle Yvonne.[65] Barcelona's Ricardo Gennert, similarly, sold "discipline"-themed photos to numerous British customers.[66] In short, Britons could purchase materials containing similar themes from producers in multiple countries and distributed through different methods.

The fact that numerous works on flagellation were originally published in French and Spanish shows that residents of France and Spain consumed some of the same materials enjoyed in Britain.[67] Transnational tastes went well beyond flagellation, however. A survey of the same catalogues and magazines that supplied Britons with flagellation pornography shows that British customers also had access to "artistic" studio nudes, photographs of "exotic" Asian and African women, and "action photos." Buyers also consumed other themes on a transnational scale. Photographs printed in American pulp fiction magazines catered to numerous tastes, including everything from nudes in conventional studio poses to topless women playing tennis and riding motorcycles.[68] In short, customers both in Britain and around the world had the ability to purchase products on diverse themes in a variety of media and originating in multiple countries. Whether they took full advantage of this variety remains unclear.

Other features found in catalogues and pornographic literature reveal attempts to market to a transnational or foreign audience. Books, like photographs and films, contained similar themes and tropes regardless of country of origin. In addition, books printed in one language were often translations of works that had originally been printed in other countries. French authors such as Sadie Blackeyes and Aime van Rod originally published their works in French, which were later translated and reissued by British and American publishers.[69] In other cases, producers printed books with a specific foreign audience in mind. The cheap pornographic novel *Confessions of a Virtuous Wife*, for example, was printed in Venice around 1930. The book's poor grammar indicates hasty or incompetent translation into English, while the inclusion of a satirical poem based on "God Save the Queen" points to an intended British audience.[70] In addition, the pseudonyms employed by pornographic authors listed in French and German catalogues often included sexual puns that would have been immediately understood by an English-speaking audience but may not have been as obvious to speakers of other languages. For example, authors listed in flagellation-themed French catalogues include such pen names as James Lovebirch and Lord Birchisgood.[71] These features, like the overall similarities found in pornographic materials, reveal the multiple levels on which producers worked with a transnational customer base in mind.

Catalogues and postcards also demonstrate the transnational character of the pornography trade. Postcards featuring nude Middle Eastern or North African women, for example, frequently contained text in multiple languages. The German-speaking photographers Lehnert and Landrock printed their catalogues and photograph descriptions in French.[72] As early as 1905, German catalogues of nude photographs listed prices in British, American, Spanish, and Italian currencies.[73] During the interwar years, Yva Richard used primarily French text in their catalogues but included prices in American dollars and British shillings. Moreover, some of their advertising included excerpts from letters written by happy customers in countries ranging from Canada to Colombia.[74] These catalogues and advertisements thus reflected the distributors' assumptions that orders would originate from both domestic and foreign sources.

TRANSNATIONALISM AND CONTENT

Despite the distinctions found between individual photographers and writers, very few national trends can be found in the content of pornography. Instead, pornographic content reflected the transnational nature of its production and circulation. Flagellation and corset fetish imagery, typically depicted as a British trend, appeared in photographs from France, Germany, Portugal, and other parts of the world.[75] When we consider literary pornography, comparisons between French works like Aime van Rod's *The Misfortunes of Collette* and American books like *Invitation to the Dance* show clear parallels.

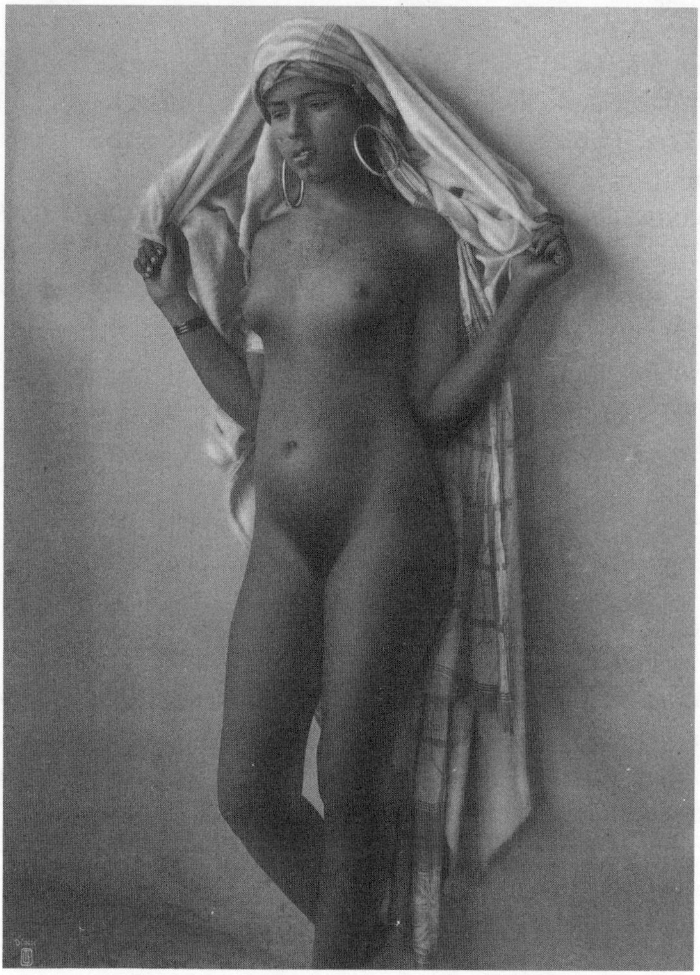

Figure 2.1 | Untitled Lehnert and Landrock photograph, Tunis, 19?.

In both of these publications, the whipping and discipline of a young woman by an older female authority figure are described and illustrated in graphic detail, but the story includes no intercourse or other sexual acts beyond the bondage and flogging imagery.[76] Given their shared themes, it is no surprise that both appeared in editions printed by Gargoyle Press, a New York publishing house specializing in bondage and flagellation stories. Similarly, Orientalist themes were featured in photographs and postcards from

Figure 2.2 | Veiled woman, Studio Manasse, Vienna.

around Europe, North Africa, and the Middle East. For example, the use of a veil on an otherwise nude woman can be found both in Lehnert and Landrock catalogues and in Viennese photographs printed in American magazines and then sold to British consumers (see figures 2.1 and 2.2).[77]

While France had a reputation for producing the highest-quality pornographic works, French photographs closely resembled those from the rest of Europe in style, composition, and content. In many

Figure 2.3 | Untitled, undated boot and corset image.

cases, the origin of early twentieth-century pornographic photos can be nearly impossible to determine.[78] In figures 2.3 and 2.4, for example, the use of whips, long gloves, and corsets, all consistent with photos produced for clients interested in flagellation or BDSM imagery, appeared in photos from both France and the United States.[79]

Several pornographic trends clearly originated in a specific location or had reputations that strongly corresponded to a particular

Figure 2.4 | Masked woman with whip. Charles Guyette, 1928.

country but which spread out throughout the transnational system. In one example, advertisements and order forms requesting German naturist photographs demonstrated a clear association between Germany and a specific style of nude photography that emphasized athletic poses and outdoor settings.[80] While German photographers may have been largely responsible for starting the naturist trend, other pornographers around the world quickly adopted the style for their own work. In one notable example, the

1934 American pseudo-documentary *Elysia: Valley of the Nude* incorporated many of the tropes commonly found in German nudist photography. Like much of the German photography sold internationally for erotic purposes, *Elysia* represented itself as a desexualized exploration of the physical and mental benefits of the nudist lifestyle. The film contradicted this alleged purpose, however, through its disproportionate use of female compared with male nudity and numerous scenes of young women adopting clearly provocative poses inconsistent with documentary filmmaking of "real life."[81] In other English-language erotic films from the 1920s and '30s, nude women in an outdoor setting occasionally ceased moving and adopted immobile poses reminiscent of German outdoor nudist photographs; in some cases, these poses appeared with title cards bearing labels like "Wood Sprites" or "Golden Tresses," both evocative of the descriptive captions often included on German nude postcards and photographs.[82]

The strong similarities between photographs and films originating in different countries indicate that pornographers in locations as far apart as the United States and Germany catered to customers with similar tastes. The use of similar imagery and themes, moreover, points to the conclusion that pornographers did not operate in isolation, but instead influenced and learned from work produced in other locations. In some cases, such as the relatively generic nude female studio pose, these styles cannot be attributed to any one geographic origin. In other examples, such as the naturist style popular in Germany or the veiled nude women of North Africa, trends appeared in one region and spread to others through transnational circuits. Regardless of origin, pornographic subgenres and trends did not remain confined to a specific cultural or geographic space. As discussed in chapter 1, individuals often shifted between roles, acting as consumer, producer, and distributor at different times. Those who began their involvement in the pornography trade by consuming materials produced in one country, such as France or Germany, before becoming a producer in another country, such as Britain, would naturally adopt the tropes and techniques gleaned from their own consumption patterns. To be clear, this is not to suggest that customers across the globe interpreted or experienced pornographic materials in the same way; indeed, the specific ways in which people in different parts of the world saw pornography certainly depended on their specific cultural and geographical context. Consistent patterns in pornographic content do, however, point to strong connections linking individuals and networks across national borders.

STATE RESPONSES TO TRANSNATIONAL NETWORKS

Officials working for the British state understood that the transnational nature of the pornography trade crippled their ability to respond effectively. While diplomacy led to some convictions of foreign dealers, in most cases it failed. As it became clear that the Customs Office and the GPO could not hope to screen all goods entering the country, the Home Office and the Foreign Office turned to the League of Nations. The 1923 International Convention for the Suppression of the Circulation of Obscene Publications sought to coordinate international legal responses to the traffic in pornography. Throughout the interwar years and into the early 1940s, convention signatories submitted annual reports regarding the circulation of obscene publications within their borders. In these reports, nearly every country downplayed the existence of a domestic trade, claiming that no cases existed or that any active pornography trade originated abroad. As a result, authorities had access to little accurate information regarding the scope of the transnational trade.[83]

The British state seems to have been exceptionally likely to misrepresent pornography circulation. For example, during the interwar years, British government estimates of the total number of pornographic items seized per year generally fell between 2,000 and 3,000.[84] Interwar newspaper articles of domestic obscenity trials, however, sometimes reported as many as 14,000 items seized from a single distributor in a single case.[85] This vast discrepancy indicates not only that government reports largely ignored the domestic trade, but that they dramatically misrepresented the amount of pornography circulating on British soil. In an additional handicap, the League of Nations convention failed to develop a single definition of obscenity or a legal framework that would apply to all signatories. As a result, diplomatic efforts to address transnational pornography networks continued to involve negotiations between representatives of two countries, often on a case-by-case basis. For example, lengthy talks between Britain and France regarding France's permissive obscenity laws resulted in disappointment when the new French law addressed visual pornography but included no measures for obscene literature, perceived by British officials as the most troubling type of pornographic material.[86]

Despite efforts toward international policies regarding obscene publications, British government actions taken against the transnational movement of pornography after 1901 consisted mainly of surveillance. As American publications began to make up an increasingly large portion of British pornography sales, several prominent New York pornographers came to the attention of British authorities. The 1937 trial of Samuel Roth, presented by the American press as New York's pornography kingpin, was closely monitored by the Home Office. Minute sheets also noted the federal criminal conviction of Ben Rhebhun, Anne Rhebhun, and Ben Raeburn of New York's Falstaff Press.[87] As in the case of Charles Carrington and other Parisian pornographers, this surveillance yielded few tangible results, but allowed authorities to claim victories against the traffic in pornography. This close attention to foreign dealers reveals a clear awareness of how pornographers were able to exploit the nature of international borders, as well as a high level of uncertainty about how to address the issue without weakening national sovereignty. As will be discussed further in chapter 6, one should not attribute ineffective official approaches to the pornography trade to either weakness or lack of comprehension of the trade's scale. Rather, the failure to develop countermeasures suitable to combat a transnational trade anchored by localized networks resulted from competing internal and international political pressures that limited the state's ability to move effectively without compromising other goals. Regardless of the causes of this ineffectual set of policies, however, the result was clearly beneficial for those seeking to move pornography through transnational networks. Viewed against the backdrop of limited international co-operation and political will on the part of the British state, the methods and decisions of transnational pornographers come into focus as logical responses to surrounding legal and economic pressures.

CONCLUSION

As demonstrated by people like João de Brito, Cyril Benbow, and Ricardo Gennert, early twentieth-century pornographers operated as members of a transnational business community anchored by localized nodes or networks. The products they sold circulated around the world, while distributors carried the pornography trade to new locations as they travelled and migrated. Their business dealings often rested on personal connections and contacts in multiple countries; these connections could be developed through common languages and cultural backgrounds, or could be based on other forms of friendship and personal acquaintance. Producers and distributors worked within established and long-lasting networks, their success dependent on reputation, personal connections, and local contacts as a point of entry into foreign markets.

In many of the cases discussed in this chapter, the pornography industry served as a means of contact between people of different cultures or nationalities. At times, this contact involved no face-to-face encounters or movement outside of either party's country of residence. Ricardo Gennert and Cyril Benbow, for example, created business connections between Barcelona and London without (to anyone's knowledge) ever meeting in person. Through the pornography trade, London distributors and customers crossed formal national boundaries to establish cultural and commercial links with Germans living in Tunisia, eastern European immigrants in New York, and French and Hungarian citizens operating businesses across the Iberian peninsula. In their understanding and manipulation of these transnational networks, early twentieth-century pornographers displayed a level of adaptability that was unmatched by the governments and law enforcement officials who sought to curb their trade.

Given the transnational nature of the early twentieth-century pornography trade, any attempt to analyze specifically "British" pornography becomes questionable at best. It is possible in some cases to identify pornography produced by British authors and publishers active in local networks, but this leaves the question of whether it was written with a British audience in mind. Similarly, evidence shows numerous examples of foreign products sold to British customers, but these products were often produced and marketed for other nationalities in addition to the British. As a result, it appears virtually impossible to arrive at any conclusions regarding a specific British psychology or sexual culture based on the pornography they produced or consumed. One can, however, use content analysis of pornography to show that British participants in the pornography trade responded and contributed to a much larger transnational sexual community. While national and regional sexual cultures certainly varied, similarities in pornography indicate that some elements were shared across borders.

The transnational element of early twentieth-century pornography networks has important implications for the study of Britain's community of pornographers and enthusiasts. Just as particular tastes brought diverse individuals into loose networks within Britain, many British buyers and sellers of pornography became involved with groups that spanned national and imperial borders. Cyril Benbow, for example, came into contact with a transnational network of people whose appreciation for corset and flagellation fetish pornography placed them outside of mainstream sexual culture. Moreover, just as the localized trade complicated British heteronormative standards by creating spaces for deviant sexual practices, transnational elements of the trade triggered anxieties through the ways in which they blurred the seemingly clear lines between national, ethnic, and imperial categories. In the next chapter, I use the context discussed up to this point to explore the crucial question of how these conditions of production shaped the content of pornographic materials.

CHAPTER THREE

"Let the Picture Tell Its Own Story"

Pornographic Content, 1900–1945

The scene begins with that classic pornographic storytelling device: the peephole. Two women, oblivious to the fact that they are being observed, undress and engage in foreplay, providing an erotic scene not only for the viewer of the film but for the Peeping Tom. This 1920s French stag loop does not, however, feature the expected lone male spy, but a man and a woman who are equally aroused by the sight of the two women having sex in the next room.[1]

In another medium, a 1922 photograph depicts a topless woman brandishing a whip while a well-dressed man cowers on the floor before her.[2] In literary pornography, examples abound of sadistic schoolmistresses and their masochistic female students operating in environments entirely devoid of men, whose absence is neither noted nor mourned.[3]

In the examples given above, early twentieth-century pornographic materials displayed features such as female-dominant sex, equitable power dynamics between genders, homosexuality, and acceptance of extramarital and non-monogamous sexuality. In short, they did not conform to heteronormative models of male sexual control and female subordination, strictly defined binary gender roles, or anything resembling early twentieth-century notions of bourgeois respectability.[4] This stands in stark contrast to widely accepted mainstream literature and film of the period, which sometimes included mild sexual content but typically reflected the values and practices promoted as normative by the state and dominant civil institutions. Pornography produced between 1900 and 1945, rather than differing from mainstream entertainment solely in its level of sexual explicitness, offered entirely distinct models of sexuality and gendered interaction.[5]

Pornography's transgressive sexual messages did not, however, stem solely from the imagery of individual pornographic items. Rather, pornography's status as a site of contestation to the heteronormative order resulted from its non-hierarchical approach to sexual variety. As will be discussed in chapters 5 and 6, heteronormative views of sexuality employed strictly defined categories of accepted and deviant sexual acts and proclivities. Early twentieth-century pornography, in contrast, did not reflect such divisions. Pornography's queer outlook did not arise just from showing acts considered "deviant." On the contrary, pornography frequently depicted intercourse between white heterosexual couples, images that encapsulated British concepts of heteronormative sexuality. As a genre, however, early twentieth-century pornography challenged mainstream values by placing these heterosexual, seemingly normative encounters alongside BDSM, homosexual encounters, group sex, and other sexual acts, thus presenting all as valid sexual options. The threat posed by pornography lay not in opposing heterosexual monogamy, but in incorporating that model of sexual interaction into a worldview that encompassed a broader range of sexual possibilities.

Early twentieth-century pornography's critique of heteronormative sexuality only becomes truly apparent in light of the underground networks that produced, distributed, and consumed it. As shown in this book's first two chapters, British participants in the broader transnational trade operated within loose collections of underground networks, their activities and products culturally and legally constructed deviant and unacceptable. This economic and cultural context provides the crucial lens through which we can understand and analyze pornographic materials from this period. In other words, we must ask what meanings and sexual values become apparent if we approach pornography not from a position of presumed heteronormativity, but as a product of marginalized and "deviant" networks embedded within transnational flows. These exact same materials would, after all, carry an entirely different set of meanings if they had been produced and distributed in full view of the British public or in spaces that enjoyed widespread acceptance. Keeping this important context in mind, let us now delve into the more specific features of pornography as a queer cultural production in the early twentieth century.

ART AND ENTERTAINMENT IN EARLY TWENTIETH-CENTURY BRITAIN

Edwardian and interwar Britons experienced a deluge of new artistic media and forms of entertainment. The wireless, which had emerged as an obscure new technology in the 1890s, became a popular commercial music and entertainment medium in the 1920s. Late Victorian and Edwardian Britons experienced film for the first time, with talkies emerging scarcely a generation later. While the British film industry did not achieve the same status as the American films, both imported and domestically produced films fundamentally altered the nature of entertainment in Britain.[6] Even older forms of media like print saw significant changes. While books had remained expensive and largely inaccessible in the mid- to late nineteenth century, cheap editions and the advent of twopenny libraries made books easier to produce and distribute to a wider range of consumers.[7] Music and dancing changed with the introduction of jazz and experimental dance styles that grew out of increasing cross-cultural and transnational contact.[8] Across diverse forms of media, the people of Edwardian and interwar Britain had access to a variety of entertainment options that previous generations never could have imagined.

Changes in the nature of British art and entertainment were not merely issues of technology or quantity. The changing possibilities these factors created for art and entertainment introduced new cultural concerns and social questions.[9] The regulatory apparatus employed for the theatre, for example, proved inadequate for the cinema, necessitating the development of an entirely new regulatory body.[10] More broadly, Britons expressed ambivalence about the social messages and values communicated across different media. Rather than being an unquestioned good, near-universal literacy was viewed by officials and many members of the middle class as a potential source of danger and corruption. The experimental literature produced during the interwar years led to several sensational obscenity trials and widespread social debates concerning censorship and the dangers of subversive fiction.[11] For some media and genres associated with non-British nationalities or people of colour, such as film and jazz, commentators questioned whether they could ever be wholesome entertainment at all.[12] Despite these concerns about new types of entertainment, little could be done to quash the popularity of cinema, music, magazines, and paperbacks. With the genie of mass media out of the bottle, there was simply no turning back. While the British state and powerful members of civil society managed to harness the propaganda potential of film and other media during both world wars, mass media also promoted messages and values that proved more troubling and difficult to control.[13] Pornographers and consumers operating between 1900 and 1945 therefore could choose from a wide variety of potential media in which to work, and those who sought to regulate the world of entertainment had never been so ill-equipped to enact serious limitations on what people purchased, read, and watched.

APPROACHING AND CATEGORIZING PORNOGRAPHIC CONTENT

Given the highly problematic ways in which pornographic content has been analyzed in both popular discourse and the academy, it is worth pausing for a moment to discuss the best way to approach smutty books and dirty pictures as a body of historical sources. As discussed in the introduction, since 1989 feminist and queer scholars such as Linda Williams and Feona Attwood have moved conversations about pornography past the pro- and con- impasse that prevailed for much of the 1980s.[14] Publications like the journal *Porn Studies* have produced critical scholarship that seeks to delve into questions of pornography intended for specific niche audiences, the effect of regulation on specific pornography markets, and analyses of race in American pornography.[15] This body of scholarship, which incorporates approaches from feminist literature, queer theory, cultural studies, and other disciplines, has created a crucial field in which pornography is recognized as a distinct genre subject to surrounding cultural trends and regulatory pressures.[16] The historical application of these approaches, however, is only beginning to emerge.

One of my major goals in this project is to combine the specificity and critical attention of porn studies scholarship with social history methods in order to arrive at a more critical, historically grounded analysis of pornography in the specific context of Britain and its empire between 1900 and 1945. Porn studies scholarship, heavily influenced by queer theory, has opened the door for this approach by emphasizing the importance of constructed categories of normativity and deviance and the ways in which pornography must be interpreted in light of those power dynamics, an approach now adapted to this particular historical case. Rather than beginning with the pornographic sample and extrapolating conclusions regarding the behavior and views of producers and consumers, I begin with the conditions of production and consumption established in the first two chapters, interpreting early twentieth-century pornography within that specific context.[17] In other words, rather than assuming heterosexual male consumers and producers and viewing all pornographic samples through that lens, I approach archival examples of pornography produced between 1900 and 1945 armed with the knowledge that pornography networks included men and women, the working poor and the middle classes, Britons and overseas participants, heterosexuals and homosexuals, married couples, and sex workers who specialized in bondage and domination.

Catering to this wide variety of sexualities, early twentieth-century pornography had enormous subversive potential. As any survey of pornography will reveal, however, in many cases these materials also reproduced rather than subverted mainstream structures of gender, class, and race. Orientalist depictions of Asian and African women, for example, clearly communicated racial hierarchies that highlighted the "exotic" sexuality of women of colour. Novels and visual materials depicting sexual exploitation of a member of the working class by one in a position of economic power similarly reproduced dominant class structures. While I argue that pornography as a whole undermined British heteronormativity, it also ignored or bolstered imperialist ideologies. As shown later in this chapter, the pornography trade's status as a queer space did not by any means render it all-inclusive or universally accepting; instead, as a transnational but still largely white western European, British, and North American community, it often reflected the systems of racialized inequality that affected other aspects of economic and sexual life in the early twentieth century. One must therefore be cautious about placing pornography as a whole into categories such as "oppressive" or "liberating," given the uneven experiences and differing perspectives even within a single network. Rather than impose a negative or positive value judgment on the entire trade, I seek instead to employ a queer lens to examine the points at which pornographic materials either broke with or reinforced normative structures and cultural views.

Contemporary pornographic categories typically fall into a set of binaries such as soft/hardcore, homosexual/heterosexual, mainstream/alt, and kink/vanilla.[18] As this survey of pornographic media indicates, these labels simply did not apply to pre-1945 pornographic ephemera. As discussed in chapter 1, pornographers and consumers did not form groups according to specific sexual proclivity such as BDSM or heterosexuality, but rather shared distribution networks and suppliers. The content of pornographic ephemera followed this trend of sexual diversity. As a result, imposing contemporary categories according to sexual act or preference runs the risk of creating anachronistic and artificial labels that would not have been recognized by consumers or producers living in the early twentieth-century British Empire. In addition, such an approach directly undermines the sexual fluidity found within this queer context, imposing binary forms of categorization on networks that specifically rejected sexual dichotomies.

Other systems of categorization can, however, be useful for thinking about the early twentieth-century pornography trade. The greatest differences between pornographic artifacts lay not in the depiction of various sexual activities, but rather in the use of different media. Focusing on differences and similarities between pornographic literature, film, photographs, and cartoons foregrounds conditions of production, distribution, and consumption. The coordination and number of personnel required to produce a film, for example, yielded different results than the far simpler task of drawing and printing a booklet of pornographic cartoons. Conditions of production also held widely varying possibilities as far as the level of realism and the types of fantasy that could be depicted, attracting customers of different tastes and preferences to different media. Identifying the constraints imposed by conditions of production and distribution allows us to more clearly identify the patterns and consistent traits found across all different pornographic media prior to 1945.

PORNOGRAPHIC LITERATURE

We will begin this survey of pornographic media with arguably the oldest and most established medium: the book. Books printed for pornographic purposes, or literary pornography, fell into two general categories.[19] The first category contained books specifically written as pornography rather than as a mainstream work. Of all pornographic media, novels contained the most explicit scenes and arguably the greatest variety of sexual acts. Most pornographic stories and novels employed first-person narration by either a male or female character and described several different sexual encounters connected by minimal plot and characterization. Some books graphically depicted sexual intercourse, oral sex, and other explicit sexual acts, while others described equally detailed but BDSM-centred images like floggings rather than intercourse.[20] Both women and men appeared as sexual aggressors in early twentieth-century literary pornography, and both typically achieved sexual fulfillment during the various encounters depicted.[21] Sexual encounters between women appeared with relative frequency, while fewer stories contained male on male sexuality.[22]

The second type of pornographic book sold in Britain and other locations connected by the transnational pornography trade can be broadly described as "the repurposed text." For this kind of pornographic literature, publishing companies like Falstaff Press and the Esoterika Biblion Society printed illustrated or edited editions of existing non-pornographic texts. The Falstaff Press's *Hindu Art of Love*, for example, consisted of excerpts from the *Kama Sutra* and other texts relating to sexuality, paired with newly produced, titillating line drawings.[23] These books generally offered more suggestive than graphic content, but still contained features consistent with pornography rather than academic study. For example, the Falstaff Press advertised a new translation of *The Perfumed Garden* that included thirty-four nude photographs in addition to the original text.[24]

Written pornography reflected a wide variety of tastes and sexual proclivities. Some texts more closely resembled "softcore" than explicit pornography, but most texts offered a wide range of sexual scenarios. Most depicted sex with very little social context and without negative consequences for sexual behaviour. In addition, pornographic novels frequently upended normative gender roles. For example, stories might depict women with rich sexual lives that included no men. Within heterosexual encounters, women often appeared as the instigator; even in cases when the woman began as a reluctant party, stories often included a switch in roles in which the female character embraced her sexuality and became the more assertive partner. For example, Sadie Blackeyes's *Miss* begins with the protagonist as a passive participant in whipping practices, but she grows to enjoy flagellation and becomes a sexually assertive flagellant.[25]

Written pornography also displayed a sense of sexual fluidity in which characters moved between heterosexual and homosexual encounters, monogamy and group sex, BDSM and "vanilla" intercourse, collapsing established sexual categories. In *The Lascivious Hypocrite*, for instance, the male protagonist vicariously experiences sex between two women, enjoys actual sexual relations with women, is happily seduced by another man, and participates in a variety of sexual acts during each of these encounters.[26] In the same way that production and distribution networks established the pornography trade as a queer space, literary pornography offered diverse sexual possibilities without mainstream hierarchical categorization.

Both the variety and prevalence of explicit content in literary pornography has clear connections to the specific conditions under which it was produced. Of any pornographic medium, literary forms had the fewest barriers to production. While high-end presses required significant investment, short stories sold in envelopes or printed in magazines cost little to produce. Even novels could be produced in low-quality paperback editions. Writers required nothing more than a pen and paper, or perhaps a typewriter, to make their contribution; moreover, writers could work a great distance from the publisher or customer, perhaps never meeting face to face. Free from the need to purchase expensive equipment, develop the technical skills to produce films or photographs, or even take the legal risk of working in the same physical space as other participants, writers enjoyed relative freedom. In addition, the possibility of producing pornography at a distance, discussed at length in the previous two chapters, opened literary pornography to participation by many who would not have enjoyed such acceptance in a face-to-face encounter; women, for example, frequently worked as writers of pornographic fiction, and many unknown writers used feminine pen names like Sadie Blackeyes and Aime van Rod.[27] As a medium that requires no special effects or advanced visual technologies, written pornography's variety of sexual acts or scenarios were limited only by the writer's imagination and the tastes of potential customers. Here we can clearly see the ways in which the broader context of the pornography trade as well as the specific conditions of production experienced by writers provide the necessary background to understand the range of available content.

PHOTOGRAPHY

Of all the pornographic media of the early twentieth century, photography was the most artistically accomplished. It also featured the most variation of all existing media of the period, including a larger body of surviving archival samples and a broader range of styles and topics than those found in books, magazines, or film. Photographers produced work that catered to virtually all conceivable sexual tastes and proclivities in the early twentieth century,

Figure 3.1 | Yva Richard in specialty lingerie, 1920s.

rendering it difficult if not impossible to make generalizations about the nature of erotic photography from the period. Photographs offered everything from studio nudes to group sex, homosexual and heterosexual encounters, kink and vanilla sex, and models of a wide variety of body types, ages, and ethnic backgrounds.

Pornography is often assumed to consist of a sexual act between at least two individuals.[28] Significant quantities of early twentieth-century pornographic photography, in contrast, consisted of nude

Figure 3.2 | Corseted French model, France, 1920–1936.

women and occasionally men in suggestive but not necessarily explicit poses. Despite the lack of on-camera interaction, these nudes still operated as counterpoints to normative sexuality. Costume and setting, for example, communicated the model's status as either sexually dominant or submissive; the frequent appearance of lone female models bearing whips and stern facial expressions conjured images of sexually assertive and aggressive women (see figure 3.1). On a more subtle level, photographs featuring nude women who

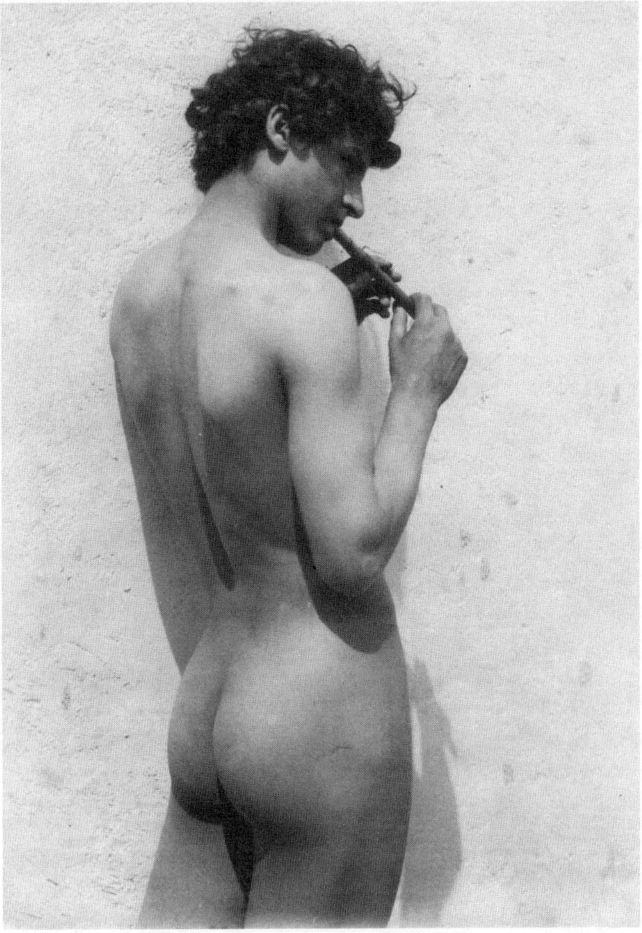

Figure 3.3 | *Au bonheur du jour*, undated. Guglielmo Pluschow.

appeared at ease with the camera (and therefore the viewer) conflicted with normative standards of female modesty and sexual restraint (see figure 3.2). Male nudes, similarly, framed the male rather than female body as the object of sexual desire, thus complicating assumed binaries of female object and male viewer (see figure 3.3).[29]

Despite the diversity of images in photographic pornography, some prominent trends can be identified. As has been persuasively argued in other studies of photography such as the groundbreaking work *Lynching Photographs*, evaluating photographs as evidence requires attention to the role played by the photographer in the event depicted as well as the material forms and venues in which the photograph circulated.[30] Attention to details of production is therefore crucial. Photographers carefully choreographed sets and costumes, with very few photographs arranged in such a way that they could have been taken spontaneously. Models often appeared in numerous poses and angles within the same setting, and photographs showed multiple models posing in the same location.[31] Photographs were often produced and sold in sets of six or more, often showing an escalating or shifting sexual encounter in several acts.[32] While some photographic pornography from the period consisted of genital close-ups or sexual acts free of context, the general importance of costume, setting, and careful arrangement of poses demonstrates that customers of pornographic photography placed great value on the photograph's implicit scenario rather than just the nudity or sex act itself. Moreover, it indicates that photographers and their models had to engage in significant communication in order to achieve the desired result, a natural consequence of pornography production operating as a set of social as well as economic networks.

As will be discussed in later chapters, various bodies in the British state held the position that photographs posed less of a social threat than books because they were less capable of communicating complex social messages. Given the importance of storylines and scenarios in photographs, however, it is clear that the messages communicated and detected through photography could be apparent to those active in pornography networks but opaque to those outside the trade. Photographs, rather than serving merely as a cheap and disposable thrill, existed as a body of materials offering a range of sexual worlds and possibilities, many of which challenged heteronormative assumptions and categories.

When we compare the distinctive characteristics of photographs and written pornography, it is once again important to consider conditions of production and distribution. Producing pornographic photographs required significantly more equipment and expertise than did literary pornography. While photography became far more accessible in the early twentieth century than it had been for much of the Victorian period, it still required a photographer skilled in areas such as lighting, composition, and photographic development. Pornographic photographs also required the co-operation of multiple actors; while self-portraits were technologically possible, such an approach would have been impractical for most pornographic scenarios. Unlike literary pornography, photographic content was thus restricted not only by the material limitations of sets and costumes, but also by the need to secure the participation of one or more models. Photographs were also easy to transport and produce in large quantities. These distinctions in conditions of production provide a clear context for understanding the differences between the content of literary and photographic materials; the expertise required to produce even the most basic photographs ensured a higher overall level of artistry, while the need to build scenarios around available props, settings, and models offered a more limited range of sexual content than was available through a writer's imagination.

FILM

Like literature and photography, early pornographic films ran the gamut from non-explicit depictions of nudes to stag loops featuring unsimulated intercourse and other graphic sexual acts. Two major categories of early twentieth-century pornographic films circulated among pornography consumers. The first and less explicit category consisted of "nudist" documentaries, burlesque dance numbers, and other films that contained nudity and innuendo but no explicit sex acts. These films carefully negotiated the boundary between pornographic and mainstream entertainment, framing their arousing content in such a way that it could serve a dual purpose depending on whether the viewer was familiar with pornographic tropes. The 1934 documentary *Elysia: Valley of the Nude*, for example, contained no explicit sexual content and included a narrative celebrating the health benefits of the nudist lifestyle, but also offered numerous scenes in which female models adopted poses intended

Figure 3.4 | Two chained women, 1936.

to emphasize sexually attractive qualities rather than a typical day in nudist life.[33]

The second category of pornographic film was the stag loop, characterized by explicit sexual acts that rendered the films clearly obscene under all early twentieth-century laws. Unlike photography, stag films had low quality and shoddy production values.[34]

While models in photographs often appeared quite convincing in their facial expressions and body language, stag film actors and actresses made little effort at enthusiastic performances. Both men and women typically performed sex acts with a mildly bored demeanour. While a handful of stag films contained detailed sets, the majority took place in minimally furnished flats or hotel rooms, often employing a stationary camera. These factors demonstrate that, despite well-known cases of influential filmmakers who got their start in pornography, such as Georges Melies and Bernard Natan, film generally attracted less talent and fewer resources than the world of photography or literature.[35]

Despite the low quality of early pornographic films, these products still worked to disrupt heteronormative categories. Like the books and photographs discussed above, film depicted consequence-free sexual acts outside the confines of marriage. The undated silent-era film *A Reunited Foursome* encapsulated the transgressive class and gender dynamics of early pornographic films. The opening title card reads as follows:

> Dear Children – Teacher will tell you a bed-time story. A husband, watching the maid preparing to retire, successfully insults her. Suddenly, his wife returns. She suspects nothing, phones her lover who arrives and does some very welcome insulting on his own account. A moan – a sigh – a gasp – discovery – denounciation [*sic*] – accusations and then – Oh Hell! – children, let the picture tell its own story.[36]

At the film's outset, the setup conforms to long-standing stereotypes about sexually available working-class women and sexually entitled elite men. This narrative is complicated, however, by the simultaneous infidelity of the lady of the house. In addition, the storyline does not frame her infidelity as a greater crime than her husband's, nor are any of the participants subjected to retribution, as would generally be the case in mainstream entertainment (discussed later in the chapter). Rather, the two couples switch partners, and all participate in the group sexual encounter, with the maid and working-class male lover displaying as much sexual autonomy as the wealthier pair.[37] In this film, therefore, the sexual act undermines rather than reinforces classed and gendered inequalities by extending the same extramarital sexual rights tacitly tolerated in elite men to the women and working-class characters in the scene.

This acceptance of female and working-class pleasure served as a key feature of pornographic films in this period. While analyses of contemporary pornographic films have understandably identified male sexual pleasure as the primary goal of on-camera sex, stag films complicate such assumptions. In films involving a sexual encounter between one man and one woman, cunnilingus frequently occupied equal or greater screen time compared to fellatio. In the 1930s stag loop *London Bridge*, for example, two-thirds of the film's running time depicts a man performing oral sex on a female partner.[38] While there is every possibility that the filmmakers still designed these scenes as a way of arousing male rather than female viewers, they nevertheless chose to portray a scenario in which female pleasure served as a crucial feature of the encounter. Moreover, this female pleasure was not delivered in the form of penetration by a phallus, but rather by oral sex. This contrasts with the assumption in contemporary pornography in which female sexual fulfillment is equated with vaginal penetration.[39]

As in the case of photography and writing, early twentieth-century pornographic film must be viewed as a broader corpus of work rather than as isolated scenes or individual films. As a whole, pornographic films were aligned with written pornography and photography in that they did not employ the clearly defined categories of the period's heteronormative sexual worldview. Same-sex encounters, BDSM, and group sex appeared with less frequency than heterosexual encounters between single men and women, but they also appeared without the visual cues and markers deeming these acts as being lower in the sexual hierarchy. As a body of materials, pornographic films offered the viewer a queer contrast with heteronormative sexuality. While the same sex acts appeared in both worldviews, mainstream materials employed deviant sexuality as a means of defining its normative counterpart while those materials produced within the queer spaces of the pornography trade allowed for sexual coexistence.

The technology and expertise required to produce a pornographic film created very different conditions than those experienced by pornographic writers and photographers. As in the case of photography, the content of pornographic film was limited by available sets, props, and performers. Unlike photography, however, film carried the additional burdens of expense, flammability, screening difficulties, and cumbersome transport. Photography's production complications were somewhat offset by easy transportation and reproducibility, but film offered few advantages besides novelty. As a result, stag films attracted minimal talent and far fewer sexual scenarios, in all likelihood due to limitations on the sexual acts performers agreed to perform in unsimulated scenes. The fact that pornographic films were produced in queer spaces ensured that its content challenged and contested heteronormative sexuality, but it did so with less complexity and an entirely different aesthetic than that of photographs or literary pornography.

COMICS AND TIJUANA BIBLES

Tijuana bibles, also known as Tillie and Mac books, were cheaply produced pornographic comics usually comprising eight pages or less.[40] They contained crudely drawn yet highly graphic sexual encounters, often featuring pornographic versions of existing comic book characters or representations of celebrities like Joan Crawford or Mae West.[41] The overwhelming majority of materials produced in this medium adopted a light, joking tone and made liberal use of crude sexual humour. The frequent appearance of misspelled words, poor grammar, and the middling quality of the illustrations indicates that Tijuana bible producers generally possessed a lower level of education or artistic skill than the pornographers working in photography or higher-quality pornographic literature.[42]

Despite the crude artistry and apparently low educational level of their authors, Tijuana bibles contained some of the most overtly political subversive messages found in early twentieth-century pornography. For example, in a clear display of patriotic and anti-fascist sentiment, the author of one comic depicted Adolf Hitler as a sexually depraved sadist.[43] Even those Tijuana bibles that did not directly engage with real political figures contained strongly subversive queer imagery. For example, the use of popular cartoon characters like Olive Oyl and Popeye reappropriated widely recognizable American cultural icons and reversed the message of the original cartoons. The original versions of cartoon couples like Popeye and Olive Oyl or Blondie and Dagwood appeared wholesome, seemingly asexual, and consistent with gender binaries of the passive female and the more assertive male. In the Tijuana bibles, however, the female character often appeared as the sexual aggressor and the male character as cuckolded or sexually dominated during the encounter.[44] Such images challenged and undermined normative Anglo-American gender roles, offering a glimpse of alternative sexual cultures in which women rather than men acted as the sexually dominant figure.

While there is comparatively little information about the specific practices involved in creating and distributing pornographic comics, we can infer some general points from the materials themselves. In some ways, comics ranked as the most accessible materials for both consumers and producers. Required to fill only eight pages and make minimal use of text, they did not need to possess the writing qualities of Anaïs Nin or other talented erotic writers. Printed on the lowest-quality paper and sometimes stapled by hand, comics did not require the expense of a printing press or a darkroom. Pornographic drawings, much like literary pornography, did not possess the limitations imposed by models' participation or even by the physical realities of human anatomy. In other words, comics offered all the advantages of the written word while also allowing for faster production and intelligibility even for the completely illiterate. The fact that comics were by no means the most popular form of pornography, on the other hand, plainly illustrates that convenience and ease of production were certainly not the only considerations shaping pornography networks.[45] Given the choice between cheap but crudely drawn comics and more expensive literary pornography or exquisitely photographed nude figures, many opted for the latter.

PULP FICTION MAGAZINES

While common in pornographic materials like photographs or Tijuana bibles, female sexual autonomy was not a universal feature of pornographic advertising and distribution. This becomes particularly apparent in a survey of pulp fiction magazines. Interwar American pulp fiction magazines, more than any other product related to pornography distribution, seem at first glance to be a paradox. On the one hand, the plots and characters of their stories invariably conformed to heteronormative morality; spunky female characters flirted with danger and sexual passion, but found true love and an engagement ring by the final page. On the other hand, the advertisements appearing in the magazines' back pages offered the types of explicit pornography that undermined those same mainstream sexual mores. In another puzzling contradiction, the drawings and photographs of bare-breasted women appearing throughout pulps like *Spicy Stories* and *French Frolics* seemed to be aimed squarely at a heterosexual male audience, yet large numbers of advertisements specifically sought female customers.[46]

The seemingly contradictory nature of racy American pulp fiction magazines can be seen in the May 1930 issue of *French Follies*. In the story "Nothing but Thrills," the flapper-heroine, Patty, runs off to Paris after rejecting the marriage proposal of a good but dull man. In her pursuit of adventure, Patty finds herself captured and sold to a lecherous foreigner named Alla Bey. After discovering that she has been drugged in an act of "Eastern trickery," Patty wakes up assuming that she has been transported to Alla Bey's harem. To her surprise and relief, she discovers that her spurned fiancé rescued her from her captor before he was able to carry out his presumably evil plans for her. Realizing the error of her ways, Patty joyfully accepts her rescuer's marriage proposal.[47]

The story of Patty's near-downfall conformed in every way to heteronormative ideals of the interwar years. It depicted female sexual independence as foolish at best and catastrophic at worst. Interactions between the innocent Caucasian Patty and the lustful Alla Bey reinforced Orientalist stereotypes of Arabs as oversexed and predatory. Finally, Patty's rescue and engagement safely

Figure 3.5 | Cover of August 1935 issue of *Tattle Tales*.

channelled her sexuality into the socially appropriate venue of the heterosexual monogamous marriage. Given the light tone of the magazine, Patty's punishment for her sexual transgression naturally fell short of a violent attack or another grim turn of events, but her frightening encounter with Alla Bey and her short-lived belief upon waking that she has been trapped in a harem clearly served a cautionary and perhaps even punitive purpose. Aside from the spare line drawings of bare-breasted women that illustrate the story, one would be hard-pressed to find a subversive moment in the tale.

60 PARIS NIGHTS

BOOKS on CORPORAL PUNISHMENT

Remarkable stories of Whippings inflicted on both sexes, disclosing the strange grip the Rod has had on men and women since the beginning of Time.

Also many other curious and absorbing volumes on strange amatory customs and practices,—unabridged, privately printed and unusually illustrated.

ILLUSTRATED booklet, handsomely printed, describing these volumes in great detail, sent free in sealed envelope to responsible adults only. Send stamp. State age. Postcards ignored.

THE GARGOYLE PRESS
Dept. PN, 70 Fifth Avenue, New York

"THE GREAT ALPHABET"

of ancient Hebrew Magic explained so anyone can use it to obtain, Love, Money, Health, Friends, Protection. The Great Alphabet was written by David and has been used for 3,000 years by those who knew its secrets. You too can use it. Send one dollar bill to MAGUS ALBUS, 2743 North 9th Street, Philadelphia, Pa., for complete instructions.

MIND READING "SECRETS"

This book explains under one cover the Most Successful Verbal, Silent and Crystal Ball Mind Reading Methods used by Famous Stage, Club and Parlor Performers of the Present Day, such as The Vaudeville Musical "Silent Thought" Transference Act, A Vaudeville Second-Sight Act, A "Complete" Original Vaudeville Mind-Reading Act, Winged Mystery—a Baffling, Sensational, Sure-Fire Mind-Reading Experiment, a Latter Day Miracle—a "Different" Sort of Sure-Fire Test, Vaudeville, Crystal-Gazing Act, Phonetic System for Silent Thought Transmission Acts, Feature Mind-Reading Act, On Answering Questions, Method of Obtaining "Sealed" Messages Written at Home by the Audience; The Blindfolded Drive, a Most Sensational Publicity Stunt; Publicity Stunts for Mind Reader; "Silent" Thought Transference and Mind-Reading Act, Written for Club Entertainers; The Chess Knight Tour, Voice Culture Instructions and a two-hour Act entitled "Gambols of the Ghosts." Illustrated and Guaranteed. Only $2.00 postpaid.

SHADE PUBLISHING CO.
1008 W. York St. Philadelphia, Pa.

HERE is a chance for men to make money on the side in spare time. If you are honest and reliable, write to us for full details. A real offer not to be passed up. (No canvassing.) Please enclose stamp. Box 254-B, Sta. F, New York City.

LADIES ONLY!

Delayed? Use famous time-tested B-X MONTHLY RELIEF COMPOUND when nature fails! *Starts working instantly!* Brings soothing, satisfying relief in some of longest, most stubborn, unnatural delays very quickly—in only a few hours in some cases! Very powerful, yet absolutely safe! *Guaranteed—Pure—Harmless.* No pain, inconvenience, or interference with duties! Constituents strongly recommended by famous doctors! Used & praised by thousands of grateful women! Double Strength, $2. *Amazingly prompt shipment!* Rushed 1st class mail, plain sealed wrapper, within 1 hour of order.
B-X Lab'tories, 1505 E. 60th St., Dept. RT5, Chicago

RARE NUDE!

Undraped & unretouched pictures of living nude models in daring positions. Each picture Postcard size & on glossy paper. Send $2 for 25 positions or $1 for 10 positions and get FREE 15 versions of Love, Gay Life in Paris, What Tommy Saw, 12 Gay Love Letters, (read 2 ways), Private Tips & The Vampire. Send stamped envelope for circular on BOOKS.
LaROMA, 4 W. 15th St., Dept H-46, New York

Genuine Spanking Photos

A rare set of 8 gloss photos showing actual chastisement of girls and young women. This is a new set, best out, and sure to please. Also 16 additional "Men Only" gloss photos and 2 extremely spicy 5x8 gloss enlargements. If this is your first order $2. Express only—cash—stamps—money order. MODERN PRODUCTS, P.O. Box 588, Dept. P, Rockford, Illinois.

"Because, dearest, as I tried to tell you before, Lyla is my sister!"

"Your sister? La, la, la, what a fool I haf been!" Renee laughed in sheer relief. She placed her right arm about Don's neck and drew his face down to her own. "I remember now, you did say zat you had a sister. She lives in Bristol wiz your mother?"

"That's right," Don told her as he placed his head upon the pillow alongside her own.

"Me, I am so happy. So happy, but tell me, mon cheri, am I forgiven for all zose nasty zings I say to you?"

"Of course, my own, — my dearest! What man wouldn't forgive a sweet darling like yourself?"

Impulsively, Don bent his head until his mouth covered Renee's soft, fragrant lips, while her dark eyes brimmed over with a breath-taking radiance. He lowered his body to a position beside her own and held her close.

"We'll be married," he whispered to her happily, "just as soon as we can. I don't want to risk losing you again out of jealousy for the scrub woman or anyone like that, — my darling high-flyin' Baby!"

He found her lips and gave her such a kiss that it defied all time, during which the stiff English nurse returned and then whirled about and left the room again,— thoroughly shocked.

TROUBLE OF HIS OWN

Said the butcher as the customer pulled up to the meat market: "I've got deviled kidneys, calves' brains, pig's feet, chicken livers an'—"

"Forget it, fellow," growled the cranky patron. "I've got a headache, eczema, fallen arches, corns, a bunion, three warts and some shopping to do. Quit complaining and give me two pounds of loin steak."

* * *

HIS FRANCHISE

Wife (introducing a gigolo to her hubby): "Meet Bill, Henry, he's my dancing partner for the evening. Why, Henry, what are you kicking Bill for?"

Hubby: "As long as I'm the head of the house, I'll foot all the Bills."

Figure 3.6 | Interior page, *Paris Nights*.

The back pages of this same issue of *French Follies*, however, provided an entirely different set of sexual messages. Advertisements offered unmistakable descriptions of pornographic products, including "action photos," Tillie and Mac cartoons, and "snappy bedroom scenes."[48] Many of the ads were marked "for men only," but as many if not more advertisements offered products like contraceptives exclusively to female customers.[49] In addition to these advertisements for pornography and other sex products, *French Follies* and other pulp fiction magazines frequently printed letters from readers interested in lonely hearts services. Like the advertisement section, the lonely hearts letters directly undermined any assumptions that the pictures of nude women found on every page meant that the magazines were intended solely for a male audience. Writers claiming to be women contributed extensively to these sections, extolling the magazine's praises and offering to exchange photographs and sexual stories with fellow enthusiasts.[50]

The seemingly contradictory messages promoted by American pulp fiction magazines can be understood by viewing the magazines' dual role as light entertainment and as a gateway to queer networks connected to the pornography trade. By making sexual encounters implicit and by toeing the line on gender roles, magazines provided their readers with mildly naughty stories and images that nonetheless stopped short of subverting established hierarchies of race, class, or gender. By leading with such content, pulp publishers sought to protect themselves against attacks on their more risqué back pages. As discussed in chapter 1, pornography consumers constantly had to navigate formalities and barriers to consumption, many of which required an insider's understanding of the jargon and accepted practices of distribution networks. Once we take into account this constant need to decode and infer meaning from catalogues and other sources of pornography, we can begin to see how users of interwar pulp fiction magazines might have handled the contradictory messages presented to them with little confusion or conflict.[51] The content of pulp fiction magazines, as in the case of other pornographic media from the period, takes on entirely new meaning when viewed through this lens, a meaning that otherwise remains obscured.

THEMATIC PATTERNS AND COMMON TROPES

The previous sections of this chapter provided an overview of pornographic content and culture as seen in different pornographic media, as well as the complications and possibilities created by the surrounding conditions of production. Now for the all-important question of what it all means, and what patterns we can discern from this mass of material. These patterns do not make themselves immediately apparent. Indeed, one's initial impression upon sifting through these piles of pornographic ephemera is of overwhelming variety. In all of the forms of pornography discussed here, consumers could choose from more or less explicit content. Films could show a nude dancer or graphic intercourse, photographs ranged from studio-style glamour shots to explicit group sex, and literature ran the gamut from the frank prose of *Fanny Hill* or *Painful Pleasures* to the coy titillation of Edith Hull's *The Sheik*. Consumers also had the options of same-sex or opposite-sex scenes, BDSM, Orientalist photography, or translated erotic classics. Heterogeneity, rather than any one sexual act or trend, thus stands out as a primary characteristic of pornography between 1900 and 1945.

While pluralism might be the most oddly consistent feature of pornography during this period, there are other elements shared across the body of materials. One feature that appeared consistently across genres was the use of humour. While some scholars have, somewhat bafflingly, discussed the "seriousness" of pornography, erotic materials produced between 1900 and 1945 displayed an overwhelmingly playful tone.[52] Consider figures 3.7 and 3.8. These are two images taken from a set of photographs produced in Portugal between 1912 and 1915. Until the set's final image, all of the photographs consist of a graphic, violent threesome between two women and one man. In all of these images, the performers adopt a serious demeanour. In the closing photograph, however, the seriousness of the set's preceding images is utterly undermined by an image of the three performers smiling and sticking their tongues out for the camera (see figures 3.7 and 3.8). Other forms of pornography, such as Tijuana bibles and stag films, consistently adopted similar methods to present sexual acts in a humorous or even satirical context.[53]

Figure 3.7 | Portuguese photograph, second in series, 1912–1915.

The prominent element of humour brings us back to queerness as practised within pornography networks. Depictions of fluid sexuality offered a pluralistic approach to sex and challenged assumptions of heterosexual marital intercourse as a morally superior form of sexual expression rather than one of many sexual options. Humour compounded this transgressive outlook, treating sexuality in a light-hearted matter rather than with the level of gravity employed in socially sanctioned sex education books or religious

Figure 3.8 | Portuguese photograph, last in series 1912–1915.

publications.[54] Queerness within the pornography trade was not merely a matter of particular sexual acts but of overall tone and outlook regarding the place of sex in society. In the eyes of the British legal and religious establishment, treating sex as anything other than deadly serious business served as a marker of sexual immorality and social decay.

On the other hand, pornography could also challenge normative assumptions by choosing not to trivialize a sexual encounter. While not found consistently across all or even most pornography, depictions of emotional connection also stand out as a recurring element of the genre in the early twentieth century. Typical discussions of contemporary pornography juxtapose the purely physical and mercenary nature of sex in pornography with the more emotional and loving depictions found in "erotica" or "romantic" entertainment.[55] Pornography produced between 1900 and 1945, however, did not correspond to such simplistic distinctions. In numerous examples, filmmakers, photographers, and models conveyed a sense of affection and emotional connection between participants. In some cases, this emotional closeness appeared as an isolated moment – perhaps captured by chance. In other cases, positive emotional connection between participants was clearly a deliberate decision on the part of the producer. One rather striking example can be found in an undated stag film called *Late Supper.* In this film, probably produced in the 1940s, the two performers engage in a variety of sex acts including intercourse and fellatio. After the man ejaculates, however, the film departs from expected genre conventions through the inclusion of a final scene in which he brings his partner a drink and they sit together in a comfortable pose that shows companionship and affection.[56]

While these examples should not be viewed as representing all early twentieth-century pornography, they demonstrate that assumptions of pornography as antithetical to emotional connection and marital happiness should be called into question, particularly in light of the role pornography apparently played in the sex lives of married and partnered couples in the early twentieth century.[57] Pornographers and consumers did not promote the simplistic polar opposite of normative relationships, with one side seeking only to satisfy lust and the other valuing love. Rather, pornographic materials offered a sexual worldview that included possibilities for a deep emotional connection, but did not situate these cases as morally and socially superior examples.

In another prominent pattern found across the different media is the element of reappropriation. Burlesque dance films, artists' model photos, and history/sexology texts all began as non-pornographic materials and became pornographic through editing or redirection to a particular audience.[58] In the case of the pornography trade, this appropriation took the form of both technology and genre conventions or characters. Technologies of printing and film production operated within heavily monitored industries and often served as tools of state or civil authority, easily seen in the British state's sustained interest in producing newsreels and other films during the First and Second World Wars.[59] Reappropriation of film, photography, and printing thus served as a reversal of "legitimate" uses of such technologies. More explicitly, the reappropriation of images of popular celebrities and cartoon characters transformed sexual acts into subversive commentary by drawing unmistakable contrasts between the non-threatening original image and its reconfigured new form. This element of reappropriation existed in all different pornographic media, providing a consistent thread of queer sentiment running through the genre.

Reappropriation also occurred within the pornography trade itself. For example, photos circulating during the 1920s depicted such images as a scantily clad woman reading a copy of *Paris Sex Appeal*, a widely known racy pulp fiction magazine.[60] A 1920s Pathé short film referenced the pornographic photography industry by showing its subject, a "nightclub girl" dancing and stripping for a camera and posing in lingerie for a photographer.[61] Filmmakers included a more overtly sexual case in the pornographic film *Lip Service* (date unknown, probably 1930s), in which a woman begins to masturbate while reading a book, suggesting that the contents are pornographic in nature.[62] Beyond American and western European products, Japanese pornography produced in the 1920s and 1930s included images of women looking at erotic cards during sex.[63] In each of these cases, references to racy magazines, books, or erotic photography served as a marker of sexual availability or a catalyst for further sexual activity.

Literary materials also contained references to other forms of pornography. The 1935 BDSM-themed *The Way of a Man with a Maid* included a lengthy passage in which a couple peruses a collection of "indecent photographs" featuring same-sex encounters between nuns.[64] In other cases, literary materials like erotic novels were illustrated with pornographic photographs, combining two different media into a single storyline. In some cases, photographs used to illustrate pornographic novels do not appear to have been specifically produced for the book and bore only a passing resemblance to descriptions of the plot and characters. For example, a London-produced edition of the pornographic novel *Sylvia: A Story of Insatiable Lust* contained photographs pasted by hand into blank pages within the novel. All of the photographs contained graphic sexual images of the same couple, but they did not closely correspond to the sexual acts described in the story.[65] This underscores the fact that pornographic publishers did not necessarily have the resources to support collaboration of an author, photographer, and illustrator all working on a single coordinated project. They did, however, have enough access to different forms of pornography that they could combine several products into one volume. The fact that some anonymous pornographer pasted *Sylvia*'s photos into each copy by hand is consistent with the small operations of people like Irene England, Charles Domec-Carre, and Richard Elias, all discussed in chapter 1.

Frequent references to other pornographic media illustrate that customers were familiar with a wide array of materials. The appearance of erotic magazines, photographs, and books in other media operated as one element of a queer visual vocabulary, communicating messages of sexual arousal and availability with little or no explanation. This assumption of familiarity with various media and their use as a feature of sexual scenes is entirely expected within the context of networks that produced, traded, and purchased large varieties of pornographic media. Such cross-pollination would be obvious to people who could choose from photographs, books, and films out of the back pages of an American magazine, or who traded materials within Irene England and Charles Domec-Carre's network. It thus becomes clear how even seemingly insignificant details of pornographic content were influenced by the distribution networks in which their creators worked.

GENDERED PATTERNS

In addition to the patterns discussed above, common features relating to gender dynamics merit special consideration. As we have seen, female sexual pleasure and autonomy were featured in a variety of pornographic materials. These materials, however, contained distinctions in the depiction of female sexuality and gender relations according to medium. As a general trend, violence appeared frequently in literary pornography, occasionally surfaced in photography, and remained virtually absent in film. Literary pornography depicted everything from spankings to brutal flagellation to rape.[66] While photographic pornography also featured BDSM and coercion themes, they appeared far less than in written pornography.[67] Moreover, these scenes were less graphically rendered and appeared in ways that emphasize the staged nature of the scenario. Film, in contrast, typically contained few if any obvious elements of violence or BDSM.

The relative need for female co-operation was a major factor in this distinction between media. Novels and cheap comics could engage in violent or dangerous fantasies without asking living models to experience actual discomfort. Photographs, which required models to enact the fantasy, could simulate some whippings, beatings, and other painful acts. Caning and whipping images, for example, rarely if ever showed real bruises or whip marks, instead depicting injuries that had obviously been painted or drawn on the model's body or onto the photograph itself.[68] Filmmakers could not depict a violent act without either inflicting real pain on a performer or carefully staging scenes that would have been beyond the capacity of those producing such low-quality films. As a result, early pornographic films rarely if ever showed male or female performers in threatening or abusive scenarios. This need to accommodate the comfort and safety of female performers stemmed directly from early twentieth-century conditions of production. As discussed in chapter 1, pornography production in Britain and most other locales tended to occur on a small scale, in informal environments, and sometimes for non-commercial purposes. While other countries like France had more well-developed publishing houses and distribution operations, the consistent presence of the same names on dealer lists and the amateurish qualities of much pornography in circulation suggests that informal and cottage-industry-style production was also common across Continental Europe. In such an environment, pornographic performance necessarily consisted of negotiated encounters that precluded the depiction of any explicit violence against models.

Surveying pornographic materials also reveals other significant patterns relating to gender. While same-sex eroticism between women is plentiful in surviving examples of pornography from virtually all periods and locations, fewer examples of male homosexual pornography remain. Some companies, such as Long Island's Photozique Studios, specialized almost exclusively on homoerotic nude photography.[69] Other remaining archival samples of photographs taken between 1890 and 1940 depicted explicit sexual encounters between men, some of which included additional queer elements like drag or the use of corsets.[70] As in the case of pornography designed for a heterosexual audience, however, homoerotic pornography included significant variety and did not closely adhere to a single model of sexual interactions between men.

As discussed in chapter 1, networks operating within the pornography trade did not display a clear divide between heterosexual and homosexual communities. This overlap between heterosexual and homosexual interests could be found in a single text like *The Lascivious Hypocrite*. A sense of sexual fluidity appeared in films as well; the oldest known case of a male same-sex encounter in a pornographic film, Bernard Natan's *Ménage moderne du Madame Butterfly*, also contains heterosexual intercourse as well as a sexual encounter between two women.[71] Few if any pornographic materials from this period clearly acknowledged the existence of homosexuality as an exclusive category entirely separate from heterosexuality. In terms of sexual acts and partners, pornographic materials deviated from the types of rigid sexual identity categories that became widespread in early twentieth-century British society. Once again, the queer elements within these materials come into focus when read against the backdrop of their conditions of production and distribution. Divisions between heterosexuality and homosexuality were, after all, a heteronormative construct; in spaces occupied by people already considered deviant, it is entirely logical that rigid categorization based on object choice would hold less meaning.[72]

Pornography also portrayed distinct variants on masculinity within heterosexual encounters. The depiction of women and female sexuality has been the focus of most analyses of pornographic content, with relatively little attention paid to masculinity. An underlying assumption of this body of work is that female sexual availability corresponds to masculine dominance and superiority, an argument that results from a binary view of men and women in systems of patriarchal power relations.[73] This view is not, however, consistent with pornography produced before 1945. In this period pornography could in fact simultaneously depict women as sexually available and men as possessing diminished or non-normative masculine qualities. While literary pornography tended to depict men as dominant and virile, photographs and films offered images of men who either struggled to perform or did so in a position submissive to that of a female partner.[74]

While many BDSM-themed erotic photographs included a female submissive, this was far from a universal trend. A significant number of photographs featured men submitting to a dominatrix or other formidable women. As in the case of depictions of female sexual pleasure, the presence of a dominant woman does not mean that the materials were aimed at a female audience; indeed, many male pornography consumers sought out these scenarios. The appearance of dominant women and submissive men offered a sexual alternative to the strictly male-dominant, female-submissive gender roles imposed by normative early twentieth-century culture. Compared with cultural assumptions of dominant, decisive male heads of household and compliant wives/mothers, images of bound men and whip-brandishing women became a highly transgressive sexual counterpoint (see figure 3.9).

As previously discussed, few early films catered directly to BDSM tastes. Films still, however, found ways to challenge normative masculinity without depicting men being bound and whipped by a woman. While contemporary pornographic films are widely derided for including male performers with enormous erections that persist through endless sexual gymnastics, men performing in early twentieth-century films often began with a flaccid penis, and many lost their erection well before the end of the film.[75] In several cases, the filmmakers made no attempt to conceal male performers' struggle to achieve erection or penetration.[76] Compared

Figure 3.9 | Three women dominating male submissive, 1935.

with stereotypical images of today's porn actors, most of the men performing in early stag films appeared middle-aged and few had muscular physiques[77] – in short, they did not project an ideal image of male virility.

Imagery suggesting queer variants on normative masculinity went beyond physical characteristics of performers, and surfaced in the storylines of the films as well. Male humiliation at the hands of women, for example, was a prominent element of pornography during this period. In one well-known stag loop from the late 1920s or early 1930s, *On the Beach*, a young man sees three women swimming nude and hides their clothes in order to force them into sex. The three women, pretending to go along with the scheme, trick the man into having sex with a goat instead. In a later encounter with the same man (who remains blissfully unaware that he has committed bestiality) one of the women stuffs a towel under her dress in order to fool the man into believing that she is pregnant. The film ends with the man in a state of extreme and richly deserved distress and the women thoroughly amused at their successful prank.[78]

This model of masculinity should not be viewed as pornography's answer to traditional male qualities. Many examples of pornography did feature assertive men who fit American and British models of normative masculinity.[79] Rather, pornography of this period offered a number of sexual possibilities, including men who lacked the qualities idealized in mainstream sexual culture. The variety offered by pornographic materials included not only different sexual acts and gendered combinations of partners, but also different models of manly or feminine behaviour. Given the documented involvement of men like Mervyn Hyde (who possessed significant quantities of cross-dressing gear and BDSM paraphernalia at the time of his arrest), the prevalence of alternative models of masculinity appears as a logical consequence of those involved in production and distribution.[80]

RACE AND ETHNICITY

Beyond thematic and gendered patterns, it is also important to consider common tropes related to race and ethnicity. Early twentieth-century pornographic materials frequently undermined heteronormative concepts of appropriate gender roles and the relative value of different sexual acts, but depictions of race conformed more directly to racialized imperial hierarchies. This was particularly true of North African and Asian nude photography, which depicted women in exotic settings and poses that directly reflected Orientalist fantasies like the harem (see figure 3.10). Pornography involving people of African descent often featured an outdoor set-

Figure 3.10 | *À la citerne*, undated. Lehnert and Landrock.

ting suggestive of a remote village, along with jewellery and accessories that conformed to early twentieth-century expectations of "backwards" tribal villagers.[81] In materials featuring homosexual encounters, racial hierarchies manifested in costume and setting choices – for example, the white man as the "active" partner and the man of colour or one dressed in pseudo-Arab garb as the "passive" partner.[82] Rarely did pornography depict interracial sex in a way that did not explicitly call attention to racialized hierarchies.

Tijuana bibles often employed blunt and obvious racial stereotypes. One comic featuring Aunt Jemima used a racist and stereotypical rendering of African-American appearance and dialect, despite the fact that such characterizations did nothing to advance the sexual scenario depicted. Another had as its title "A Sailor Finds Out if It's True What They Say about Chinese Girls," referring to long-standing Western myths that Asian women possessed horizontal vaginas.[83] Both in presentation of body types and in depiction of cultural characteristics, these comics reinforced images of Asian and African-American women as more highly sexual than Caucasian women. They also made the assumption that women of colour are more sexually available to white men.[84]

Read alongside highly subversive messages of gender and sexual orientation, pornography's reproduction of widely accepted racial hierarchies seems puzzling. These trends, however, closely conform to available information about who would have typically participated in the pornography trade. While evidence clearly indicates that British, western European, and American men and women participated in the pornography trade with relative frequency, records contain far less evidence of people outside of these regions producing pornography within the same networks. As discussed in chapter 2, intercepted letters indicate that African colonial subjects did purchase foreign pornography in some cases, and the example of Carmen Corti shows that women of colour living in Britain were involved in the trade.[85] Despite these few notable examples, however, both the transnational trade and local British pornography networks were configured around assumptions of Caucasian Anglo-Americans and western Europeans as the most important population of customers and producers. While various aspects of the pornography trade specifically targeted female customers, pornographers displayed little obvious interest in catering to an African or Asian customer base or in inviting them to participate in the production end of the trade. In other words, the typical producer and consumer may have chafed under the constraints of monogamy or female passivity, but few sought an alternative to colonial sexual hierarchies. Even as they displayed a variety of queer features, pornographic materials were by no means all-inclusive or egalitarian. Instead, following the patterns of representation and participation in the production end of the trade, pornography operated simultaneously as a tool of queer critique and of imperial oppression.

SUBJECTS AND SPECIALIZATION

This survey of patterns in content raises questions of how the pornography trade came to adopt this particular blend of sexual variety, queered gender categories, and imperialist imagery. These themes and patterns did not simply spring from the minds of individual pornographic producers, but rather followed marketing and production patterns. One of the most important elements of the content of early twentieth-century pornography involves the easy mix of themes and tropes. This thematic fluidity appears not only in the content of pornographic ephemera, but in the circumstances under which this pornography was produced and circulated. In a striking contrast to modern-day pornography studios, early twentieth-century producers and suppliers did not typically specialize according to theme. While some provided more products in a particular medium, such as books rather than photographs, this trend did not depend on the sexual content of the material.

Despite evidence demonstrating that producers and distributors catered to a wide range of sexual proclivities, the photo albums left behind by early collectors indicate high levels of specialization according to taste. One American album, for example, contains a disproportionate quantity of photographs depicting acts of bestiality. Notations made by the Kinsey archive observe that while bestiality accounted for less than 1 per cent of the material seized by German authorities of the period, it comprised the majority of photographs in that particular album.[86] These specialized albums serve as examples of the different sexual proclivities that interacted within the spaces of the pornography trade. A customer might be interested in only a specific type of material, such as bestiality, but he or she nevertheless would have interacted with a network of people with entirely different sexual tastes. Such interaction inevitably led to cross-pollination of sexual concepts and trends, even if some individual participants remained interested in one narrow type of pornography.

Like consumers, artists and distributors rarely divided along heterosexual and homosexual lines. While there is little evidence available for British producers, Continental photographers blurred the boundaries between heterosexual and homosexual pornography. Italy-based photographers Guglielmo Pluschow and Vincenzo Galdi, who both followed Prussian photographer Wilhelm von Gloeden's example of photographing large numbers of homoerotic nudes in the classical or Arcadian style, also produced pornographic photographs of women. Galdi in particular sold numerous erotically charged photographs of male-female couples or of women exposing their genitals for the camera.[87] Studio Manasse, which primarily photographed nude women, also produced the occasional erotic photograph of the nude male body.[88] As in the case of the Benbow-Hyde network, connections between producers and distributors of erotic photographs originated in a shared connection to the pornography trade rather than an interest in particular genders, styles, or sex acts.

Even marketing materials did not generally cater to specific sexual tastes or populations. A 1920s photographic catalogue produced in Great Britain describe photographs ranging from "young woman pissing and enjoying herself with her fingers and instruments of various kinds" to "torture and flagellation" to "two young boys."[89] The producers of the catalogue assumed that a customer who desired heterosexual flagellation pornography would be comfortable ordering from a catalogue that also catered to those interested in images of young boys or a woman urinating.[90] A French catalogue from the same period similarly described postcards depicting men, women, Caucasian, and "Oriental" figures.[91] As in the Benbow and Hyde correspondence, these materials point to the conclusion that networks of pornographers and consumers did not divide along lines such as specific sexual taste, but rather brought together consumers and distributors through a common interest in pornographic materials. Producers likely had other motives for this scattershot approach to themes and content, and those motives almost certainly involved financial practicalities. While there is little information available about the profits made in a typical pornography operation, we know from most of the cases discussed in the first two chapters that the industry could support a modest lifestyle at best. A producer or distributor seeking to maximize profits would not, therefore, have a strong incentive to specialize in a narrow pornography sub-genre likely to have a smaller pool of interested customers. Selling and marketing a broad variety of sexual acts and themes would have been the most logical business strategy for pornography operations. Regardless of intent, however, pornographers still created networks offering a broad variety of sexual possibilities. The queer content of early twentieth-century pornography thus acted as both a reflection of and a reinforcing factor in the networks making up the transnational trade.

COMPARATIVE MAINSTREAM CASES

In order to place early twentieth-century pornography's queer character in a comparative frame, one need look no further than mainstream films and novels of the 1920s and 1930s. Fiction that was perceived as promoting acceptable moral characteristics maintained the importance of heterosexual monogamous marriage and, more broadly, heteronormative respectability. Novels and films of the period frequently depicted characters who violated these standards, but such violations resulted in either a penalty or an eventual redemption. This is not to suggest that mainstream films, plays, and novels unfailingly promoted the values of the respectable middle class; novelists, filmmakers, and artists all introduced moral ambiguity and found ways to question social norms, sometimes at high risk to their careers and social lives.[92] Surveys of literature and film do, however, reveal clear limitations and boundaries regarding what messages could be promoted about gender and sexuality.

Beyond the realm of pornography, films and books that fell outside of the boundaries outlined above also ran the risk of being labelled obscene or morally dangerous. *The Well of Loneliness*, found obscene by a British court in 1922, cannot by any stretch of the imagination be considered pornographic. Even the judge's ruling on the case acknowledged that it contained no arousing content. Rather, the book's obscenity rested on the fact that the "invert" protagonist survived and remained happy at the end of the book. The mere existence of homosexual attraction did not necessarily render the work obscene; rather, in the eyes of the court, author Radclyffe Hall's failure to condemn a homosexual character to misery and loneliness amounted to an endorsement of an immoral lifestyle. As the presiding magistrate wrote in his lengthy ruling, "I can imagine a book dealing with this subject matter as a tragedy, the tragedy being that there may be people so afflicted who try their best to fight against this horrible vice, find themselves impelled in that direction or unable to resist those tendencies, with the result of the moral and physical degradation which indulgences in those vices must necessarily involve."[93]

In other words, the fact that Hall located tragedy in society's lack of acceptance rather than in her characters' failure to resist their impulses rendered obscene a story that might otherwise have been found morally acceptable by the court.

By comparing the ruling on *The Well of Loneliness* to widely accepted mainstream entertainment, we can start to map the heteronormative boundaries dictating the types of messages literature could safely promote. Lillian Hellman's play *The Children's Hour*, staged first in New York then in London in 1936, courted some controversy but also critical acclaim. The implied homosexual attraction of one protagonist, Martha, to her fellow schoolteacher, Karen, surfaces following a false allegation of a sexual affair between the two women. Martha, wracked with guilt over her attraction to Karen, commits suicide at the end of the play.[94] While *The Children's Hour* differs from *The Well of Loneliness* in that Hellman rendered the homosexual attraction one-sided rather than reciprocal, the more important distinction lies in the fate of the protagonist. As the very different reception of these two works indicates, mainstream characters could engage in activities perceived as immoral, provided they paid the price.

Mainstream cinema operated under even more stringent conditions, but internal tension and subversive elements were by no means absent. Films depicted infidelity, the burden of domesticity, and other elements that directly or indirectly challenged accepted sexual norms. Despite this potential for subversion, however, the content of pre-1945 British films leaned heavily toward upholding middle-class respectability, heteronormativity, and compliance with the state's domestic and imperial agenda.[95] While content and message differed depending on genre and specific time period, several broad trends dominated the screen. Early melodramas presented female characters as juxtaposed "virgin and whore" archetypes, with the respectable domestic woman winning the male protagonist's heart.[96] Sexually promiscuous women, while sometimes portrayed as sympathetic victims of exploitation, generally ended the film alone or destitute. Male sexuality also had to be constrained; while men enjoyed considerably more leeway and sexual autonomy than women, films still promoted their monogamous marriage with a "good" woman and demanded that the temptation to infidelity be overcome or punished.[97] Moreover, male protagonists adhered to a particularly middle-class model of masculinity that depended on strength and dominance but not excessive violence or cruelty. Male characters frequently achieved this ideal masculinity through the civilizing influence of a respectable woman.[98] In both Hollywood films screened in Britain and films produced by the British film industry, homosexuality always signified moral decay or danger.[99]

While many British filmmakers voluntarily promoted these messages, they also operated under significant legal constraints. The British Board of Film Censors screened and awarded audience certificates based on the film's content; their standards and regulations therefore serve as a map of the boundaries of respectability and morality in British society. Some elements, such as nudity and cruelty to animals, could not be shown onscreen under any circumstances. Other regulations, however, depended on the overall message of the film.[100] For example, films could depict interracial relationships, provided that such unions ended badly. Several films featuring interracial relationships resulted in the suicide or tragic death of at least one party, and no film passed by the British Board of Film Censors prior to 1939 depicted an interracial couple who managed to reach the end of the film alive, happy, and with their relationship intact.[101]

Several popular British films from diverse genres illustrate the constraints of heteronormativity on the film industry. The 1934 historical drama *The Rise of Catherine the Great* juxtaposed two models of femininity: the capricious, overbearing, and casually sexual Empress Elizabeth, and the demure, humble, and devoted wife Catherine. The film depicted Catherine's rise to power as a necessary but reluctant act of self-defence against a philandering and psychotically abusive husband rather than an act of calculated political manoeuvring. Only Catherine's lack of ambition, delicate femininity, and devotion to her husband made her eventual ascent to the throne of Russia palatable for film censors.[102]

In a much lighter vein, the musical comedy *First a Girl* (a 1935 adaptation of *Viktor und Viktoria* and predecessor to the Blake Edwards classic *Victor/Victoria*) depicted a plucky shopgirl named Elizabeth who teams up with an aspiring Shakespeare performer and experienced female impersonator, Victor, to develop an exceptionally convincing "female impersonator" act. While this film would appear at first glance to challenge gender norms in its double-layered cross-dressing, the filmmakers scrupulously avoided any hint of homosexuality or queer gender identities outside of the theatrical realm. Victor, for example, engages in female impersonation purely for the money rather than actual desire and displays a clear attraction to a female character. In addition, Elizabeth abandons her act upon winning the love of a handsome man, neutralizing any issues that might accompany a heterosexual man entering into a relationship with someone who publicly presents as male.[103] By making all characters unambiguously heterosexual, the film rendered cross-dressing unthreatening and ultimately supportive of rigid gender binaries, serving as a testament to the limited possibilities for filmmakers who sought to directly challenge heteronormativity.

Mainstream films also promoted consistent messages regarding race and sexuality. Racist sexual stereotypes can be clearly seen in the popular 1937 film *The Bitter Tea of General Yen*, an American Frank

Capra production approved for distribution in Britain. In a fairly unusual move, this film depicts a romance between a Caucasian missionary and a Chinese man named General Yen. The impact of the interracial relationship was softened, however, by the fact that the male lead was played by Danish actor Nils Asther, while Asian actors played all other Chinese characters in the film. Following established patterns for interracial romance in the early twentieth century, the relationship ends in predictable tragedy when General Yen poisons himself. In addition to the typically cautionary ending to the romance, the film's secondary female character, the beautiful but devious concubine Mah Li, behaves in a manner consistent with Western concepts of "inscrutable" Asian femininity.[104] In accordance with the social and legal constraints of early British cinema, films like *General Yen* could depict interracial attraction but had to warn viewers that such relationships came with dire consequences.

In short, there was nothing unusual about the fact that pornography depicted homosexuality, female sexual autonomy, and interracial relationships. Such themes appeared in mainstream cinema with great frequency. The difference between how these themes were treated in pornography and mainstream content, however, lay not only in the explicitness of the scene, but in the moral message attached. The sexually aggressive women of Hollywood film noir and British melodrama either converted through marriage or faced penalties for their sins in the form of unplanned pregnancy, abandonment, or death. The women of pornography, in contrast, initiated sexual encounters with total impunity. Pornography's interracial sexual encounters, while in many ways reproducing stereotypes of Black or Asian sexuality, did not condemn through tragedy as mainstream entertainment did. While both male and female characters in pornography could enjoy homosexual encounters, even the slightest hint of homosexuality in mainstream literature and film had to be accompanied by clear moral condemnation (preferably in the form of an agonizing demise) in order to avoid charges of obscenity.

These differences must be understood in terms of how mainstream and pornographic materials were produced and distributed. Mainstream British filmmakers worked with the full knowledge that they would have to submit their finished product to a censor; in the case of American filmmakers, they could face serious consequences for running afoul of the Hays Code. Beyond this formal regulation, filmmakers also had to contend with the possibility that their reputations would suffer or that they might face condemnation in the press if they misjudged sexual norms and gender roles or pushed boundaries too far. Pornographers, on the other hand, worked in already-marginalized spaces. Having been constructed as deviant simply by virtue of producing sexually explicit work, pornographers had little incentive to play it safe. To be clear, I do not argue that this was a conscious decision or deliberate rebellion; rather, I wish to call attention to the ways in which pornography complicated normative categories and assumptions, and how this contestation logically followed from conditions of production, distribution, and consumption.

CONCLUSION

Let us imagine a habitual pornography consumer in early twentieth-century Britain. What did this person see when they looked at nude photos or read a risqué story? As many of the examples provided in this chapter illustrate, pornography often contained subversive gender interactions and sexual images. It could also, however, reproduce mainstream hierarchies. One example of pornography might embrace assertive female sexuality while another reinforced Orientalist fantasies of lustful beys and submissive harem girls. In other words, we can reasonably imagine that our imaginary pornography consumer would have seen a variety of desirable sexual practices and liberated gender roles as well as constant reinforcement of imperial ideologies and white supremacy. One thing this imaginary viewer would not have seen, however, would be a signal illustrating that some sexualities or practices had greater value than others. Given the porous boundaries between roles like consumer, distributor, and producer, it then becomes all too easy to imagine this fictional viewer reproducing the same set of themes and unstable categories in their own work. We can only speculate about what message, if any, pornographers wanted to communicate, but we can point to the larger corpus of early twentieth-century pornography as the creative space in which they worked and learned. That space clearly fostered a queer sexual outlook with distinct norms and principles rather than a mere vulgar copy of normative sexuality.

The major goal of this chapter has been to look at pornography against the backdrop of the groups that produced, distributed, and consumed it. Each medium offered its own limitations and possibilities for the kind of sexual scenarios that one could depict. Different technologies required different levels of participation by performers, particularly women. Comparisons drawn between printed matter, photography, and film clearly indicate that performers did not function as puppets. Violence commonly found in printed matter seldom appeared in situations requiring a model's participation, and the emphasis placed on female rather than male sexual pleasure depended heavily on the medium. Customers also shaped the content of pornography, making requests for specific poses and sexual acts. Recognizing that pornographic content was to a large extent negotiated between customers, producers, and performers rather than unilaterally imposed from above by a single participant further reinforces the importance of thinking about how pornography was made and whose views and desires were reflected in the finished product. We must remember, however, that participants in the pornography trade did not have uncontested authority over what they produced, where it was distributed, and what could be purchased. In the next three chapters, we turn to the question of how state and civil authorities viewed and reacted to the trade and its subversive products, and how their actions dictated the spaces within which these materials were created.

CHAPTER FOUR

"No Public Danger, but a Matter More for Pity"

The British Press and the Pornography Trade

On 8 July 1936, the *Times* of London reported that Old Street magistrate Herbert Metcalfe had ordered the destruction of 14,582 photographs, pamphlets, and books seized from the Bethnal Green shop of Maurice Sugarman. Prior to the destruction order, Sugarman had pleaded guilty to charges of selling packets of obscene photographs by post and had been offered the choice between three months' imprisonment or £75 in fines and fees.[1] Given the variety and large quantity of materials seized, one might expect that the story would have received extensive coverage in British newspapers. Instead, the story of Sugarman's conviction appeared on page 16 and ran only 126 words. Moreover, the article employed a neutral and reserved tone rather than the sensationalism all too frequently employed in journalistic coverage of pornography in various historical contexts.

The *Times*'s coverage of the Sugarman case provides a useful example of a national trend in early twentieth-century journalistic approaches to pornography and obscenity cases. While newspapers used sensationalist tactics to compete for an ever-larger population of readers, their coverage of pornography cases tended toward measured and even dull reporting. Rather than emphasize potential moral danger, journalists routinely described pornography cases with such remarks as "no public danger, but a matter more for pity."[2] This approach to pornography is perplexing on two levels. First, late nineteenth-century journalists like W.T. Stead had frequently produced sensationalist exposés of smut peddlers, pieces that triggered public outrage and supported the goals of the social purity movement; dramatic coverage of pornography therefore had well-established and recent precedent in the British newspaper industry.[3] Second, as I have discussed at length in previous chapters, there is every indication that the size of the pornography trade increased rather than decreased between 1900 and 1945, with new forms of distribution emerging after the departure of publishers like Charles Carrington. While the Society for the Suppression of Vice (SSV) reported seizing roughly 140,000 pornographic photographs and prints in the forty-year period leading up to 1872, during the 1920s a single case could easily yield over 20,000 photographs.[4] Networks connecting local customers and distributors in the British Isles and their counterparts abroad ensured a steady supply of foreign pornography, while local producers made modest but important contributions to the market. Moreover, the early twentieth century saw the emergence of pornographic film and other new technologies that could have served as perfect fodder for a moral panic. In other words, this trend toward less alarmist coverage occurred in a context that in many ways appeared ripe for an explosion of anti-pornography sentiment.

Rather than following a reduction in pornography consumption or a general move toward less sensational reporting, journalistic restraint regarding issues of obscenity and pornography resulted from the newspaper industry's need to strike a balance between competing discourses of morality, sexuality, and controversial policy questions like censorship and imprisonment. In addition, business interests stood to lose profits from censorship or other close official scrutiny of printed matter, particularly given the newspaper industry's own connections to pornography distribution through the mechanism of printed advertising. Due to the increased importance of maintaining both a diverse readership and high advertising revenues, post-1900 journalists occupied a precarious position. On the one hand, sex scandals and moral outrage could be a boon for newspaper sales. On the other hand, any large-scale campaign attempting to eradicate the mail-order pornography trade would eventually have to contend with the importance of the classified pages and advertisements found in every British newspaper. In addition, editors who sought to push the boundaries of public acceptability could find their own papers prosecuted in the event of increased vigilance against sexual content. In response to these surrounding social and economic pressures, British newspapers adopted a measured tone in reporting obscenity cases, balancing moral condemnation with warnings about the dangers of censorship and excessive policing. Journalists also emphasized elements of the trade that redirected focus away from the domestic newspaper industry and placed blame for pornography distribution on foreigners and immigrants. The British press's approach to the issue did not result solely from factors internal to the newspaper industry, but rather was aligned with the ideology of other powerful social actors. These changes in the treatment of pornography must, therefore, be analyzed against the backdrop of the press's relationship with other actors like the state and the anti-vice movement and with an eye toward how these changes affected the shape of the pornography trade's British networks and their transnational counterparts.

Early twentieth-century newspapers varied significantly in their politics and readership, raising questions of whether they should be discussed as a single body of evidence. Despite differences in journalistic style, the political leanings of newspaper owners, and other factors, post-1900 ownership of British newspapers became heavily concentrated in the hands of a small number of magnates. As a result, large numbers of newspapers reflected similar views on various political and social issues.[5] While not every newspaper approached the issue of pornography in an identical fashion, some trends appear consistent regardless of circulation size, political position, or status as a national or provincial paper. As will be discussed in chapter 6, pornography was not a subject of partisan debate within Parliament or other state bodies. A paper's allegiance to Conservative, Labour, or other parties therefore had little effect on their coverage of the pornography trade.

While this widespread political consensus on pornography might explain the lack of obvious party-line distinctions in newspaper reports on the issue, the newspaper industry was divided by other factors. Status as a national or regional paper, for instance, led to widely varying emphases, styles, and coverage of different issues. Publications printed for particular social groups also carried distinctions in content.[6] Despite this heterogeneity within the newspaper industry, post-1900 coverage of pornography as an issue proved remarkably consistent. The editors and owners of papers may have disagreed on economic policy, imperial concerns, and other major social and political questions, but these distinctions fell away when it came to coverage of pornography-related arrests or scandals. For this specific study, therefore, it makes sense to view newspapers broadly and as a single body of materials.

The newspaper industry played a crucial role in the regulation, dissemination, and policy debates surrounding pornography, but it also approached the topic in a way that proves problematic for historians. While the police, government officials, and the legal system all to some extent conflated sexualized obscenity (pornography) with materials obscene on moral or political grounds, all of them drew practical policy distinctions that constructed pornography as a distinct and identifiable form of obscene publication. Newspapers, in contrast, rarely made any distinctions between different forms of obscenity. As a result, analysis of newspaper coverage of obscene publications is necessarily ambiguous and includes some coverage concerning materials that would not have been considered pornographic by authorities of the period. Despite this fact, newspaper coverage of the issue affected both state policy and the shape of the pornography trade regardless of whether the specific case under discussion involved pornography or another form of obscene material. As a result, it is crucial to include these ambiguous cases rather than restrict analysis solely to stories concerned with clear examples of pornography in order to fully understand the newspaper industry's role in policy and the development of pornography networks. We will now take a closer look at specific shifts in the British newspaper industry and how those changes affected their coverage of pornography as a social issue.

HISTORY OF THE BRITISH NEWSPAPER

The newspaper industry achieved its greatest level of cultural and political relevance in British society between 1850 and 1950. Particularly after 1900, newspapers became a mass-marketed product aimed at a broad variety of classes, ages, and genders rather than a narrow group of elites. Post-1900 newspapers were thus both a tool of social control and a potential form of subversion that could represent and appeal to marginalized people.[7] The early twentieth century's "New Journalism" required newspapers to strike a precarious balance between the conflicting interests of parties ranging from the working classes to members of Parliament. Newspapers could neither appear insensitive to the needs of the masses nor employ enough working-class populist rhetoric to antagonize advertisers and business interests. Newspapers had to support parliamentary action and the state's imperial agenda while simultaneously attacking the foibles of hated individual government officials, a goal that proved vulnerable to miscalculation.[8]

An ideological shift occurred in the newspaper industry between the 1880s and the 1920s, rejecting "upliftment" of the masses in favour of populist journalism that purported to represent the views of its broad readership.[9] Some historians attribute this shift to the rise of propaganda theory during the First World War, which added a negative connotation to the concept of deliberately influencing the public. As a result, newspapers began to present themselves as a medium that represented rather than influenced public opinion, however far they fell short of that goal in practice.[10] Others have pointed to economic explanations for changing philosophies of news reporting and the rise of "New Journalism" under newspaper magnates like Lord Northcliffe, owner of numerous papers including the *Daily Mail* and the *Times*. This high concentration of newspapers under a single owner, coupled with improvements in transportation and faster print technology, all contributed to a farther reach and greater demand for British newspapers than had ever existed in the past. Northcliffe increased this demand still further through methods designed to attract the widest possible readership. Under the banner of New Journalism, editors and journalists carefully calibrated everything from headlines to the physical layout of the papers to appeal to the masses.[11]

Under Northcliffe's direction, sensationalist reporting and gimmicks like contests attracted working-class readers and increased sales. London-based papers expanded across Britain, pushing provincial papers out of business. Most importantly, the business strategy of Northcliffe and his rivals depended heavily on attracting as many advertisers as possible, vastly increasing the revenue derived from advertising compared to newspaper sales. The introduction of advertisers as a major force in the newspaper industry added a variety of business interests for politicians and journalists, who were those most directly concerned with the messaging of newspapers.[12] Changes in mass media coverage of pornography were therefore not an isolated occurrence, but rather were bound up in larger cultural and economic pressures leading to changes in how reporters approached a range of issues.[13]

Gender and sexuality were major sites of contestation in the early twentieth-century newspaper industry. Competition between different models of morality and sexuality could be seen in the need for newspapers to appeal to as wide a readership as possible. Northcliffe's papers recognized that sexual content attracted readers, particularly youths and members of the working classes, but too much discussion of sex would repel middle-class and professional audiences. As a result, constant class-based tension surrounded the depiction of sexuality in post-1900 newspapers. This tension occasionally flared up into controversy as newspapers experimented and pushed the boundaries of acceptable newspaper content.[14] Similar tension emerged between competing discourses of gender norms. Edwardian and interwar newspapers, which needed to attract female as well as male readers, had to contend with shifting gender roles such as the advancement of women's suffrage. While newspapers continued to reflect ideals of domesticity and patriarchal family structures, journalists could not completely ignore changing views of gender without alienating female readers.[15]

In sum, the newspaper industry underwent crucial changes in its role in British society from the late nineteenth to the mid-twentieth century. Reporting became more sensational, advertising revenue increased dramatically, and newspaper readership expanded to include both elite and mass audiences. While it is beyond the scope of this project to pinpoint every factor leading to this transformation, the newspaper industry clearly developed a far different relationship with the early twentieth-century public than had existed in previous years. In the specific area of coverage of pornography sales and consumption, changes were also apparent.

These shifts, however, did not follow the same trajectory as the rest of British journalism. Rather than becoming more sensationalized, stories of pornography consumption became more neutral and were accompanied by warnings against moral panic or judicial excess. In addition, stories shifted blame for pornography circulation from the urban poor to foreigners and hypocritical elites. In other words, something about pornography set it apart from the bulk of other sexual scandals and vices covered by newspapers. By situating journalistic coverage of pornography cases in the context of expanded readership and Northcliffe's New Journalism, we can identify the specific concerns and relationships between the newspaper industry, the British state, civil actors, as well as the ways in which pornography operated in the spaces between these interests.

NINETEENTH-CENTURY NEWSPAPERS

One of the most striking features of this shift toward cautious and neutral reporting on pornography was its speed; during the late 1890s, the newspaper industry still firmly adhered to older sensationalist narratives of pornography as a threat, but by the Edwardian years they seem to have changed their position. Prior to 1900, the newspaper industry served as one of the main proponents of obscenity prosecutions and the eradication of pornography. Journalists forged strong relationships with purity campaigners and reform organizations like the National Vigilance Association (NVA), painting their prosecution efforts in an overwhelmingly positive light. Government officials who introduced anti-obscenity measures enjoyed similarly benign coverage, while law enforcement officers perceived as lax on issues of obscene publications could be subjected to stinging criticism. While a variety of narratives surrounded the pornography trade, the most common threats identified by the nineteenth-century press involved the corruption of youth and the contamination of English national character by the morals of the inferior classes, a population of working poor that also happened to fall outside of expected newspaper readership.

The journalists and editors of the *Pall Mall Gazette* embodied the nineteenth century's "crusading" approach to journalism, frequently playing up the moral and national threat posed by obscene publications. Stories about the circulation of "street literature" often appeared in the paper's first two pages and included lengthy analyses. Headlines included such eye-catching and inflammatory examples as "How Bad Books May Destroy States" and "The Nuisance of the Streets."[16] These articles displayed several consistent features. In the most important pattern, they linked the sale and consumption of obscene publications to widespread social degeneration rather than simply to individual harm. For example, one article demanded the suppression of obscene publications on the following grounds: "It is both legitimate and necessary to oppose the circulation of writings which may attack public morality, for nations who respect women and who are pure in their sentiments grow and prosper; whereas those in which immorality reigns, on the contrary, decline and fall."[17] In addition to promoting narratives of national decay, *Pall Mall Gazette* articles displayed a deep admiration for purity organizations like the SSV. Journalists described obscenity convictions secured by the organization using terms such as "reflecting the highest possible credit" of the SSV, or "the mischief done [by the accused] to the morals of society was incalculable."[18]

Alarmist coverage of the pornography trade was not limited to crusader publications like the *Pall Mall Gazette.* National and provincial papers ranging from the *Times* to the *Northeastern Daily Gazette* all characterized obscene publications as a potentially devastating threat to society. Journalists from a variety of newspapers described obscene publications using phrases like "the most loathsome blight that can fall upon [young people's] lives" and "wretched garbage."[19] The moral threat identified in this heated coverage depended heavily on class. Accused pornographers described in the press generally worked as street hawkers or owned small shops on the Strand.

Reports of those corrupted by pornographers' wares, in contrast, focused on such practices as hawking obscene publications in respectable neighbourhoods.[20]

Nineteenth-century newspapers also identified highly gendered threats posed by obscene publications. Details such as allegations that a pornographic photographer had thrown catalogues over the walls of a girls' school bolstered claims of the threat posed by the accused.[21] Heavily gendered concern also applied to young men and boys. An article in the *Times* concerning a convicted dealer of pornographic photos emphasized the horror of knowing that the man's trade had "carried on to poison the morals of hundreds of lads."[22] Journalists, while acknowledging that women and girls consumed obscene publications, clearly viewed indecent literature as particularly threatening to young males. While young males constituted the group most likely to be personally corrupted by purchasing or viewing obscenity, journalists saw threats to women in the apparent decreased respect for womanhood promoted by the publications.[23]

While relations between the newspaper industry and the social purity movement remained largely positive through the end of the nineteenth century, interactions between journalists, police, and government officials could be tense. Articles frequently accused the police of indifference or incompetence in the enforcement of obscenity laws. An 1884 article in the *Dundee Courier*, for example, expressed the hope that a public anti-obscenity lecture delivered by a prison chaplain might result in the police being "quickened into greater activity."[24] On other occasions, purity campaigners and journalists joined forces to lobby for direct intervention on the part of the Home Office to stop the obscene publications trade.[25] These articles questioned the state's commitment to battling the obscenity threat while simultaneously bolstering the moral authority of journalists and purity campaigners.

Taking a comparative look at nineteenth-century coverage of pornography tells us several things. First, it plainly illustrates that the newspaper industry did not remain consistent in its approach to pornography as a social issue. Moreover, as the evidence below indicates, shifts in tone and style could occur within a remarkably short period of time.[26] Second, this discussion of the relationships between mass media, the state, and private organizations reveals the capabilities of the newspaper industry when disrupting the pornography trade suited their interests. During the period in the late nineteenth century when the press enjoyed close relationships with the social purity movement, the British state passed far more anti-obscenity legislation than was ever passed in the first half of the twentieth century.[27] In addition, enforcement of these laws became so severe that it resulted in the aforementioned exodus of prominent British pornographers to the Continent to avoid prosecution.[28] Given the newspaper industry's demonstrated ability and willingness to disrupt pornography operations in Britain, we now turn to the question of why they largely abandoned such efforts after 1900.

TWENTIETH-CENTURY OBSCENITY CASE COVERAGE

In the first decade of the twentieth century, newspapers began to adopt a far calmer tone regarding issues of pornography distribution. Obscene publications cases rarely appeared on the first few pages, and were often relegated to brief paragraphs buried in the law enforcement or police sections. In a representative example, the trial of a man accused of printing over eight thousand copies of German nude photos per month garnered a less prominent placement on page 7 of the *Western Daily Press* than a heartwarming photo of a sheepdog cuddling with a tabby cat.[29] Heated language and lengthy quotes from magistrates bemoaning the social evils of obscene publications noticeably decreased. Journalists continued to place blame on police incompetence and foreign influence, but these ideas did not accompany demands for greater censorship or direct intervention by Parliament or the Home Office.

It is important to recognize that changes in obscenity case coverage did not constitute acceptance or defence of obscene publications. Pornographic photographs and books still served as a marker of immorality. In some articles, possession of obscene publications was used as a titillating detail in an otherwise unrelated story. In coverage of a heavily publicized 1911 Italian murder trial, for example, a priest's collection of obscene postcards received frequent mention despite its lack of direct relevance to the case.[30] In other articles, journalists made similar references to obscene publications, using discoveries of nude postcards or obscene books to increase interest in a story.[31] Despite the perceived relationship between obscenity and immorality, however, the presence of obscene publications appeared as more of a colourful detail than a major aspect of surrounding criminal activity.

The decline of heated anti-pornography rhetoric, combined with reduced criminal penalties and the diminishing relevance of vice societies (discussed in chapters 5 and 6), created an environment far more conducive to the quiet growth of pornography networks than had existed in the nineteenth century. While frequent use of pornography as an aside designed to mark its owner as morally inferior reinforced cultural views of pornography as an obvious yet unexamined evil, the lack of fervent calls for enforcement reduced the chances of serious anti-pornography campaigns. As long as pornographers and customers stayed out of the public eye, the newspaper industry refrained from pushing to have them rooted out. Silence was not, however, the newspaper industry's only reaction to the pornography trade. In addition, the ways in which journalists reported those cases that seemed to warrant discussion also contained features that undermined the possibility of serious anti-pornography efforts and worked against the emergence of moral panics.

In one of the most striking changes to emerge in early twentieth-century coverage of obscene publications, journalists began to include hints of sympathy for defendants. While pre-1900 coverage had rarely featured any statements from accused pornographers, twentieth-century journalism offered glimpses of the defendants' views. Newspaper articles dedicated particular attention to cheeky retorts to the prosecution's questioning. For example, one article in the *Daily Mail* emphasized a shopkeeper's total co-operation in the police investigation of her shop before including her casual remark that "the police were her best customers."[32] In another example, Gloucester defendant Dorothy Kernahan responded to a magistrate's questions about postcards sold in her shop by handing him a commonly sold periodical and pointing out that such (apparently comparable) materials were freely available in every shop.[33] Other articles emphasized defendants' claims that their postcards and magazines could be considered no more obscene than nude paintings found in elite art galleries.[34] This shift in coverage had the effect of humanizing defendants in contrast to the inflammatory descriptions provided by magistrates. Significantly, journalists identified the defendants in most of these cases as working-class street hawkers or lower-middle-class booksellers, many of them female. Rather than reflecting strictly male and middle-class views by quoting purity campaigners and magistrates, the inclusion of statements by defendants provided glimpses of diverse voices and viewpoints completely absent from nineteenth-century coverage. Given the expanded readership of post-1900 newspapers, this increased attention to female and working-class voices seems to have been a deliberate attempt to appeal to as many readers as possible.

In no way did reporting these rebellious statements qualify as journalistic endorsement or acceptance of the pornography trade. Newspapers more than compensated for these humanizing portrayals through their oft-repeated imagery of corrupted children and foreign smut-peddlers. These glimpses of unapologetic behaviour, however, constituted one of the few moments in which an accused pornographer or collector could express their views beyond the confines of pornography distribution networks. Neither newspapers nor the state ever allowed pornography supporters a recognized position in public discourse, but statements made in court or while confronted by police nevertheless publicly circulated the message that many pornographers were prepared to assert their views and defend their trade in the face of state authority.

APPROACHES TO RACE, GENDER, AND AGE

Despite the shift toward humanizing British defendants and downplaying the threat posed by pornography, journalists highlighted certain aspects that posed moral and social dangers. Immigrants and foreign producers received significant attention. Journalists consistently reported immigrant defendants' nationalities, even when this information had no relevance to the case. A 1900 article, for instance, placed unnecessary emphasis on the defendant's Italian background.[35] In some cases, even British-born children of immigrants were characterized as foreign. A 1935 edition of the *Western Morning News,* for example, specifically described convicted bookseller Louis Phillips as the London-born son of Russian immigrants.[36] Overseas pornographers also received coverage in British newspapers; the *Dundee Courier*, in one instance, reported on the criminal conviction of one Napoleon Hayard, the alleged "king of the Paris street hawkers."[37]

Journalists also placed greater emphasis on products of foreign origin than those produced domestically. The press frequently applied the ambiguous label "foreign" to descriptions of seized publications and photographs, rarely including more specific information regarding the origin of the materials.[38] Use of the word "foreign," rather than signalling a specific origin, worked as shorthand for obscenity and depravity; a 1923 article in the *Nottingham Evening Post,* for instance, made use of the phrase "abominable foreign filth."[39] Some articles went so far as to claim that all pornographic materials came to Britain from abroad, denying any evidence of domestic production.[40] As in the nineteenth century, France appeared as the default source of depravity and major producer of obscene publications.[41] Unlike nineteenth-century coverage, however, post-1900 newspapers also acknowledged obscene publications originating in Germany, Spain, the United States, and other countries.[42] While journalists clearly widened their understanding of the international pornography trade beyond France, they did not display a clear awareness of the transnational movement of pornographers and their goods around the globe. Rarely, for example, did journalists point out the existence of a colonial trade. Nor did they report on cases of British pornographers involved in an overseas market. In general, the newspaper industry sought to absolve Britain of responsibility for production of obscene publications, painting the country as an island of sanity and sexual morality surrounded by unsavoury foreign influences.

In discussing pornography distribution and consumption, newspapers adopted a surprisingly gender-neutral stance after 1900. While the protection of women and young girls had been a staple of nineteenth-century anti-pornography writings, it did not appear as a prominent feature of news coverage between 1900 and 1945. Twentieth-century newspapers continued to classify youths as a vulnerable category, but adult women no longer appeared as major candidates for corruption. This cannot be attributed to a lack of awareness of female customers; in numerous articles, journalists reported women and girls purchasing obscene publications. In one example, a husband in a divorce case submitted evidence that his wife, in addition to being an alcoholic, possessed numerous obscene photographs. While this piece of evidence succeeded in winning the judge's sympathy, the wife's gender received no emphasis, suggesting that a husband's pornography consumption would also have been considered a marker of deviance.[43] In addition, cases in which a witness reported seeing a defendant selling pornography to young people included youths of both sexes, with neither boys nor girls receiving greater attention.[44] This indicates an early twentieth-century shift toward structuring the risks of pornography solely in terms of age rather than through a hierarchy that combined age, gender, and class.

Early twentieth-century newspapers also appeared largely indifferent to gender in their discussion of distributors and producers appearing in court. Numerous cases included female defendants who owned bookshops or sold pornography through other means, yet these accused pornographers received no special attention from journalists compared to their male counterparts. Even an article involving obscene magazines purchased from a fifteen-year-old female clerk made no more than a passing reference to her age.[45] Numerous other stories reported on female shopkeepers or hawkers charged with distributing obscene books or photographs.[46] Several articles addressed obscene publications charges made against married or cohabiting couples, placing no greater emphasis on the male or female half of the pair. In one example, police charged a husband and wife with selling grossly obscene photographs. The subsequent article paid little special attention to the wife's participation, choosing instead to emphasize the fact that both members of the couple were hearing-impaired.[47] As these examples make clear, journalists fully understood that women participated in the obscene publications trade. The businesslike tone of articles reporting on female pornographers indicates that discourses surrounding obscene publications did not include concepts of pornography as inherently hostile to women. More importantly, however, journalists reporting on female pornographers and customers displayed no interest in stoking moral panic in the ways that nineteenth-century journalists had often done when choosing how to frame gendered issues related to obscene publications.

In addition to gender, nineteenth-century coverage had depended on age as a category by which to judge vulnerability to corruption. Post-1900 newspapers did not abandon concepts of children as a group that could be harmed by obscenity. In fact, articles frequently judged the severity of the alleged crime and potential for damage according to the likelihood that a youth could gain access to the materials.[48] Journalists did, however, temper their rhetoric and include greater recognition of young people's active involvement in the pornography trade. While nineteenth-century coverage had depicted children as accosted or seduced by pornography hawkers, post-1900 coverage acknowledged the more realistic possibility that curious young people might seek out mail-order pornography. Many of these articles concerned the arrest or prosecution of a dealer who came to the attention of authorities after a child or youth had been caught in possession of pornographic wares. In a typical example, a Leicester police officer discovered that young people throughout his village had acquired modified opera glasses that displayed an obscene photograph when held to the eye. The article noted that the prosecution of the vendor responsible for distributing the glasses followed from the discovery that he had sold to children, but included no histrionics on the evil effects attributable to obscene materials.[49] In another case, the *Times* reported on an incident in which a schoolboy ordered a packet of obscene materials from an ad in a comic book, resulting in the subsequent prosecution of the supplier. Notably, this article included attention to the great lengths the boy went to acquire the materials (including signing the name of the school's headmaster on the order form) rather than depicting the supplier as preying on innocent children, as had often been the case in Victorian-era coverage.[50]

Early twentieth-century coverage also recognized that young people acted as sellers, reporting arrests and prosecutions of "boy shopkeepers" and teenage girls who worked in tobacco shops.[51] These vendors, while identified as young people, were not depicted as unusual. One can infer that average readers would have viewed the fact of a sixteen-year-old selling pornography as unfortunate but not particularly shocking.[52] In newspapers' treatment of underage customers and hawkers, we can see the influence of changing ideologies of youth and childhood. While shielding children from sexual knowledge had been a major middle-class concern in the nineteenth century, the first half of the twentieth century saw growing support for educating children about sexuality.[53] This education remained extremely limited, leaving many people unfamiliar with the biology of sexuality and pregnancy until well into adulthood. While nineteenth-century parents viewed sexual ignorance as appropriate for children, early twentieth-century parents more frequently treated it as a problem that needed to be addressed.[54] In addition, post-1900 physicians and sexologists began to question the accepted belief that masturbation was a threat to children. While popular notions of masturbation as immoral remained in place, it was generally seen as much less of a danger than it had been in the nineteenth century.[55] In short, the early twentieth century saw gradual cultural change that rendered the idea of sexual curiosity among children as a problem, but not one on the same scale as in the Victorian period. The involvement of teenagers and children in pornography consumption or sales therefore shifted in status from national crisis to unexceptional youthful indiscretion.

FEAR OF CENSORSHIP

While early twentieth-century newspapers altered their coverage of pornography, they continued to frame it as a social problem. No element in mass media went so far as to declare pornography harmless. Newspapers did, however, balance discussions of the threat posed by pornography with warnings against censorship. In a direct reversal from Victorian-era coverage, newspaper editorials insisted that existing legislation contained sufficient tools to deal with the pornography trade, and that creating additional censorship boards or other regulations could only limit free expression.[56] Moreover, while nineteenth-century papers had castigated legislation for not going far enough, interwar opinion began to criticize the broad and sometimes ambiguous wording of the regulations and feared the possibility that they could be used to impose greater controls on publishing.[57]

Home Secretary from 1924 to 1929, William Joynson-Hicks, often referred to in the press as "Jix," was a particularly reviled supporter of censorship. While late nineteenth-century press coverage had included the highest praise for politicians and officials who opposed pornography on moral grounds, interwar newspapers mocked Jix as prudish and anachronistic in his views on modesty and sexual decency.[58] This is particularly notable considering that Joynson-Hicks did not support new legislation but merely exercised his discretionary powers as Home Secretary in a way many considered to be excessive.[59] While newspapers did not dismiss the supposed threat posed by obscene publications, the opinions of journalists and readers had clearly shifted to a point at which moderate opposition to pornography sales, manifested in such enforcement methods as arresting those who publicly displayed pornography or sold it to children, became far more palatable than extensive censorship or aggressive policing of the mails.

COMPARATIVE CASES

Given this abrupt shift in tone regarding the coverage of obscenity cases and the pornography trade, one might conclude that the early twentieth-century journalistic profession simply turned away from sensationalist rhetoric in favour of more sober and balanced reporting. By comparing coverage of pornography cases with other topics, however, it becomes clear that sensationalism still reigned in the reporting of numerous social issues. Articles about the white slave trade continued to appear, the coverage maintaining the same hysterical rhetoric prevalent during the nineteenth century. League of Nations conferences addressing the white slave trade received extensive coverage, much of which quoted the most lurid and frightening claims made by delegates. A 1927 article appearing on the front page of the *Nottingham Evening Post*, for example, included an extensive and alarming list of methods by which traffickers supposedly tricked young girls into the trade; dangers to young girls included pursuing a career on the stage and seduction by foreign men.[60]

Obscene publications and the white slave trade received similar treatment by social reformers and legal bodies like the League of Nations, both of whom combined the two issues into single conferences and publications.[61] Newspapers, however, had very different approaches to each. Here, the role of advertising and obscenity laws appear as important factors. Newspapers stood to lose nothing from campaigns against white slavery. Indeed, stirring up fears about an epidemic of trafficked white virgins could only increase sales. Unless the coverage became too lurid or graphic, newspapers would lose no advertisers and would not be targeted for legal action. Obscene publications campaigns, in contrast, could easily backfire against the newspaper industry if regulation efforts turned to the issue of newspaper advertising or other forms of censorship.

Journalists did not restrict sensationalist coverage to the white slave trade. Alcohol, cocaine, and opium were treated as devastating threats in mainstream newspaper coverage. Like pornography and the white slavery narrative, cocaine and opium could be persuasively framed as a foreign threat. Both served as a marker of the racial Other, whether through stories of sordid Chinese opium dens or "coloured musicians" arrested for possession of cocaine.[62] Alcohol, in contrast, had a substantial domestic market and significant numbers of British producers whom newspapers could alienate if they were perceived as hostile to alcohol consumption. Despite these factors, the temperance movement received support from the press during the First World War and the interwar years; protests by brewers' unions and others opposed to temperance were far less effective than the widespread fears that drink could harm the war effort by affecting industrial efficiency.[63] In addition, the increasing importance of female readership may have been a factor. Prior to and during the First World War, women's organizations spearheaded numerous temperance efforts, becoming involved in political lobbying, child neglect prosecutions, and the institutionalization of alcoholics.[64] As a medium seeking to attract female readers, newspapers could demonize alcohol in a way that would have been impossible to apply to pornography without leaving the industry vulnerable to the side effects of censorship and regulated advertising. The sensationalism found in stories about alcohol and drug abuse, like the white slave trade, raises the question of why the press abandoned historical precedent by not employing similar tactics in their coverage of obscenity issues.

THE DE MARNEY CASE

The 1906 prosecution of *Judy* editor Edward de Marney may be partially responsible for decreases in alarmist coverage of the pornography trade relative to other issues. On 19 December 1906, de Marney appeared at the Central Criminal Court under charges of violating the 1884 Post Office Protection Act. While no obscene matter could be found in the pages of *Judy*, the advertising section contained ads for distributors of pornographic books and photos operating in Munich, Paris, Amsterdam, Berlin, and other European cities.[65] The case's lead detective testified that he had been aware of de Marney's business since 1901 and had warned him against printing the advertisements on several occasions. Upon receiving photographs ordered from the contacts listed in *Judy*'s advertising page, the police determined them to be grossly indecent. The court found de Marney guilty, despite a total lack of evidence that de Marney himself had ever dealt with or handled obscene publications.[66]

De Marney's case had troubling implications for the newspaper industry. Previous allegations of obscenity in journalism, such as sordid details included in coverage of divorce cases, involved allegedly obscene content printed in the newspaper itself, an issue that could easily be dealt with through self-policing.[67] Even previous cases involving obscene advertisements involved advertising contraceptives and other products likely to be seized under various obscenity laws. With the de Marney conviction, however, newspaper owners and editors faced the possibility of prosecution even for innocuously worded advertisements offering "books" or "photos." Given the number of classified ads printed on a daily basis, thorough investigations would have been virtually impossible and at the very least would have severely affected the industry's advertising revenue, which was more important than ever in the early twentieth century. While the case received little public comment, one can easily imagine that it served as a rude awakening for editors who had been less than diligent in vetting their advertising sections.

Following the de Marney case, newspapers made little mention of how mail-order pornography operations advertised their wares. While many pornographers advertised in photography periodicals, art publications, and pulp magazines, advertisements also appeared in widely available newspapers. For example, classified ads for items like "French postcards," "rare books," and "photographs of the positions of matrimony" appeared in newspapers ranging from the *Illustrated Police News* to the *Essex Chronicle*.[68] Cyril Benbow's distribution efforts involved posting ads in papers like the *Sunday Times* and the *Daily Mail*; these ads mentioned books and articles alongside key terms like "corset" and "wasp-waisted," which indicated BDSM and corset fetish imagery.[69] The language used in some of these advertisements was sufficiently ambiguous to make regulation nearly impossible, even if editors had wished to do so. Rather than attempt to confront the clandestine communication occurring within their papers, members of the press opted to ignore the subject of British pornographic advertising altogether.

The British press had one major exception to their general rule of minimizing the importance of newspaper advertising in pornography distribution: the case of foreign papers. A 1923 article in the *Nottingham Evening Post*, for example, presented a sympathetic and supportive image of the Home Office's attempts to combat the growth of pornographic films. Home Office officials specifically blamed foreign papers for the spread of the films, a claim presented as plausible in the newspaper coverage.[70] Several articles emphasized the role of French newspapers and magazines in the dissemination of obscene publications. This tactic had two advantages. First, it reinforced the narrative of obscene publications as a foreign rather than domestic product. Second, it deflected attention away from British classified advertising and put pressure on foreign publications that sold papers and magazines to the English-speaking public. This strategy had obvious benefits for the British press, which depended on undermining the competition without compromising their own advertising revenue. Such policies also benefited domestic British producers and distributors seeking to advertise their wares within the country.

The press often facilitated the operations of the obscene publications trade outside the boundaries of the classified advertisement. Some government officials and purity campaigners held the press responsible for publicizing authors and titles, which then increased sales. Even under the guise of condemning a book, lurid descriptions communicated to readers which new books or magazines contained exciting or sexualized content. On numerous occasions, police and Home Office officials expressed concerns that prosecuting a minor breach of obscenity law could backfire if the press chose to publicize the case. In 1901, for example, Scotland Yard investigators advised the undersecretary of state against prosecuting a purveyor of nude mutoscope images, arguing that a failed prosecution would serve only to advertise the product to potential customers.[71] While it appears unlikely that the press made a practice of deliberately promoting obscene materials, they were clearly aware of their role in its distribution.

Evidence of the press's role in publicizing pornography went beyond anxious police memos. Publishers and authors clearly understood the advantages of having their work publicized through fiery condemnation. In August 1933, W.K. Fudge of the Mitre Press wrote to the editor of the *Daily Mail*, inviting the paper to "write an attack on [an unpublished] novel" and noting that a magazine recently condemned by the paper had enjoyed a major increase in sales.[72] While obscene books "scooped" by the paper tended to be borderline or "racy" books rather than explicit pornography or photographs, any publicity for one book would bring attention to the rest of the items in the publishing company's catalogue. For example, catalogues for the Esoterika Biblion Society of London and New York contained both racy classic literature like *Arabian Nights* and explicit literary pornography like *Autobiography of a Flea* and *The Way of a Man with a Maid.*[73] A publicized legal challenge to literature like *Arabian Nights* would, therefore, attract customers to the more explicit pornographic items. By providing free publicity, newspapers facilitated pornography distribution and provided customers with the necessary information to obtain pornographic literature and images, all without sacrificing their image as respectable family newspapers. In fact, articles written in a condemnatory tone, even if they ultimately did more to advertise than attack pornographic books, actually bolstered the newspaper industry's moral credentials.

NEWSPAPERS AND SELECTIVE PORNOGRAPHY COVERAGE

Early twentieth-century newspapers tended to focus on specific concerns rather than the full variety of issues related to pornography; aside from their emphasis on foreign pornography, they also dedicated significant attention to the failings of legal authorities. As in the late nineteenth century, relations between the police and the newspaper industry could be contentious. Police departments served as convenient scapegoats for the continuing growth and success of the pornography industry. Accusations from the press usually involved claims of police incompetence or indifference, but journalists occasionally made more serious allegations of corruption. These more pointed challenges generally originated in left-wing newspapers, most of which did not hesitate to report on state negligence. A 1929 article in the *New Statesman,* for example, implied that the London Metropolitan Police sold seized pornography and pocketed the profits rather than comply with court orders for destruction. The accusation caused enough of a stir that the superintendent of police responded to inquiries within ten days, outlining the specific destruction methods and procedures followed in obscene publications cases.[74] As this incident indicates, law enforcement officials feared the consequences of ignoring the newspaper industry's claims.

In some cases, journalists spurred police investigations by uncovering aspects of the pornography industry that had previously escaped the attention of law enforcement. Between 1920 and 1931, newspaper stories triggered half a dozen investigations into the production and screening of pornographic films on British soil. In many of these exposés on the underground pornographic film trade, journalists pointed to inaction by police and government officials as a sign of corruption. For example, a 1923 article in *John Bull* claimed that an Indian prince had brought French and German pornographic films into London, exploiting his immunity from customs checks. The prince then allegedly screened these films for Members of Parliament.[75] A 1924 article from the same publication claimed that pornographic films were being produced in London at the request of a peer. The role of this influential peer seemingly explained why the police had failed to follow up on a report filed by a witness.[76] Police found no evidence of either of these alleged pornography operations, and it appears quite likely that *John Bull* was merely printing sensational rumours. These incidents, however, reveal the powerful influence of the newspaper industry, which had the ability to pressure the police into investigating previously non-existent cases. In addition, the emphasis on foreigners (particularly foreign people of colour) and antagonism toward elites characterized obscenity case coverage during the interwar years.

Not all of the police investigations resulting from press coverage failed to produce results. In some cases, journalists uncovered genuine pornography operations that had previously escaped official notice. One of the investigations triggered by stories of an underground pornographic film circuit, a 1923 case against Kinematograph Agencies, probably uncovered a genuine pornographic film operation. The case's lead investigator, Inspector Draper, secured samples of pornographic films from his informant in the operation. The subsequent investigation suggested that films produced in London could be purchased by customers in India or South America. The case later collapsed due to a failed sting operation, but the samples obtained by Draper indicate that the newspaper industry did successfully conduct genuine investigations into the pornography trade rather than simply printing rumours.[77] Significantly, these sensational reports did not involve the domestic mail-order trade and featured a heavy emphasis on foreign sales.

These incidents reinforce the point that the newspaper industry facilitated the growth of specific practices and spaces within the pornography trade. Their coverage of foreign producers and unusual cases channelled official attention toward specific types of distributors, including some who were completely fictional. Elaborate claims of Indian princes watching pornography with MPs, in addition to being almost certainly false, bore no resemblance to the real operations of the pornography trade's transnational networks. Discussion of foreign pornography made little mention of mobile British and foreign citizens who moved across borders and distributed materials within complex transnational circuits. Nor did journalists identify the significance of mail-order and non-commercial exchange of materials between Britons and small-scale enthusiasts in other countries.

Similarly, in pressuring the London Metropolitan Police to take greater action against nefarious kingpins, newspapers ignored the fact that Customs and the Post Office accounted for 95 per cent of pornography seizures, placing the vast majority of pornography operations beyond police jurisdiction.[78] Moreover, this focus on pornographers who bore a resemblance to the organized crime lords of popular fiction did nothing to address the far more common scenario of people like Richard Elias, who produced photographs on a cottage-industry scale. As a result, while the police faced occasional pressure from the media to take greater actions against pornographers, none of this pressure directed them toward small, domestic mail-order operations, non-commercial exchanges, or customers who ordered small quantities from foreign catalogues. Protected by exaggerated images of pornographer-princes and non-existent organized criminals, small-scale pornography production and distribution networks could operate in relative safety and obscurity.

While the press deflected attention from most people involved in the pornography trade, it increased scrutiny of others. In addition to the highly improbable cases discussed above, the press made some other exceptions to their general policy of measured and calm reportage. These exceptions generally featured people who had been upstanding members of the community prior to an arrest.

Journalists and editors delighted in exposing the sins of clergymen, military officers, and schoolmasters, including far more salacious detail than typically appeared even in the prosecutions of major dealers. In 1913, for instance, press reports on a vicar charged with enclosing an obscene image in a graphically sexual letter to a young woman included numerous statements by magistrates emphasizing the "disgusting" nature of the case.[79] Five years later, a former schoolmaster serving as a lieutenant in the officer training corps received similar coverage when he faced charges of mailing obscene postcards and photographs to young women. The press focused on his military rank, position in the community, and his pathetic public declarations that "I have prayed to God every night to give me a clean heart."[80]

The appeal of these stories is not difficult to surmise. Despite the relative democratization of popular culture and a greater working-class presence in all areas of British public life in the early twentieth century, concepts of sexual morality still carried heavy class divisions. Middle-class professions and marriages still appeared as the normative ideal toward which the working class should strive.[81] Articles reporting that a cleric, the pinnacle of middle-class moral fortitude, had been caught sending dirty pictures to young girls could serve as a powerful challenge to the middle-class monopoly on respectability. By depicting such people as atypical rather than representative of their class, newspapers could make an appeal to the working class without alienating their middle-class readership. These stories, while exposing the variety of people who consumed pornography, ultimately served to reinforce heteronormativity categories and standards. In emphasizing the shocking nature of a cleric or schoolmaster being involved in pornography, the press communicated the message that respectability and pornography were mutually exclusive categories. While many individuals did in fact live outwardly respectable and normative lives while privately engaging in pornography production or consumption, the press constantly reinforced the binary between the normative and deviant sexuality, thus encouraging the growth of clandestine networks and queer spaces.[82]

In addition to these marked changes in class politics and deep concerns over the consequences of censorship, colonial readership must be considered as a factor in the changing newspaper coverage of the pornography trade. Early twentieth-century British newspapers were not written for a domestic audience alone, as they circulated throughout the colonies of the British Empire. Moreover, British and colonial papers enjoyed a symbiotic relationship; colonial papers supplied domestic British papers with international news, while copies of the *Times* or the *Daily Mail* delivered news of British politics and society to colonies all over the world.[83] This served an obvious imperial function, seeking to bind the British Empire together into an "imagined community" through a common print culture.[84]

This global newspaper readership could, however, be a double-edged sword. British newspapers with a colonial readership risked damaging the moral reputation of the metropole through reporting on an active British pornography trade. On every issue from drug abuse to white slavery, British newspapers emphasized external rather than internal threats to British sexual morality. The same held true in reporting on the pornography trade. Pornography had to be constructed as strictly foreign not only for British self-image, but for colonial audiences. In taking this approach, the British newspaper industry pursued the all-important goal of maintaining British moral superiority over both Continental Europeans and colonized peoples, but also took public focus away from those localized elements of the pornography trade that might have been effectively pursued through domestic policy actions.

THE PRESS AND PORNOGRAPHY NETWORKS

These changes in the mass media's approach to pornography had a significant impact on the shape taken by pornography distribution networks. On an entirely practical level, classified newspaper ads served as one of the major mechanisms of contact and communication within the trade. More importantly, however, British mass media framed the threat of pornography or lack thereof in such a way as to deflect popular and state attention from British networks' main forms of interaction. In failing to aggressively publicize the purported medical and psychological harms of pornography, the press robbed the anti-vice movement of one of its main arguments for strict pornography regulation.[85] The tendency to promote images of pornography as a foreign vice dovetailed with the British state's comforting assurances that pornography posed only a minor threat and that it originated almost entirely in other, less moral countries.[86]

The mass media also facilitated the growth of British and transnational pornography networks by continuing to support models of normative sexuality in which pornography could exist only as a form of deviance. While twentieth-century newspapers might have challenged images of pornography as a major evil, at no point did the industry question the basic premise of obscene materials as a social problem. Nor did they engage with the issue of pornographers and consumers as a community or profession. The press thus played a major part in constructing a sexual culture in which space existed for networks trading in deviant sexual materials to emerge, but which allowed pornography absolutely no place in mainstream public discourse. Free of serious campaigns against pornography but without any possibility of public acceptance, discreet illegal interaction became the most viable option for producers, distributors, and consumers. Having constructed the practice of pornography as deviant, the newspaper industry inadvertently laid the groundwork for the pornography trade to develop queer spaces and networks.

CONCLUSION

As the early twentieth-century British pornography trade became increasingly integrated into an intricate transnational system, the newspaper industry quietly backed away from alarmist and sensational coverage of obscene publications. While never openly declaring pornography harmless, journalists began to raise serious questions about the acceptability of censorship in the name of eradicating obscenity. In contrast to the nineteenth-century alliance between the newspaper industry and social purity campaigners, post-1900 news coverage of social purity causes could be tepid and occasionally hostile. Newspapers also deflected attention from the domestic mail-order trade, focusing on immigrants, foreign dealers, and low-level street hawkers. In short, the early twentieth-century newspaper industry's approach to obscene publications reflected an expanded readership that held increasingly fragmented and contested views on moral issues like obscene publications. None openly argued for the acceptability of pornography, but the old narratives of the threat posed by pornographic materials had begun to crumble and had not yet been replaced by an equally compelling alternative.

The factors behind this shift can be found both within the specific economic conditions of the early twentieth-century newspaper industry and in broader cultural trends in British society. Due to events such as the de Marney case and trends like the use of increasingly risqué imagery to attract readers, the press found itself vulnerable to attack under British obscenity law. Any major panic surrounding obscene publications would, therefore, pose a considerable financial and legal threat to journalists, editors, and even owners. In addition to legal self-preservation, newspapers also shifted their coverage of obscene publications cases in response to the unprecedented presence of women, young people, and members of the working class among daily newspaper readership. One-sided approaches to obscenity cases, reflecting a strictly anti-vice viewpoint, could not appeal to such a diverse population of readers.

While newspapers did not abandon older and stereotypically middle-class views of obscene publications as a social problem, they did broaden their scope to include voices and perceptions of accused pornographers, many of whom were women and/or working class. While the moral inferiority of the urban poor had been a major explanation for the nineteenth-century trade, such an explanation could not appeal to a readership that expanded beyond the middle classes. Pointing to foreigners rather than small shopkeepers or the working poor as the main sources of the obscene publications trade allowed journalists to condemn pornography without alienating large segments of their broad readership. The newspaper industry's weak and ambivalent position on pornography signalled a broader cultural shift in which competing discourses of sexual morality began to challenge views of pornography and sexuality that had gone largely unquestioned in the second half of the nineteenth century. On a practical level, this ambivalence robbed anti-pornography forces of a potentially powerful ally, leaving pornographers and their consumers in certain spaces free from the high level of unified opposition they had faced in the nineteenth century. In the next two chapters, I explore the distinct but related reasons for the lack of concerted anti-pornography efforts among the newspaper industry's former anti-obscenity allies: anti-vice organizations and the British state.

CHAPTER FIVE

"No Background of Moral Standard"

Vice Societies, Morality, and Anti-Pornography Campaigns

In 1927, members of vice societies from around the world attended an international conference on the suppression of the traffic in women and children.[1] Pornography, perceived as a related issue, appeared as part of the agenda. During a speech to the delegates, a German representative named Dr Ninck described the pornography trade as a "chain of international organizations" in which members "form[ed] circles for the purpose of exchanging or lending out obscene publications from mere lust and without thought of profit."[2] Dr Ninck seems to have understood the early twentieth-century pornography trade rather well. He recognized it as a system of loose networks and transnational connections, many of which blurred the lines between economic and social interaction. Moreover, Dr Ninck was not alone in his astute comprehension of the pornography trade, as several of his colleagues in the international anti-vice movement also observed the importance of specialized jargon, transnational communication, and other practices distinctive to the pornography trade. As reported in an anti-vice publication from the following year: "The English Press has its critics but we are assured that no newspaper or periodical in England would insert advertisements of this kind if the meaning were obvious to the uninitiated. A limited number may appear but they would be understood, should they appear, only by a small number of informed persons."[3]

Vice societies' surprisingly good grasp of the nature of pornography in the early twentieth century did not, however, translate into a comprehensive program of action against pornographers and consumers. While anti-pornography rhetoric circulated in public discourse and prosecutions occurred with regularity, no state organization claimed pornography as its top priority. Time, energy, and resources instead went toward social problems like prostitution, white slavery, venereal disease, and illegitimacy. This lack of concerted effort against pornography, which contrasted sharply with the strong anti-pornography efforts of the mid- to late nineteenth century, can be explained by several factors. First, while vice societies' positions on sexual morality remained the tacitly accepted normative standard, changing views in the press and the general public made the moral threats identified by vice societies appear less alarming or relevant than other social issues like poverty or unemployment. This proved particularly true of pornography. During the first few decades of the twentieth century, changing medical and popular opinions regarding the effects of obscenity rendered its status as a threat ambiguous and indirect. Second, competition for diminishing funds and support encouraged vice societies to narrow their activities to limited "signature" campaigns designed to appeal to donors and mark out each group's own area of expertise. As a social concern lacking the urgency or appeal of more dramatic issues like the white slave trade or colonial brothels, pornography did not feature as a central campaign and thus fell through the cracks between the different organizations.

Finally, political and legal measures that might have more effectively disrupted the trade conflicted with social trends like British opposition to censorship and demands for a less draconian criminal justice system.[4] This contributed to the growth of spaces in which pornographers and consumers could produce and exchange pornographic materials. People active in the trade experienced enough marginalization to encourage the formation of their own networks, jargon, and social practices, but not such severe persecution by anti-vice forces that participating in the trade became a significant risk. Vice societies and their allies continued to play a critical role in policing normative boundaries and constructing certain identities and practices as deviant, but these efforts no longer revolved around anti-pornography efforts after the turn of the century.

The following sections map the major vice societies and their relationships to the state and civil society. I then explore the ideology of anti-vice campaigns, identifying both the commonalities and fissures between different individuals and organizations. Finally, I situate the specific issue of pornography in the wider context of anti-vice politics and worldview. As this analysis shows, the anti-vice movement reflected a widely accepted middle-class view of sexuality and morality, but this set of sexual ideals began to lose its sense of urgency and relevance in the midst of early twentieth-century social and political upheaval. In short, few openly questioned the basic principles at the core of the anti-vice movement, such as the necessity of monogamous marriage or the negative effects of prostitution and pornography. At the same time, however, few sought active involvement in vice society campaigns or even lent token amounts of financial support. The anti-vice movement should therefore be viewed as a reflection of heteronormative sexuality and an actor in its production, but one whose influence became increasingly attenuated over time.[5] The social position and resulting actions (or lack of them) taken by vice societies and their allies served as a major contributing factor in determining the practices and spaces the pornography trade could occupy with relative impunity, along with which actions were risky and thus to be avoided.

PRIVATE ORGANIZATIONS AND SOCIAL POLICY

Vice societies have a long and storied history in Britain. During the late nineteenth century, they played a critical role in increasing public support for the anti-pornography policies that largely destroyed pre-1901 production. More broadly, they acted as arbiters of bourgeois heteronormativity, dictating the forms of sexual deviance that would be aggressively pursued and those that would be tacitly accepted. Vice societies did not, however, have unquestioned authority over British sexual norms. Rather, they had a complex and occasionally tense relationship with the British state and with other elements of civil society like the press. Moreover, these relationships changed significantly during the Edwardian years. This brings us to questions surrounding precisely what role vice societies played in producing and reinforcing normative categories in British society and how that role shifted in the twentieth century.

The first issue that must be considered is the nature of vice societies' participation in social debates surrounding normative sexuality. Large vice societies engaged in highly publicized national and international campaigns, often in partial collaboration with the state. Moreover, both vice societies themselves and various organs of the state accorded these organizations an important role in the politics of sexual morality. One vice society report described the division of labour between state and vice societies as follows: "It had been held that the function of Governments was to report on facts, and that of the voluntary associations to report on efforts" relating to traffic in women and children.[6] State documents offered a similar perspective, presenting vice societies as an integral (if occasionally exasperating) participant in policing correct standards of sexual morality.[7] On the level of social and political significance, therefore, vice societies played an important part in creating legal and social barriers to participation in the pornography trade.

The second element that must be addressed concerns whether vice societies served as a useful reflection of heteronormativity in Britain or if their views deviated significantly from widely accepted social norms. They failed, after all, to effectively combat the pornography trade and had mixed results with their other campaigns. Moreover, some historians have depicted the early twentieth century, particularly the 1920s, as a time of sexual revolution, with the rise of the New Woman and the emergence of free-love advocates like Dora and Bertrand Russell. Through this lens, social purity organizations appear as anachronistic throwbacks to the Victorian era.[8] Historians like Lesley Hall, however, have made far more convincing arguments that this "sexual revolution" was in fact limited to a small group of elite intellectuals and artists.[9] Among the general population, sexual norms continued to revolve around monogamy, marriage, and compulsory heterosexuality. In some respects, sexuality became even more constrained after the First World War. Police crackdowns on homosexuals, for example, increased during the 1930s, while eugenics supporters sought to regulate interracial sex and reproduction among the allegedly unfit.[10] These views aligned with those of vice societies, but the more important indicator of their dominant status can be found in an almost total lack of organized resistance to their core principles on the part of the press, the general public, or rival organizations. Given this lack of opposition, their inability to disrupt the pornography trade did not reflect a loss of status as the standard bearers of British heteronormativity. The diminished importance of vice societies instead reflected a cultural and political context in which the imposition of normative sexuality came into conflict with other goals and principles such as fear of censorship, a desire to see pornography as a strictly "foreign" problem, and shortages of monetary resources. In short, the lack of support for anti-pornography initiatives does not mean that Britons rejected the sexual values of vice societies. Rather, as in the case of pornography's diminished status in the British press, this relative indifference simply indicates conflicting priorities. Vice societies still, however, played a critical part in producing heteronormative and deviant identity categories and behaviours, thus creating spaces for queer contestation to emerge.

NATIONAL, INTERNATIONAL, AND LOCAL ORGANIZATIONS

While countless local organizations sought to combat vice in the years between 1900 and 1945, a small number of large societies dominated national and international anti-vice campaigns. These organizations shared a common outlook on the dangers of pornography and agreed on most points regarding sexual morality and social hygiene. On the level of daily operations and campaigns, however, clear divides emerged between these major organizations. The three most important societies concerned with pornography were the National Vigilance Association (NVA), the Public Morality Council (PMC), and the Association for Moral and Social Hygiene (AMSH).

Founded in 1885, the NVA remained the oldest and most influential anti-vice society in Britain through the first half of the twentieth century. While it had initially been highly involved in investigating and prosecuting vice, including pornography distribution, by 1900 it began to redirect its attention to international campaigns against the white slave trade. It spearheaded efforts to organize the first international conference on the topic; this and later conferences included attention to pornography as a closely related social problem.[11] Domestically, "station work" became its signature campaign. With the stated goal of rescuing trafficked girls, station workers patrolled railway stations looking for young women who appeared to be lost, threatened, or at risk in some fashion.[12] Lobbying efforts typically involved international or national rather than local bodies, including the Home Office and the League of Nations.

The emphasis on national and international lobbying extended to the NVA's anti-pornography efforts. NVA annual reports and publications like the *Vigilance Record* discussed few instances in which the NVA investigated a pornography case, prosecuted an offender, or otherwise became directly involved in fighting the pornography trade. Instead, its domestic anti-pornography efforts took the form of organizing delegations to present the Home Secretary with reports of their work or their proposals for new anti-obscenity legislation.[13] Internationally, the organization's main concern centred on ensuring that different countries developed similar legislation and policies regarding vice to allow for a coordinated effort against it.[14] In short, the NVA's main influence on sexuality took the form of policy formation rather than day-to-day policing and outreach.

The PMC, founded in 1899, approached vice in a very different way. Aside from its activities in the National Committee (discussed below), the PMC operated almost entirely in the domestic realm. Unlike the direct outreach practised by the NVA in the form of station work, the PMC focused on lobbying, public education, and directing anti-vice complaints to the appropriate local authorities. Rather than national or international bodies, their most frequent political collaborators were local borough councils.[15] While the PMC also dedicated more attention to prostitution than pornography, it engaged in more direct efforts against pornography and other forms of vice than did the NVA. For instance, PMC members patrolled areas reported to contain brothels, bottle parties, or pornographers. They collected indecent materials like American and French pulp magazines, storing samples in their official papers (purely for research purposes, of course).[16] In some cases, it collected evidence for criminal prosecutions. For example, in 1941 one member observed and obtained photographs of a book stall that purportedly sold indecent publications, a level of investigation that went well beyond reporting a perceived infraction to the police.[17] After investigating alleged vice, PMC representatives would then bring evidence to the local borough council or directly to the police. The PMC's own patrol summaries, however, clearly demonstrated its lack of interest in pornography compared with other forms of vice. One 1940 patrol summary, for instance, listed sixty-one disorderly houses and twenty-three bottle parties reported to the police, compared with only two indecent publication cases during the same time period.[18]

A newer organization, AMSH, provides an instructive comparison to older anti-vice groups. Described by Lesley Hall as "perhaps the most feminist and libertarian of the social purity organizations," AMSH deviated from the NVA and PMC in that it made gender equality a central concern of the organization.[19] Of all the major organizations, AMSH displayed the least concern with pornography. Like the NVA, its efforts overwhelmingly focused on forming deputations for lobbying government officials, printing informational leaflets, and holding public meetings. It also engaged in fact-finding missions, after which it would present its collected evidence to the relevant governmental authority. Unlike the NVA and PMC, AMSH also provided grants for foreign organizations. In all of these efforts, AMSH remained heavily focused on prostitution and venereal disease rather than the broader array of moral questions addressed by the other organizations.[20] They also displayed far more concern with vice in the colonial context than did any other national organization.[21] In short, AMSH represented a newer generation of anti-vice campaigners who regarded pornography as a secondary concern from the moment of the organization's inception rather than as a formerly crucial issue that had gradually diminished in importance.

Despite these different areas of specialization, British vice societies co-operated within the body of the National Committee. The British National Committee, in turn, collaborated with similar national committees from other countries active in anti-vice campaigns. Together, these groups formed the International Bureau for the Suppression of the Traffic in Women and Children, which held its first conference in 1899.[22] As the name of this organization suggests, the International Bureau focused on trafficked prostitutes. It also dealt with a variety of other forms of vice, including pornography.[23] As a body comprising representatives from diverse organizations, the National Committee espoused views common to all groups or arrived at through consensus. The publications of the International Bureau, in turn, reflect the shared viewpoints and points of disagreement among the anti-vice forces of different member states. As will be discussed later in this chapter, the values of British anti-vice forces enjoyed broad consensus within the larger community of vice societies around the world.

Small rescue and social hygiene organizations operating at the level of the borough or diocesan branch engaged in entirely different activities than the national and international organizations. Here, anti-pornography efforts were virtually non-existent. Although they employed the language of anti-vice organizations with terms like "vigilance, "rescue work," and "moral hygiene," local groups participated in direct community involvement rather than legislative lobbying or conferences.[24] Meetings of the Charing Cross Blue Lamp Committee, for instance, focused on employment for former prostitutes and unwed mothers, grants for treatment of venereal disease, and hospitalization for the ill.[25] The Stepney branch of the London Diocesan Council for Rescue Work similarly dedicated funds toward shelters for homeless young women, runaways, and others perceived to be at moral risk.[26] As other historians have argued, the growth of local aid societies during the 1920s and 1930s resulted in part from the British state's shift toward decentralizing welfare services and providing aid through local bodies rather than through a central Poor Law authority.[27] Anti-vice efforts thus became increasingly entangled with welfare and employment services on the local level.

This bureaucratic decentralization cannot, however, fully explain the ideological gaps between local and national organizations. Rather, the lack of attention to pornography at the local and diocesan level stemmed from significant ideological distance between the older and wealthier vice societies and those concerned with direct community aid. It also resulted from the priorities of religious institutions. Many of these smaller community aid organizations received funding from the Diocese of London, including the contents of the collection box. Organizations like the NVA also counted bishops and other clergymen among their ranks but did not enjoy the same kind of widespread institutional support offered to organizations that assisted "fallen women" or runaways in Hammersmith or Southwark.[28] While these local aid organizations may have accepted the narrative of larger vice societies regarding the causal connections between pornography and other problems like illegitimacy and prostitution, they clearly did not feel that this connection was strong enough to warrant direct action or resources, unlike the nineteenth-century vice societies that so ably drove Charles Carrington and his ilk from British shores.

IDEOLOGY OF VICE SOCIETIES

While local organizations focused on practical aid, the larger anti-vice groups devoted greater attention to articulating and actively promoting a specific moral worldview. Several different ideological strands shaped their views of sexual vice in general and pornography in particular. By the early years of the twentieth century, the ideology of the anti-vice movement had adopted elements from Christian philanthropy, women's suffrage campaigns, and imperialist concepts of racial hygiene. Christianity formed the basis for much anti-obscenity rhetoric, often existing in tension with the explicitly interfaith nature of bodies like the National Committee.[29] In one memo, the PMC put forth the following argument: "The question of what is obscene is fairly easy for those who accept

Christian Moral Standards ... But it must not be overlooked that those who accept Christian Moral Standards are vastly in the minority in this country."[30] In discussions of public campaigns and sexual education for young people, the need to integrate Christian positions on sexuality appeared as a consistent theme.[31] These references to Christian values, however, rarely if ever accompanied any kind of theological discussion or explanation of how Christian views deviated from those of other religious groups or of society at large. AMSH writers claimed on one page of their newsletter that their support of "fundamental moral principles" existed independently of any particular religious creed, then on another described the fight to end prostitution and venereal disease as "the obligation which rests upon Christian people" resulting from acceptance of the Christian gospel.[32] Appeals to Christian morality rarely accompanied specific scriptural references, instead operating as a nebulous term for good and moral behaviour.

Opposition to sexual vice also stemmed from the suffrage movement and women's activism. Prior to serving as general secretary of AMSH, Alison Neilans had been highly active in the movement for women's suffrage.[33] In addition, AMSH members traced their intellectual and moral heritage to Josephine Butler and her campaigns against the Contagious Diseases Acts. Like Butler, they argued against compulsory VD examinations, lack of accountability for male vice, and other instances of gender inequality.[34] Citing women's apparent moral superiority, the NVA frequently called for greater numbers of female magistrates, detectives, and patrol officers in order to better combat sexual vice.[35] Outside of these professions, vice societies called for women to act as positive influences on their men by leading through moral example. As one *Vigilance Record* contributor argued, "The vast majority of men are, and probably will always be, from a moral point of view, what women demand of them."[36]

Views on gender relations, while more clearly articulated than their Christian perspective, also suffered from serious inconsistencies. The NVA and PMC clashed with activists like Margaret Sanger and Marie Stopes, remaining resolutely opposed to the advertisement of contraceptives.[37] Speakers at PMC conferences voiced concern over the growing independence of young women and girls, arguing that their physical and social mobility rendered supervision difficult.[38] The NVA published numerous stories of foolish young women who became engaged to unsuitable men (usually foreigners), at which point the association stepped in to prevent the union.[39] All of these organizations vacillated between images of the strong female moral compass and those of women who could not be left to their own devices without fear of moral ruin. The anti-vice movement therefore presented somewhat incoherent concepts of gender, promoting a vague cluster of traits signalling moral or immoral women but without deeply engaging in practical questions concerning the applications of such traits in the political or economic realm.

British cultural supremacy and imperialism also left their mark on vice society philosophies. In vice society literature, cities like Rangoon or Port Said appeared as moral cesspools threatening to contaminate Europeans in general and British women in particular.[40] British citizens who travelled to the colonies were in constant danger of corruption, while foreigners threatened to bring moral corruption to British shores. Ethnic labels often served as shorthand explanations for immoral behaviour. The case of a girl sold into prostitution in Egypt, for example, included by way of explanation that the girl's Christian father had died, leaving her with her immoral "Jewess" mother.[41] As in the case of their Christian rhetoric, however, racialized concepts of vice remained poorly defined and lacking the kinds of detailed racial hierarchies employed by eugenicists, resulting in a vague sense of British moral superiority juxtaposed against foreign vice.

Despite these examples of imprecise and ambiguous theoretical language, the vice society worldview depended on clearly defined sexual categories. Sexual behaviours could be either healthy or unhealthy, good or bad, safe or dangerous. Sexual intercourse within a monogamous heterosexual marriage was not only "healthy" because it precluded the possibility of VD, it also earned "safe" and "moral" status due to its alignment with normative concepts of good sexuality. This focus on categorizing sex according to deviant or normative labels clearly resembled the discourses of sexuality and eugenics that had prevailed in Britain and Continental Europe since the nineteenth century.[42] Vice societies, however, lacked the precision and systematic approach of prominent sexologists like Richard von Krafft-Ebing, Havelock Ellis, Magnus Hirschfeld, or Sigmund Freud, all of whom developed complex theories of sexual behaviour and identified an enormous variety of sexual pathologies.[43] Moral reformers instead tended toward a binary view of sexual categorization, with acts and practices classified as normative or deviant based on loose references to medical and scientific research but without the rigorous use of an underlying theoretical framework.

What are we to learn from these contradictions and inconsistencies? Rather than signifying irrelevance or conflict, the ideological incoherence of vice societies actually serves as a testament to their status as groups that actively constructed the "common-sense" normative view accepted throughout British society. Without organized public opposition to their moral positions, they had no need to develop comprehensive religious or theological arguments. "Christian" could instead operate as shorthand for a widely recognizable model of respectability and sexual restraint. Without challenges regarding thorny questions of female sexual autonomy, similarly, they could continue to claim status as champions of women due to brothel raids and station work. Pornography and other forms of vice could be categorized as "bad" sexuality without any clear medical or philosophical explanation of their effects. In all of these cases, borrowed terminology and theoretical language lent legitimacy to categories developed on the basis of their subjective position relative to heteronormative practices and standards. Since they aligned with widespread common-sense ideals, the inconsistencies and logical gaps in vice society thought suffered few direct attacks. This is not to suggest that the ideas of vice societies had no challengers. On the contrary, the press sometimes derided their methods, state officials denied them funding and assistance, and much of the general public clearly viewed them with indifference. Their fundamental ideology and sexual views, however, remained uncontested in the public sphere. The clandestine realm of pornography networks, consisting of practices and materials constructed as diametrically opposed to normative sexuality, thus found itself restricted to limited physical, economic, and discursive spaces removed from the mainstream respectability promoted by vice societies.

TRANSNATIONAL MORALITY

The domestic actors and forces that produced normative and deviant categories in British society also interacted with anti-vice societies of different nationalities. Like the pornography trade itself, the anti-vice movement was highly transnational.[44] This went beyond formal co-operation and attempts to establish international law. Rather, the meetings and publications of the International Bureau indicate widespread agreement on sexual morality despite the vast cultural differences between the participants. At the 1927 international conference, for example, delegates from a variety of countries including Germany, Hungary, Britain, and Spain all agreed on a series of proposals and moral positions regarding indecent publications and other sexual matters.[45] *Vigilance Record* articles monitored the legislative and political measures taken in other nations, praising prosecutions and other actions taken against vice.[46] Correspondence between American and British vice society campaigners indicates agreement on topics like obscenity and birth control.[47] The production of sexual categories in British civil society should not, therefore, be understood as an entirely national phenomenon. Rather, normativity was produced not only through national interactions between state and civil society, but within transnational circuits.

This transnational heteronormativity appears at odds with the theme of pornography and sexual immorality as foreign threats. On the one hand, British vice societies consistently blamed countries like France for the pornography trade, often by linking immorality to French cultural views. On the other hand, anti-vice campaigners collaborated with and praised members of the French National Committee, such as the crusading anti-vice campaigner Senator Berenger.[48] Delegates to international conferences appeared to agree on all salient points regarding prostitution and pornography, yet declared vaguely defined "cultural differences" to be an insurmountable obstacle to any international program of sex education for young people.[49] These cultural differences did not, however, refer to distinctions between British, French, and Russian delegates to anti-vice conferences, but to differences between the vice societies, governments, and general population of their respective countries. Chapter 6 will discuss areas of conflict between the British state and civil society regarding the pornography trade, but for the purposes of this chapter, one fundamental difference between state bodies and social purity organizations was that anti-vice groups worked as largely transnational actors, while the British state acted in an international context. This meant that while there was widespread consensus about issues like pornography within the transnational anti-vice movement, enforcement of these normative standards was limited by the national interests of the various states.

COMPOSITION OF VICE SOCIETIES

The NVA and PMC had a significant upper-middle-class and aristocratic presence on their executive boards. The executive board of the NVA included such notable figures as Lady Nunburnholme and the Lord Bishop of London, and they collaborated with Lord and Lady Gladstone on some campaigns.[50] The PMC also included the Lord Bishop of London as one of its officers, along with influential individuals like Chief Rabbi of Britain Hermann Adler and child "rescuer" Dr Paul Barnardo.[51] While many of the listed subscribers to the NVA or PMC donated less than £1 a year and therefore could have been relatively low-income individuals, the names listed on executive committee minutes clearly indicate elite leadership.[52] Their counterparts in Russia, Spain, and France followed the same pattern, including titled elites and members of government among their delegates.[53]

Women played an active role in all of the national and international anti-vice societies. They often appeared at the highest levels of organization leadership and served as delegates at conferences. At a 1935 conference in Holland, for example, nine of the twenty-four delegates were women.[54] Alison Neilans was the head of AMSH, and Lady Nunburnholme and Mrs Neville Rolf had significant involvement with NVA campaigns and international conferences. While most documents spoke of these women and others involved in vice societies in glowing terms, private correspondence reveals gendered tension with male members of their organizations.[55] A letter from an NVA member to Chairman Sir Ewart Greaves, for example, recounted a dispute in which Lady Nunburnholme accused him of trying to prevent her from attending a conference and participating in other activities. Similar issues emerged with Mrs Neville Rolf. In assessing the situation, another letter writer complained to Greaves that "it seems impossible to deal with these women because they will insist on imputing motives."[56]

While working as an essential part of the anti-vice movement, women nonetheless remained vulnerable to the same accusations of irrationality and emotional behaviour deployed against women in other professional and philanthropic settings. This aligned with the standards of femininity promoted by vice societies, which allowed for public actions like respectable employment and voting, but maintained the importance of "traditional" feminine qualities such as submission to male authority. Moreover, these ideals stood in stark contrast to the gendered interactions appearing in pornographic materials, which directly challenged accepted notions of appropriate female behaviour or interactions between the sexes. In other words, the cultural and social differences between vice societies and the pornography trade act as a microcosm of the larger tensions between British normativity and queer counterpoints found within deviant or marginalized categories. In both cases, we can draw connections between the social interactions and working conditions of those involved and the kinds of gendered messages that appeared in their materials. Vice societies valued female contributions only if the women displayed normatively feminine qualities like dutiful service rather than aggressive leadership, a value reflected in the aforementioned conflict between the strong female moral compass and fears of feminine aggression or independence. Pornography networks, which included women in integral roles from studio/bookshop owner down to the level of the avid female consumer, produced materials that often worked to complicate or disrupt normative gender hierarchies.

PORNOGRAPHY IN VICE SOCIETY IDEOLOGY

Vice societies incorporated pornography into their larger worldview of vice, prostitution, and exploitation. Discussions at the Seventh International Conference included statements regarding the use of pornographic photographs by prostitutes, who allegedly used the images to stimulate clients.[57] Explicitly articulating the divide between normative and deviant sexual expression, a pamphlet published by the PMC claimed that pornography led to "artificial stimulation of the sex instinct so that it will be urged into lust instead of its right and natural outlet, namely, genuine love and a happy and mutually responsible married life."[58] The language of excessive stimulation of sexual appetites also appeared in AMSH literature, which argued that pornography led to prostitution and VD through overstimulation.[59] Others claimed more deliberate use of pornography as a contributing factor in prostitution: "Objectionable books and pictures are well-known weapons in the armory of the seducer; they are well-known cog wheels in the machinery of the white slave trade."[60] In the vice societies' view, pornography was not a threat for its immediate effects but rather because it acted as a "gateway" to extramarital sex and prostitution. Notably, they viewed women as equally if not more vulnerable to pornography's seductive properties, indicating an awareness that women consumed pornography and that it was in no way an exclusively male enterprise.[61]

The PMC also theorized the relationships between pornographic materials of different mediums. In one publication, they promoted the concept of the vicious circle, described as follows: "Dirty pictures stimulate the appetite for dirty books, and dirty books stimulate the appetite for dirty pictures."[62] As in their discussion of the relationship between pornography and prostitution, the danger of consuming a variety of pornographic media lay in the potential for escalation rather than in the isolated act of consuming any one particular picture or obscene book. Given this focus on pornography's threat as part of a process or gateway to other acts, it comes as no surprise that discussions of pornography never addressed specific sex acts or other matters of content. Instead, threats appeared entirely dependent on real-world actions taken by consumers after exposure to escalating amounts of pornography.

In addition to prostitution, vice societies drew a direct causal link between pornography and rape. In a series of articles on the "black peril" in South Africa, NVA writers claimed that the rape of white women resulted directly from the sale of pornography to African men.[63] Reporting on the South African seizure of pornographic Stanhopes (miniaturized photographs embedded in glass or plastic), one vice publication claimed the following: "Recent occurrences indicate that natives who have committed outrages on white women were brought into contact with such baneful influences."[64] Vice societies thus constructed disparate threats posed by pornography based on the race of the consumer. While they drew direct connections between African pornography consumption and rape, they identified more nebulous threats in Asian and Middle Eastern pornography consumption. AMSH, while almost entirely ignoring domestic British consumption of pornography, took the time to anxiously report on the circulation of obscene publications in India.[65] Even "borderline" materials could be a threat. As one contributor to the *Vigilance Record* argued, "There is no comparison between the harm that can be done in England by bad films and the harm that can be done in parts of India or Africa, for instance."[66]

As explained by anti-vice campaigners, the danger of pornography lay in the fact that sex appeared without appropriate social context. Describing racy stories in American magazines, one NVA correspondent stated: "There seems to be no background of moral standard, and not the faintest suggestion of the existence of religion."[67] Anti-vice campaigners did not, therefore, object to specific sexual acts or even graphic depictions. Rather, their objection to pornography lay in its concepts of the role sex should play in social life. As discussed in chapter 3, an absence of significant social context or consequences for sexual behaviour constituted one of the most important characteristics of early twentieth-century pornography.[68]

Consequence-free sex served as a queer critique of normative sexuality; from the vice society perspective, that removal of context and hierarchical ranking of sex acts appeared as a dire threat to "acceptable" sexuality. According to the vice societies, context-free sexual materials led to promiscuity and prostitution for white viewers, but among people of colour the same sexual scenario threatened to inflame passions to the point of violence.

The indirect threats posed by pornography stood in contrast to the immediate dangers perceived by nineteenth-century purity campaigners, particularly in the form of masturbation. During the mid- to late nineteenth century, popular medical opinion had blamed masturbation for a wide variety of devastating physical and psychological afflictions, which created enormous incentive to keep children and adolescents away from potentially arousing materials.[69] Over the course of the early twentieth century, however, Havelock Ellis and other experts raised a series of challenges to the notion of masturbation as a health risk.[70] This reinforced the lack of attention to masturbation in vice society literature in general and their anti-pornography tracts in particular. In short, changing social views on adolescent and adult sexuality eliminated what had previously been the most pressing concern related to pornography consumption, reframing pornography's threat as one affecting social norms and practices rather than the integrity of the individual body or mind. While many responded strongly to this new idea of pornography as a social threat, it clearly did not have the same kind of visceral impact as older justifications for fighting pornography.

During the 1920s, members of the NVA and other organizations in Britain and abroad began to seriously discuss the possibility of sex education as an antidote to pornography consumption. At a 1927 conference, several members reasoned that sex education would take the allure out of sex and render pornography unappealing.[71] Within Britain, the NVA suggested Mary Ware Dennett's *Sex Side of Life* as a model of how to approach sex education for young people.[72] This is a revealing choice; while clear and frank in its description of sexual intercourse, Dennett's pamphlet embedded all descriptions of sex within a marital, heterosexual, and reproductive context. Sex, as described by Dennett, meant the following: "It means that a man and a woman feel that they *belong* to each other in a way that they belong to no one else; it makes them wonderfully happy to be together; they find they want to live together, work together, play together, and to have children together, that is, to marry each other; and their dream is to be happy together all their lives."[73]

As this quote indicates, vice societies did not advocate total sexual repression; on the contrary, they viewed both male and female sexual satisfaction as an important element of marital relationships. This was, however, the only acceptable outlet for sexual activity, a context that provided no room for pornography use by either party.[74] In fact, many viewed pornography as entirely antithetical to marriage. For example, in 1928 a judge presiding over divorce proceedings allowed attorneys to import and legally view pornographic works in order to use the husband's alleged consumption of such works as evidence against him.[75] If marriage served as a shorthand for normative sexuality, pornography operated as a stand-in for deviance. As far as vice societies were concerned, the rigid boundaries between these categories had to be maintained, with no acknowledgment of the possibility that pornography might play an important role in some marriages.

DOMESTIC AND TRANSNATIONAL PORNOGRAPHY CAMPAIGNS

While it did not engage directly in prosecutions or investigations, the NVA lobbied on issues of domestic pornography distribution. In a typical case, the NVA sent a deputation to the Home Secretary's office in 1912 to discuss the emergence of indecent kinematograph images.[76] In a much more publicized example, one hundred representatives from the NVA and other vice societies formed a delegation in 1929 to present Home Secretary William Joynson-Hicks with a proposed bill to increase penalties for selling indecent publications to children under eighteen.[77] Few of these delegations or proposed bills resulted in changes to policy or legislation; they were seen merely as symbolic achievements.[78] Aside from these lobbying activities, the NVA remained uninvolved in the day-to-day work of investigation and prosecution. Even their information on rates of pornography distribution and consumption depended heavily on correspondence initiated by members of the public. In 1915, for example, the Bristol branch of the NVA concluded that the circulation of pornography must have declined based on the fact that they received fewer public complaints during that year.[79]

The PMC, in contrast, participated in direct investigation and prosecution of pornographers throughout the early twentieth century. Rather than seeking out pornographers or consumers, the PMC generally responded to a complaint by a concerned citizen. For example, in 1942 a young female servant brought examples of obscene materials to the PMC offices, explaining that they had been given to her by a hawker in the East End. The PMC sent the samples to the police, along with information on known publishers in the area.[80] As this example demonstrates, PMC action against obscenity usually had to be instigated by an outside party. In addition, the PMC typically pursued cases in which pornography was publicly visible rather than distributed through the more clandestine methods discussed in chapters 1 and 2.[81] Despite this reliance on informants, the PMC officially discouraged members of the public from investigating pornography, stating: "It is highly inadvisable to encourage or embark on the search for specimens of obscene literature. Apart from the danger of contamination to those taking part, this work is better done by those with wisdom, competence, and experience … i.e. the Public Morality Council or reputable Church Department."[82]

Domestic efforts against pornography occurred in a sporadic and piecemeal manner. Groups like the PMC reacted to complaints, but did not actively pursue the trade on their own initiative. Lobbying efforts were focused on symbolic, ineffective, or unnecessary measures rather than policy changes based on an informed assessment of the pornography trade's methods and practices. This disorganized and ineffectual approach to the domestic pornography trade points to underlying assumptions regarding obscenity. It had to be addressed, certainly, but it did not warrant the same kind of attention dedicated to runaway girls or brothels. Attempts to address pornography domestically also indicate a belief that the responsibility for fighting the trade lay with the state. As will be discussed in the next chapter, however, the British state also lacked the incentives and resources to attack many aspects of the domestic trade in a systematic fashion, rendering the circulation of pornography a social problem that everyone agreed had to be dealt with but that no one was prepared to take up as a cause.

Vice societies displayed far more enthusiasm about international campaigns than domestic efforts. Transnational anti-vice policy hinged upon hopes of effective international law and co-operation, particularly after the establishment of the League of Nations. All member committees of the International Bureau adopted as one of their primary responsibilities the task of bringing proposed legislation and international conventions to the attention of their respective governments.[83] These efforts included resolutions by the National Committee declaring support for the ratification of the International Convention for the Suppression of the Traffic in Women and Children.[84] The NVA and PMC organized frequent international conferences, including preparatory conferences whose sole purpose was to allow delegates to prepare for the subsequent larger conference.[85] Conference publications reflected a widespread belief that issues like human trafficking, prostitution, and pornography could be solved only through coordinated international action.[86] In this sense, the anti-vice movement displayed a far more perceptive understanding of the transnational nature of the trade than did state officials of the period.

Despite high levels of international co-operation and a heavy investment in the potential of international law, anti-vice campaigners persisted in framing pornography and other forms of vice as "foreign" problems. In one piece of NVA correspondence to a concerned citizen, the writer suggested that the problem of indecent books sold in France stemmed not from differences in law or enforcement, but from the fact that "the attitude of the average Frenchman is markedly different from that of the average Englishman."[87] Another British vice society publication outlined four categories of obscene materials, the last and worst of which was the grossly obscene (pornographic) publication, which the author insisted nearly always originated abroad.[88] Despite their emphasis on international co-operation, British anti-vice campaigners did not hold all countries equally accountable. Britain appeared primarily as a victim of the trade and thus needed only to prevent foreign intrusion rather than fight a well-organized domestic industry or address the possibility of Britons polluting other nations.

AMSH paid little attention to domestic pornography consumption, addressing the issue only in relation to international vice. Their correspondence with the Calcutta Vigilance Association, for instance, contains numerous references to large quantities of obscene publications circulating in India.[89] Despite this concern, however, AMSH took no apparent formal action. In their publications and correspondence, brothels and venereal disease took clear precedence over issues like pornography. As the Calcutta example demonstrates, AMSH members discussed pornography as a threat only when it intersected with their larger imperial agenda, which involved demonstrating British moral superiority through the "rescue" of female colonial subjects.[90] As in the case of the newspaper industry, framing pornography in this way created significant blind spots in anti-pornography policing; vice societies may have brought additional scrutiny to the colonial trade, but they also largely ignored the practices and spaces making up British pornography networks. Vice society rhetoric therefore offered no incentive to pursue mail-order pornography, non-commercial exchanges, or the more discreet shopkeepers, thus allowing for the growth of pornography in those spaces.

FEAR OF THE BORDERLINE

Rather than focus their anti-obscenity efforts on truly pornographic materials, vice societies displayed a consistent sense of anxiety surrounding "borderline" books, photographs, and films. As a contributor to a 1928 issue of the *Vigilance Record* stated, "We hold the view, very strongly, that 'borderline' indecencies do infinitely more harm, in the long run, than frank obscenities."[91] This category included "racy" American magazines, lewd humour, and mainstream films containing sexual innuendo.[92] Anti-vice activists also suggested that borderline materials could eventually lead to a demand for pornography and render obscene materials acceptable among the mainstream.[93] Jix supported his calls for legal action against obscene publications by publicly stating: "I can deal with the bad cases, but I cannot deal with the borderline cases and it is the borderline cases which lead on to the bad ones."[94]

Fear of the borderline aligns with the clandestine nature of pornography in Britain during the early twentieth century. Anti-vice campaigners understood that pornography's legal status and content limited its influence on the mainstream, as it remained confined to clandestine spaces. Borderline cases, in contrast, had the potential to reach large audiences. By focusing their attention on maintaining the purity of mainstream culture, however, vice societies inadvertently nurtured the growth of queer spaces in pornography networks. Their policing of the borderline, seen in areas like censorship of cinema, created strict boundaries and increasing distance between the standards of mainstream entertainment and practices acceptable in the world of pornography. Those artists and writers active in the borderline had incentive to err on the side of caution in order to avoid censorship and prosecution; those operating within the realm of pornography, however, had no chance of legal mainstream acceptance and therefore could work outside the constraints of heteronormative conduct. Underground networks of pornography producers and consumers, in short, did not emerge in a vacuum; they were born at least in part out of efforts to maintain British cultural purity.

OTHER VICE CAMPAIGNS

Having established that pornography did not hold a central position in post-1900 vice campaigns, we will now turn to those issues that did preoccupy reformers. By comparing the status of anti-pornography efforts with campaigns that received more direct attention and resources, we can begin to understand the position of pornography in the worldview of early twentieth-century Britons. The issues that received greater attention and resources – including the white slave trade, female sexual promiscuity, and interracial relationships – were those that threatened concepts of British cultural supremacy and racial purity, both of which were closely tied to ideals of sexual restraint.

Prostitution, as well as its more inflammatory variation, "white slavery," consistently dominated anti-vice campaigns on the national and international level. Brothel raids formed the bulk of the street-level work performed by the PMC. The NVA's station work also operated under the banner of fighting the white slave trade, as their publications implied that the girls assisted would have either turned to prostitution or been approached by a white slave trader had a station worker not intervened. The British National Committee dedicated nearly all of its attention to international prostitution, focusing on cases of alleged trafficking and white slavery involving young British women.

One of the most consistent features of prominent campaigns across the different organizations was an emphasis on foreigners and colonial subjects. The white slave trade, for example, depended heavily on images of non-British men seducing or kidnapping young British women. Similarly, the brief flare-up of panics like the South African Black peril appealed to white British fears of Black male sexuality.[95] Even when not discussing a specific crime, anti-vice campaigners identified foreigners as a general moral problem. NVA reports highlighted the involvement of foreigners even when nationality had no bearing on the case, such as in a story about an indecent assault.[96] Beyond criminal prosecutions, the reports classified interracial relationships such as those between "coloured" seamen and white women in Cardiff as a social problem.[97] They also endorsed legislation imposing severe penalties for foreigners who committed crimes on British soil.[98] Any form of vice that involved race mixing or perceived threats to eugenic purity earned significant attention.

The second feature to regularly catch the eye of anti-vice campaigners was non-normative female behaviour. Wartime NVA publications dedicated considerable attention to the perceived problem of sexually aggressive girls becoming involved with soldiers, describing "the persistent way in which many young girls have forced their attention upon the soldiers in the streets."[99] NVA attacks on mainstream books and films, similarly, often focused on sexual autonomy and agency in female characters. Even station work, while framed as a form of assistance, identified young women travelling alone as a sign of potential sexual danger.[100] Despite the inclusion of both men and women in their messages of sexual chastity, vice societies clearly expected women to be more sexually restrained, less independent, and less aggressive than their male counterparts. As scholars like Ashwini Tambe have argued, British and specifically English female chastity often served as a marker of racial superiority in colonial discourses, resulting in greater sexual regulation of British women compared with other Europeans or indigenous women.[101]

These trends point to the anti-vice movement's role as the guardian of mainstream, middle-class, white, heteronormative values in British civil society. Their campaigns focused on sexual and social practices that challenged established power structures, including those of racial hierarchies and gender categories. They placed particular importance on the maintenance of British sexual norms as they related to concepts of racial and cultural superiority, many of which involved female chastity. Pornography production and consumption, while challenging to heteronormative sexuality, lacked the immediacy and public visibility of these more alarming causes. Only pornography that appeared in public spaces or fit narratives of foreign contamination had the potential to gain serious traction with anti-vice campaigners. As members of the NVA pointed out, since pornography production and consumption had for the most part moved behind the closed doors of private homes and businesses, it did not attract the same attention as other campaigns.

LIMITATIONS AND RESTRAINTS ON ANTI-PORNOGRAPHY CAMPAIGNS

All major vice societies reported declining funds in the early years of the twentieth century. The NVA, PMC, and AMSH depended mainly on donations from subscribers, the vast majority of whom gave £1 or less per year. In 1901, total receipts for the PMC (including subscriptions and proceeds from publication sales) amounted to £1,124. By 1907, total receipts dropped to £670, dropping again in 1912 to £520.[102] Although receipts for the NVA remained higher than those of the PMC, it still experienced financial struggles. In 1935, it received £2,034 in donations and subscriptions; this amount was insufficient, and it eventually resorted to selling stock to cover expenses. Even with the stock sale, the organization ran an overdraft of £791 for that year.[103]

Vice society members offered various explanations for the decline in funding. In public appeals for funds, the NVA pointed to economic downturns and the rationing of financial resources during the First World War and the Great Depression.[104] They also frequently reported on the deaths of older wealthy patrons, some of whom were described as long-standing supporters of the organization. Beyond economic hardship, explanations for the need for increased funds relied on claims of increased costs through services provided; an appeal for funds from the NVA, for example, claimed that the special appeal for £2,000 was designed to meet the needs of "ever-increasing" numbers of girls coming to London from other parts of the country.[105] This claim was not, however, backed by clear data regarding expenditures, and the organization provided little evidence that the number of girls in need of "rescue" had grown.

Internal minutes offer a different explanation for the fall in donations to the NVA. One memo suggested that donors had begun to divert their attention toward the problem of unemployment and as a result donated to new organizations rather than to the older and more established charities.[106] Other NVA members blamed their funding woes on the state of national politics. In this and other instances, members of the NVA demonstrated their understanding of their own diminishing appeal among the general public. They did not, however, agree on how to address the issue. Their inability to spur public interest can be seen in a dispute that erupted over a fundraising letter referencing a deceased former donor. While some NVA members argued that such a move in the immediate aftermath of the man's death could be perceived as tasteless, the fundraiser argued that the use of a famous name offered a rare opportunity to appeal to the public.[107] Decorum, so highly prized by vice society members, could nevertheless be sacrificed on the altar of financial necessity.

The financial problems experienced by the NVA and the PMC offer useful insight into public opinion on social problems. Without opinion polls or other surveys to document public reactions to the anti-vice movement, financial support serves as the best indicator of popularity or lack thereof. Anti-vice campaigns on issues such as white slavery, pornography, and brothel keeping did not resonate with either small-scale donors or the wealthy subscribers who had formed the backbone of NVA funding in its early years. The public did not express outright opposition or hostility to the vice society mission, but nor did they feel compelled to lend monetary support at anything approaching pre-1900 levels. Those with disposable income and a desire to improve society through charitable efforts quite simply did not choose the anti-vice movement as the best venue for those efforts.

The specific cases and issues discussed by vice societies in their fundraising and awareness documents represented attempts to tap into the social problems that resonated with the wider public. The *Vigilance Record*, the main publication of the NVA, reported on a wide variety of sexual issues and anti-vice campaigns. By examining the prominence and relative frequency of reporting on pornography compared to other social issues, one can determine pornography's place in the concerns and priorities of the NVA's readership. Surveys of the issues covered reveal a steady decline in coverage of obscene publications after 1900, with particularly low levels of interest during moments of major upheaval like the First World War and the Great Depression.[108] Issues from 1904 included seventeen articles addressing obscene publications, most of which involved prosecutions on British soil.[109] In 1910, the NVA published fourteen articles on the topic.[110] The 1927 issues included only eight articles on obscene publications, and by 1929 the number was down to three.[111]

As discussed in chapter 1, the pornography trade remained far more active and visible during the Second World War than during the First. This did not, however, translate into greater levels of vice society activity against pornography after 1939. Indeed, pornography fell even lower on their list of priorities after the war began. For example, while PMC records show that anti-pornography stings continued through 1941, they had declined in number and constituted a small fraction of total activities.[112] By the following year, discussion of pornography and obscenity by members of groups like the NVA largely vanished from official reports, replaced by more relevant wartime concerns such as forced prostitution in occupied nations.[113] This is not to suggest that the demands of wartime led vice societies to set aside moral panic or campaigns against vice in favour of economic and military practicality; other issues like "good time girls" and the sexuality of soldiers remained a major preoccupation.[114] As these moments of receding interest in the pornography issue illustrate, however, vice society ideologies and campaigns against pornography bore little to no relationship to the actual scale of the trade at any given moment. Rather, civil efforts against pornography depended almost entirely on economic context and the perceived urgency of other issues that came to vice societies' attention.

Compared to pornography, other issues clearly held greater appeal. White slavery remained the most consistently promoted cause throughout the first half of the twentieth century, despite increasing official skepticism that the phenomenon existed at all.[115] While anti-vice campaigns through the 1930s insisted on the existence of a vast network of trafficked white women, an official Metropolitan Police memo from 1936 bluntly stated the following: "Wild statements as to the 'White Slave Traffic' appearing in the papers are, needless to say, hopelessly exaggerated. There is no evidence whatever of any 'White Slave' case."[116] While white slavery persisted as a staple of anti-vice campaigns, promotional materials also seized upon more ephemeral moral panics that received attention for a year or two before vanishing from discussion. For example, a flurry of articles from 1936 discussed the "lorry girl menace," referring to the perceived sexual promiscuity of female truck drivers.[117] In 1920, massage houses enjoyed a brief moment in the spotlight as the latest moral scandal.[118] Internal memos and letters indicate that temporary emphasis on specific issues did not merely reflect changes in the concerns of NVA members. Rather, they corresponded with issues that would appeal to potential donors. For example, one member of the organization suggested in 1933 that certain issues should be "worked up" in a funding appeal.[119]

Ironically, anti-vice societies may have undercut their own need for funds and political support through the persistent use of triumphalist narratives claiming that they had radically improved the condition of British morals. Publications from both the NVA and the PMC insisted that they had had a measurable impact on vice in Britain, although they placed the beginning of Britain's moral improvement at different dates, each of which coincided with the commencement of that organization's activities.[120] Both agreed that the Victorian years had been a morass of vice and depravity but had very different views regarding whether 1885 or 1899 marked the start of Britain's miraculous moral recovery.[121]

This triumphalist approach to vice reveals distance between the narratives of the anti-vice movement and the beliefs of British society at large. The early twentieth century in general and the interwar period in particular saw the emergence of widespread concerns regarding moral and social decay. Controversial phenomena like the New Woman and the relaxation of some sexual norms seemed to signal the dissolution of social mores, exacerbating narratives of cultural degeneration.[122] Newspapers and other media reflected this anxiety, printing nervous claims that "pagan morality" was on the rise.[123] This put the anti-vice movement in the odd position of being the foremost proponent of battling sexual vice while simultaneously offering one of the least alarming assessments of its grip on society. The explanation for this difference in opinion lies in the relatively narrow focus of vice societies. While the NVA and PMC dedicated their attention to a few key issues, popular opinion encompassed more widespread and ambiguous phenomena like changes in female dress and demeanour. A specific, narrow topic like the visible presence of prostitutes in London could easily appear to improve at the same time that other elements of British morality seemed to be in decline. In this lack of attention to mainstream views, vice societies revealed themselves as a respected but increasingly disconnected and ineffectual participant in debates surrounding social norms.

Tension between different vice societies also impeded their efforts. While they did collaborate within the National Committee and in some other contexts, vice societies jealously guarded their areas of specialization. The dangers of infringing on another organization's territory can be found in a stern letter from AMSH to a grant applicant who sought funds for a project that would have been more appropriate for the NVA. In another example, AMSH responded to a complaint regarding advertisements for pornography in French publications by passing the information along to the NVA for further action.[124] In a similar case, Mr Sempkins of the NVA and Mr Cohen of the Jewish Association for the Protection of Girls and Women (JAPGW) debated over which organization would be better suited to pursue an obscene publications complaint based on a variety of factors such as the location of the publications and the most likely legal strategy.[125]

Territorial spats between the NVA, PMC, and AMSH emerged within the National Committee in 1928. Mr Sempkins and Mr Tyrer of the PMC struggled over who would provide reports on obscene publications to the National Committee. JAPGW's Mr. Cohen sought to act as a peacekeeper between the two, as he wrote to Sempkins: "I am quite sure that [Tyrer] still has great suspicion in his mind that an attempt is being made to steal his plunder. I have had two long letters from him, and I wrote him a longer one trying to appease his mind."[126] He then counselled Sempkins to leave the matter of obscene publications to the PMC, as they had addressed it with great enthusiasm. Cohen assured him that similar considerations would be given to the NVA, with projects like station work being left to them alone.[127] Finally, Cohen closed with a statement regarding the likely difficulties they would face from AMSH, since that organization "[was] only dealing with the theoretical aspect of the question."[128]

Notably, the infighting between members of the National Committee did not reflect ideological or cultural differences in opinion. Even in the midst of territorial spats, members of the anti-vice movement maintained a broad consensus on important causes and moral questions. Instead, their disputes were procedural and territorial in nature. Despite differences in political and religious affiliation, the various vice societies agreed on what behaviours and practices should be considered social problems. They did not, however, agree on how to address those issues, who should be responsible for them, or who should get public credit for successes. In this highly fractured and competitive environment, unified action on an issue like pornography proved difficult at best.

In the face of these funding limitations and internal conflicts, pornography remained a cause for concern, but one of diminishing importance. It appeared as a topic of debate and interest in international conferences, committee minutes, and public documents. Despite this apparent desire to eliminate pornography, however, none of the major organizations discussed in this chapter allocated significant funds to the cause or played an active role in the pursuit of pornographers. As public support waned and funds diminished, vice societies sacrificed some public campaigns and prioritized others. The NVA turned its attention to international conferences, limiting its domestic activities largely to its station work. The PMC remained more actively involved in anti-obscenity work, but also prioritized other projects like the investigation of brothels. Newer organizations like AMSH and local diocesan rescue branches did not include pornography in their programs at all, despite the circulation of popular wisdom linking pornography consumption to their central concerns of illegitimacy and prostitution.

Vice organizations appeared to grasp, on some level, the ways in which the pornography trade fostered competing perspectives on sexuality. As mentioned previously, conference speakers like Dr Ninck recognized crucial elements of the trade, such as transnationalism and the non-commercial exchange of materials within networks. References to the "adroit organization" of pornographers and their use of houses rather than shops for their pornography operations suggests comprehension of the cottage-industry scale of production and distribution.[129] Anti-vice campaigners also clearly understood the methods of communication used within pornography networks, frequently addressing the circulation of advertisements for obscene materials in national newspapers.[130] This comprehension went further, however, than simply grasping the mechanics of local and transnational distribution. Vice society publications displayed awareness that the pornography trade had shifted from the quasi-public, shop-based nature of Victorian distribution to the cultivation of networks centred on private spaces and long-distance communication. They understood fully that international borders had little meaning for pornographers and customers, and that they adeptly exploited transportation and communication technologies to avoid all conventional detection methods.[131] As one unusually forthright NVA memo stated: "Pornography, so quick to transform itself and so clever at seizing any means for increasing its profits, has by no means been behindhand in deriving benefit from these facilities of expansion ... Its commerce is no longer confined to the narrow bounds of one country."[132]

This adaptability compared unfavourably with state response, described as limited and ineffective. Here we see that the NVA fully grasped the paradoxical nature of a pornography trade that operated as part of a transnational enterprise yet existing mainly within the private sphere.

At no point, however, did vice societies attempt to engage with pornography networks as organized groups. Pornographers and consumers, similarly, mocked "prudish" people, but did not directly attack vice societies either in their pornographic materials or in their statements to legal authorities. This lack of direct engagement points to the very real limitations of pornography networks and the formidable cultural power of vice societies even in their early twentieth-century state of diminished relevance. Like homosexual communities, BDSM practitioners, and other marginalized sexual groups, pornography networks had sufficient cultural space to organize clandestinely but not to publicly pursue greater rights or openly challenge mainstream norms. As such, vice societies quite understandably did not perceive the trade itself as a threat.

CONCLUSION

Early twentieth-century vice societies lacked the will, resources, and public support to dedicate significant attention to eradicating the pornography trade. All anti-vice crusaders voiced unambiguous opposition to pornography, yet took little action against it. This resulted from a combination of factors, including poor funding, waning public support, and the greater appeal of causes like the white slave trade in campaigns and fundraising ventures. At the most basic level, however, the problem with fighting pornography was that the threat it posed lacked immediacy. Nineteenth-century narratives of pornography as an immediate and devastating threat to youth gave way to images of sexual obscenity as a nebulous danger that might lead young people to real sexual danger at some point in the future. This is not to suggest that pornography enjoyed acceptance. On the contrary, anti-vice campaigners and the general public neglected to even consider the possibility that it might be harmless. Within a weakened and internally divided anti-vice movement, however, pornography had little potential as a galvanizing force or the basis for a major campaign.

The importance of vice societies, however, goes beyond their failure to crush the pornography trade. Vice societies worked to construct early twentieth-century Britain's normative, if contested, view of human sexuality. The wealthy elites who comprised the NVA, the PMC, and AMSH promoted a sexual worldview full of clear divisions and classifications. Healthy and natural sexuality consisted of mutually fulfilling sexual intercourse between married heterosexuals. Unhealthy and psychologically damaging sex, in contrast, occurred for profit, between strangers, or between those of the same gender or different races. The fluid sexual categories found in pornographic materials and within the social interactions of the pornography trade stood in stark contrast to the clearly delineated boundaries and established systems of classification employed by the mainstream. This study of the anti-vice movement thus provides multilayered insights into the pornography trade. It offers a portrait of the heteronormative sexual worldview that the trade reacted against, forming a major part of the context explaining why such queer spaces could and did flourish in early twentieth-century Britain. We now turn to the final chapter, in which these cultural mores and policy proposals intersected with the coercive power of the state.

CHAPTER SIX

"The Ultimate Decency of Things"

The British State and the Policing of Pornography

On 25 February 1910, the Office of the Undersecretary of State replied to a controversy surrounding the dissemination of foreign mail-order pornography with the following statement: "I am in favor of doing openly what is being done by the Post Office to stop this traffic in obscene materials, but as it has been kept secret hitherto at the request of the GPO [General Post Office], I do not think it desirable to take any action which might lead to its becoming public through the person whose letters are stopped."[1] This policy of searching packages from known or suspected overseas pornographers provides an ideal example of how the British state conceptualized and attempted to deal with the threat of obscenity; they viewed pornographic materials as a foreign contagion, one best dealt with by screening items as they passed into the country from overseas. This case also points to some of the limitations of the state's attempts to police the pornography trade. In concealing the search and seizure of postal packages containing pornography, British state officials indicated the high value they placed on discretion and the prevention of any public controversy that might ignite interest in the trade, even if such policies ultimately impeded their ability to conduct prosecutions or police localized networks.

While various bodies within the British state expressed concern about pornography and enacted policies to oppose it, they focused only on narrow aspects of the trade. Sales of foreign origin, publicly visible transactions, and the distribution of pornography to children all appeared as top priorities. The clandestine circulation of pornography within underground distribution networks, in contrast, rarely elicited a response. In short, officials within the British state appeared perfectly willing to allow a localized pornography trade to exist and even interact with transnational networks as long as it did not openly tarnish Britain's image as a society of sexual restraint and propriety. Even when supported or pushed by powerful civil actors like the NVA, state officials consistently resisted the development of new legislation or increased policing of the pornography trade.

Some scholars of twentieth-century pornography have emphasized the effectiveness of British censorship and anti-obscenity policies, going so far as to argue that the British state created Paris's expatriate dirty books trade while successfully hunting pornography networks both at home and abroad.[2] While I in no way dispute the strength of certain state policies and the overall importance of expatriate publishing communities, the anti-pornography enthusiasm of the early twentieth-century British state has been wildly overstated. As discussed in chapter 1, the rabid anti-pornography sentiments of the 1890s noticeably diminished during the Edwardian years and never again approached their previous fervour. As in the case of mass media and journalism, this decline in anti-pornography efforts should be understood as a consequence of internal divisions and competing policy agendas rather than as weakness or acceptance of pornography. As discussed in the previous chapter, the actions of the British state reveal conflict and inconsistency rather than a united front against pornography.[3]

Following this emphasis on fluidity and internal negotiation, I now map the points at which local and national state officials came into conflict with other state actors or with civil institutions like the press and the anti-vice movement, thus creating the spaces in which the pornography trade operated. The British state's goals vis-à-vis the reinforcement of heteronormativity, as well as its disagreements with the press and anti-vice movements, can only be understood by examining their competing domestic interests and differing relationships with transnational and international actors. As discussed in the previous chapter, vice societies operated in a co-operative, mutually reinforcing transnational environment. Heteronormative concepts and standards produced in these transnational circuits were manifest on the national level, with the result that anti-vice campaigners from Britain to Uruguay agreed on most major issues concerning sexual morality.[4] The British state, while accepting and promoting the same normative principles, did so with different goals and interests, most of which were dependent on the maintenance of state sovereignty rather than more fluid forms of transnational negotiation and regulation. As a result, state authorities had a fundamentally different outlook on the transnational trade than that of the press or their anti-vice allies in civil society.

The British state's regulation of sexuality has often been shaped by a desire to project a specific cultural or moral image to international rivals or allies. As has been amply documented in studies of colonial and domestic prostitution, the British colonial state actively cultivated images of British sexual restraint and respectability contrasted with oversexed Continental Europeans and colonial subjects.[5] Maintaining heteronormative categories and hierarchies thus served the interests of the pre-1945 British state, but only when performed in publicly visible formats or in opposition to foreign cultural influence.[6] On the other hand, enforcing heteronormative standards against domestic pornographers or those employing more discreet methods threatened efforts at public respectability precisely because such efforts would invite scrutiny of previously hidden sexualities and sexual discourses operating within British society.

Just as the British newspaper industry avoided identifying British citizens as actors in the pornography trade due to the assumption that this information would be available to foreign and colonial readers, the state avoided actions that would call attention to domestic pornographers and consumers. Highly active international co-operation, similarly, would have required greater consideration of the complexities of the domestic trade's position as a node in a transnational system. At a minimum, attention to these transnational complexities would have challenged images of Britain as a victim of foreign obscenity rather than as host to an active element of the transnational pornography trade. Anti-pornography policies carrying the possibility of these negative side effects were therefore ignored or dismissed outright.

State reluctance to follow the anti-vice movement's program of international coordination dovetailed with domestic obstacles to pornography regulation, including public opinion against censorship and in favour of a reformed penal system based on rehabilitation rather than incarceration. Just as state officials acted with an eye toward Britain's international reputation, those involved in domestic policy betrayed deep insecurities regarding British self-image. Their policies indicate that respectability and sexual normativity, while important, could not be imposed at the expense of such ideals as an apparently free press and a "rational" justice system. Moreover, as discussed in chapter 4, the increasing political and social participation of the working class meant that the state could not scapegoat them in campaigns against sexual deviance without seriously threatening the desired image of Britain as an inclusive and well-ordered society.

Despite a widely shared goal of public respectability, national and local state actors often had different perspectives on the measures that should be taken against obscenity. Other tensions emerged between domestic and colonial state entities, as well as between offices tasked with high levels of international co-operation and those who operated only on British soil. Pornography networks thus benefited not only from conflicts between state and civil actors, but from disputes within the British state itself. These disputes and contradictions fit within a larger process of rapid changes in the relationship between the British state and its citizens in the early twentieth century, changes that granted increased autonomy and protection to some groups while boosting scrutiny of others.

THE STATE AND SEXUALITY

Compared with the revolutionary upheaval and intense violence experienced by their Continental counterparts, the Edwardian and interwar British state apparatus was highly stable. The state's relationship to different elements of British society, however, underwent subtle but important shifts during the early twentieth century. During the Edwardian years, groups like middle-class women and the working poor sought not only to join the electorate, but to become actively engaged in the political process.[7] These efforts would not come to full fruition until the interwar years, when women achieved full suffrage and the growing political sway of the working classes led to the first Labour government.[8] While the Edwardian years brought economic prosperity, the series of economic crises that followed the First World War drove up unemployment and caused immense financial strain to such a degree that armed revolution seemed a legitimate possibility. In response, several successive administrations of different political orientations were forced to introduce new forms of welfare such as unemployment insurance and decentralized poor relief administered through municipal governments.[9] By the outbreak of the Second World War, the British state had become answerable to and involved with social groups that had been completely absent from the political realm only fifty years earlier.

Figures within the British state also had to contend with a changing international landscape. While still controlling the largest empire on earth, British officials feared the growing power of their European rivals. The First World War, while ultimately a victory for Britain, was a bloodbath of a previously unimaginable scale. Within the colonies, independence movements gathered strength, while the Dominions increasingly began to resemble peers rather than subjects in international politics. Ireland was wracked first by the Anglo-Irish War and then its own civil war, both of which were an international embarrassment for the British state.[10] Prior to the First World War, British foreign policy focused on maintaining global supremacy while avoiding entanglement in foreign conflicts. During the interwar years, however, maintaining the peace became the paramount concern. To this end, Britain's foreign policy shifted toward international accords and involvement in the newly formed League of Nations. Despite acknowledging that the prevention of another major European conflict would require a framework for co-operative international diplomacy, however, the British state's embrace of the League of Nations was always hesitant. While it accepted the League of Nations in theory, the sacrifice of British sovereignty seemed too high a price to pay in practice. As a result, British foreign policy during the interwar years was characterized by half-measures and contradictions.[11]

State policies toward the pornography trade thus existed in the context of a growing and diversifying political system that undermined existing internal hierarchies just as the nation faced challenges abroad. This resulted in an anti-pornography policy as hesitant and contradictory as the British state's interwar foreign policy, an ambivalence made all the more striking by the fact that the state theoretically had the ability to enforce sexual morality far more severely than it did in practice. While civil organizations and the press played an important role in the production of sexual normativity through the promotion of social and cultural standards, the state wielded the far more tangible threat of violence and imprisonment as a means of enforcing sexual norms.[12] The state's ability to disrupt groups and practices constructed as deviant can be clearly seen in actions taken against interwar Britain's homosexual communities. As historians like Jeffrey Weeks have thoroughly documented, homosexual men of the 1930s enjoyed a relatively open sexual culture in elite and artistic circles. At the same time, however, working-class homosexuals active in streets and other public venues experienced considerable police harassment.[13] Compared to the 1930s, male prostitutes working in the 1880s reported fewer concerns about legal authorities.[14] The significance of legal action against homosexuals in interwar Britain can be clearly seen in the decision of elite homosexual men to either remain celibate or relocate to more permissive countries.[15] In this case, the British state displayed its capacity to constrain the development of sexual communities to narrow venues and dramatically limit their ability to operate across class lines and other social boundaries.

Given this evident ability to disrupt sexual practices or communities when given incentive to do so, the relative lack of attention to pornography cannot be reduced to weakness or incompetence. Nor can it be explained as a new ideological commitment to sexual privacy. Rather, as in the case of civil actors such as vigilance societies, the state had interests and concerns that conflicted with any realistic attempt to police the pornography trade. This reinforces the point that the imposition of normativity did not always align neatly with other aspects of the British state's agenda. Rather, in some circumstances the state actively policed the boundaries between normative and deviant sexuality only when it served a particular domestic or foreign policy interest.

Much of British state officials' reluctance to police the pornography trade and their struggles when attempting to do so resulted from their status as national actors trying to regulate transnational flows. As discussed in previous chapters, transnationalism refers to the flow of cultural forms and material objects across and between national borders.[16] Studies of international politics, in contrast, have generally focused on the interactions of actors representing the interests of nation-states.[17] This distinction is not a case of mere semantics; rather, it points to two entirely distinct modes of global interaction that coexisted in early twentieth-century Britain. While both forms of interaction created economic and social links between nations, they had entirely different relationships with the economy and the state. As seen in numerous cases discussed in this project, the British pornography trade operated within a larger transnational system whose actors had little regard for national or imperial borders.

As international rather than transnational actors, the organs of the British state operated not only with a different set of interests, but with entirely different options and constraints. While correspondence and packages of pornographic materials could cross borders freely on their journey from Spanish or American or Hungarian distributors to British customers and vice versa, British authorities had to pursue official diplomatic channels in an attempt to secure the co-operation of their foreign counterparts. This resulted in the development of types of commerce in which pornographers and consumers could engage with relative impunity. Different bodies within the state grappled with these issues using a variety of methods. All, however, were hindered by the fact that the pornography trade simply did not play by the rules that the British state was bound to follow. Let us now take a closer look at how various organs within the British state confronted pornography, and how they grappled with the limitations imposed by law and official policy.

POLICE DEPARTMENTS

Along with the Customs Office, the London Metropolitan Police (the MET) was the state body that interacted most frequently with pornographers. Other city police departments across Britain had their own encounters with the world of pornography, but none approached the numbers, media scrutiny, or legal significance of the MET. Their investigations focused on bookshops, tobacconists, and street hawkers, but they hesitated to intrude into the private homes and mail-order businesses that served as the foundation of the trade. Instead, the majority of official action centred on publicly visible or otherwise disruptive cases. The 1929 investigation into shopkeeper Isaac Sugarman, for example, resulted from the display of obscene pamphlets in his shop window.[18] Other pornographers came to police attention by hawking photographs and pamphlets in public markets.[19] Even investigations of more discreet pornography distributors tended to involve a public place open to a variety of customers. Shop owner Kitty Lichtenstein, for instance, did not display her wares in the shop window but kept photographs and envelopes of pornographic stories behind the counter and easily available for public sale.[20]

Along with cases depending on public visibility like shop window displays, the police had a marked tendency to target immigrants and visiting foreigners. As discussed in chapter 1, immigrants frequently participated in the pornography trade. Their participation cannot, however, account for the clear hostility and suspicion directed at them by the London police. Instead, suspicion emerged around those whose speech or appearance marked them as a non-British Other. Sugarman and Lichtenstein both immigrated from Eastern Europe, while numerous other pornography investigations focused on immigrants from Portugal, France, and other countries.[21] The nationality of foreign suspects often appeared in official documentation even when irrelevant to the case. Some British-born suspects were also identified in police documents as Jews or other minorities.[22] In addition, police assignments appear to have been based at least in part on the assumption that pornography might originate abroad. Inspector Draper, the officer responsible for the bulk of pornography cases through the 1920s, was specifically identified as a French speaker in official memoranda, which may have contributed to his apparent specialization in obscenity investigations.[23]

Despite efforts taken against immigrants and publicly disruptive pornographers, the London Metropolitan Police generally made little attempt to uncover aspects of the pornography trade that had not been brought directly to their attention. Like the Home Office and other state entities, police often expressed frustration with vice societies and other members of the public who considered pornography a more serious problem. Police complaints about these members of the public typically rested on unrealistic expectations for prosecution and definitions of obscenity that could not be successfully argued in court. For example, police received sporadic complaints about a nude statue outside of the British Medical Association (BMA) offices over a twenty-year period. From the start of the complaints, investigating officers expressed doubts that an obscenity prosecution would be successful or even necessary.[24] As in the case of the Home Office incidents discussed below, much of this frustration stemmed from the more stringent definitions of obscenity employed by vice societies, which generally fell far short of the standard required for a conviction. Police often perceived the cases identified as problematic by vice societies as insufficiently disruptive to the public to warrant action, even if the item technically violated obscenity law. In discussing the 1908 decision not to pursue action against the statue in front of the BMA, for example, one official simply noted, "Curiosity has subsided. There are no crowds."[25]

The role played by the police in attempts to limit the pornography trade depended in part on specific locale. London served as Britain's most important hub for pornography distribution, but obscenity surfaced as a concern in cities across the country. Most municipalities reported little to no active pornography trade; of roughly 120 boroughs surveyed in 1929, only two (Brighton and Newcastle-on-Tyne) described the pornography trade as being on a "fairly large scale," with over half of boroughs reporting no activity at all.[26] Those boroughs reporting obscene publications cases for the 1929 League of Nations survey carefully framed their few cases with assurances that their area had little activity to speak of. The chief constable of Preston, for instance, followed his description of a man selling cigarette cases adorned with nude photographs with the following remark: "There is no reason to believe that such obscene publications have been sold on a wide scale in this Borough ... And my Officers have instructions to pay particular attention in this respect."[27]

While it would be entirely reasonable to conclude that less densely populated areas of Britain would have a smaller trade than that of London, the easy flow of people and mail renders it highly unlikely that any police force truly had the inclination or ability to keep their borough free of pornography. In fact, in several documented cases, pornography seized outside of London originated in another location. The pornographic trinkets seized in Preston came from a Welsh distributor, while Glasgow police intercepted packages mailed from France.[28] Despite the fact that pornographic goods clearly circulated throughout the British Isles, local police outside of London rarely reported more than two or three cases per year.[29] Just as various nation-states sought to maintain an image of sexual respectability in the eyes of their rivals and allies, the local levels of the British state dedicated their energies toward maintaining the appearance of public order while ignoring more clandestine forms of pornography circulation.

A handful of British police forces went against this trend, calling for increased legislation or resources to deal with obscenity. Law enforcement officials from Guernsey, for instance, demanded additional legislative measures to deal with the circulation of pornography on the island.[30] Notably, the higher levels of the British state opted to ignore these more alarming assessments in favour of those by entities like the London Metropolitan Police, who generally supported the narrative that the British legal apparatus had all the tools required to deal with a relatively inconsequential pornography trade. The 1931 report to the League of Nations, for example, held that "in the experience of this country, grossly obscene wares are much rarer now than they were a few years ago," attributing this trend to dedicated enforcement of legal regulations.[31] The existence of competing views of the pornography trade among law enforcement, coupled with the decision of the higher levels of the British government to ignore such competing narratives, suggests that the allocation of resources and attention to obscenity depended more on maintaining the appearance of public purity than on the realities of pornography circulation in any given location. This narrow emphasis worked to keep pornography underground and out of the public eye, but it also facilitated the growth of spaces in which participants exchanged pornography on a small scale, behind closed doors, or through discreet mail-order services.

THE JUDICIARY

Even pornographers who faced arrest or prosecution for their activities might benefit from these conflicting perspectives on obscenity and regulation. Post-1900 pornography distribution cases saw a marked decline in legal penalties compared to similar cases in the nineteenth century. In a typical example from the 1890s, the court sentenced pornographers Thomas Henry Thompson and George Bridger to six months of hard labour and a fine of £50 each for the distribution of indecent prints.[32] In contrast, when Frederick Barrett accosted a plainclothes police officer with his pornographic prints in 1909, he received only one month of hard labour.[33] Numerous other defendants received no more than a small fine and had their stock destroyed by order of the court. Repeat offender Maria Donderis, for example, paid one pound three shillings and served no prison time for selling obscene Spanish books in 1911.[34]

This trend went far beyond pornography-related crimes. British incarceration rates began a steady decline during the late nineteenth and early twentieth centuries, dropping from an all-time high of 118 incarcerations per 100,000 in 1880 to 24.6 per 100,000 in 1919.[35] While it is beyond the scope of this project to undertake a comprehensive study of the forces behind the prison reform movement, the fact remains that the early twentieth-century British state and public turned against the kinds of harsh prison sentences that drove nineteenth-century British pornographers to seek refuge in Paris or Brussels.[36] This again underscores the importance of Britain's image at home and abroad. Early twentieth-century judges and MPs spoke openly of the failures of the "separate system" that had prevailed during the Victorian period, contrasting these examples with new and enlightened techniques designed to reform criminals; as Sir Wemyss Grant Wilson, director of the Borstal Association, told the *Evening Telegraph* in 1927, "the object should be to turn out a better man and not a bitter man."[37] British state officials may not have been willing to accept an image of the nation as a place of tolerated pornographers, but nor could they abide an international reputation or self-image as a country that would subject those same pornographers to years of brutal hard labour.

In addition to the general trend toward fewer prison sentences for offenders, the judiciary also began to adopt a more limited view of obscenity than that of the police or even the Home Office. Memoranda from the police or Director of Public Prosecutions often expressed concerns that materials considered obscene by a complaining civilian or even an inspector might not be found obscene in court.[38] Several incidents confirmed that this concern was justified. For example, a 1930 Metropolitan Police investigation against Henri Bonnaire resulted in a prosecution before magistrate Sir Chartres Biron. Of the 125 photographs police submitted as evidence, only seven were declared obscene by Sir Chartres.[39] This has particular significance considering that the police and other state entities had already adopted a more limited definition of obscenity than had much of civil society. The gap between what an NVA campaigner believed should be prosecuted and what the court would find obscene could therefore be considerable. In a clear illustration of this problem, the 1932 Annual Report of the PMC stated that of the over one hundred cases brought to the attention of the authorities by the organization during that year, only four had resulted in convictions.[40] These conflicts between the police, the judiciary, and other actors within the British state reveal a significant arena in which conflicting interests and views between state bodies worked to the advantage of those active in pornography networks, who often escaped legal penalties even after running afoul of vice societies or police.

THE HOME OFFICE

State concerns with pornography did not remain confined to the realm of law enforcement or criminal prosecutions. The Home Office in general and the Office of the Secretary of State in particular frequently addressed issues surrounding the pornography trade. Like most state bodies, the Home Office focused on downplaying the domestic trade, characterizing pornography as a foreign problem, and avoiding high levels of publicity or controversy on the issue. These emphases appeared in their policies surrounding the post and customs offices, as discussed at the beginning of this chapter. The use of customs officers allowed for the screening of possible foreign mail-order pornography, while the secrecy of the project minimized public awareness of their tactics.

Minimizing publicity was alternately justified as a way of preventing pornographers from knowing that packages had been detected, and as a way of stopping the press from advertising the existence of new and exciting works. Avoidance of publicity extended beyond keeping mail searches secret. In several instances, the Home Office advised against prosecuting distributors of racy novels, arguing that a trial would serve only to advertise the publication. In 1932, for example, correspondence between the Home Office and the Director of Public Prosecutions concluded that the distributor of an obscene book called *The Lamb* should not be prosecuted due to the fact that the book did not hold wide appeal, but that it might become more widely known if the subject of a public trial.[41]

The importance of minimizing publicity extended to shielding prominent individuals from prosecution. In 1927, the office of the Undersecretary of State learned of a package containing an altered edition of Frank Harris's *My Life and Loves* (including an extra chapter) that had been intercepted on the way to Church of Ireland

Reverend William Kerr of Trinity College Dublin.[42] While much of this work reads like a pedestrian coming-of-age tale, it contains numerous sexual escapades from the author's life. The original Paris-printed edition also featured nude photographs and illustrations throughout.[43] Moreover, mail-order booksellers willing to offer the book typically featured it in catalogues alongside similarly banned works like the *Kama Sutra* and *Nell in Bridewell.*[44] In short, few state officials of the time would have seriously believed that Kerr could have ordered the book in complete ignorance of its contents. Internal memoranda and correspondence concerning the case, however, emphasized the necessity for discretion and delicacy to avoid "compromising the Reverend gentleman too much."[45] When gently questioned by authorities, Kerr insisted that he had known nothing of the book's contents. This explanation satisfied all authorities in the Office of the Undersecretary of State, and they closed the investigation.[46] Here, the suspect's social prestige and the need to avoid public scandal or increased political tension with Irish authorities trumped the need to fight the pornography trade.

COLONIAL AUTHORITIES

Conflicts also emerged between various organs of the British state and those involved in colonial administration. This tension typically centred on the perceived laxity of colonial authorities. Jamaica, for example, neglected to pass legislation consistent with Britain's approach to the regulation of obscene publications, compelling the Home Office to assert in 1938 that laws regarding the importation of pornography still applied to Jamaica due to its colonial status.[47] In other cases, lack of action against colonial pornography consumption resulted from lax enforcement rather than the absence of legislation. During the 1920s, letters from the Dominion Division of the Home Office to the Commissioner of Accra and the Governor of Lagos informed both men that letters from within their jurisdiction had been intercepted on the way to known pornography dealers in France. The Dominion Division's letters anxiously noted that Home Office warrants could not be legally used to open packages from the colonies or Dominions, and that responsibility for enforcement therefore lay with colonial authorities.[48] Officials based in the metropole often experienced frustration with colonial officials, who seemed unable or unwilling to take action against vice in their jurisdictions. In 1949, for example, the Colonial Office contacted Nigerian authorities with an inquiry regarding discrepancies between the official low figures on prostitution and pornography compared with the situation on the ground as reported by visitors.[49] In this sense, imperial holdings like Jamaica and Nigeria acted in a manner consistent with European nations who minimized their own domestic trade despite clear evidence of active pornography networks. Their actions elicited greater alarm, however, because visible sexual immorality in the colonies could be construed as a reflection of British weakness or loss of influence.

As discussed in chapter 5, the consumption of pornography by colonial subjects triggered serious public concerns about the transnational trade.[50] While minimizing publicity was considered more important than preventing consumption on British soil, restricting sales and consumption appeared as the top priority in the colonial context, where American and European pornography became available to people of colour. The unusually persistent attempts to secure the American prosecution of New York's Falstaff Press, for instance, clearly centred on the fact that the company's circulars had made it into the hands of "Europeans as well as Natives in East Africa."[51] This anxiety also translated into more severe penalties against colonial offenders. In contrast to the light fines and brief sentences given to British pornographers, South African authorities responded to the 1911 explosion of "Black peril" hysteria by sentencing a Bulawayo distributor to one and a half years in prison and a £300 fine.[52] In short, while colonial officials resisted taking serious efforts against the transnational pornography trade, this reluctance ended when pornography in their jurisdiction became the subject of British public outcry. Despite these moments in which public opinion identified pornography as a problem in specific colonial locations, the general indifference of colonial authorities created space for a well-documented, thriving trade in places like Port Said.[53]

INTERNATIONAL NEGOTIATIONS

As the organ of the state tasked with diplomatic efforts, the Foreign Office was one of the few organizations in a position to grapple with the transnational aspects of the trade. Their activities illustrate that dealing with a transnational trade using international methods generally amounted to a frustrating and inefficient process with few concrete results. Actions by the Foreign Office focused on two main areas. First, they worked with foreign governments to secure expulsions or prosecutions of individual pornography producers. Second, they tried to influence the development of anti-obscenity legislation in foreign nations like France and Germany in order to stem the flow of pornographic materials at their alleged source. The ongoing and ineffectual nature of their negotiations with the French government appeared repeatedly in Foreign Office letters from as early as 1901, suggesting that the French should "once more" be approached about the pornography issue in their country.[54]

Some foreign negotiations proved successful. After years of his publications appearing in Britain, the Foreign Office managed to secure the expulsion of infamous pornographer Charles Carrington from his home in France.[55] In another case, French citizen Leon Branch stood trial in the French Consular Court of Egypt largely at the behest of the British government.[56] As discussed in chapter 1, however, both of these cases occurred early in the Edwardian period, with very few similar successes occurring in later years. Even so, British officials pursued alternative avenues such as pushing for new foreign legislation. In 1929, for example, the Foreign Office successfully encouraged the French government to pass new anti-obscenity laws. Despite this apparent success, the result disappointed British negotiators due to the fact that the new law applied only to visual rather than literary materials.[57] As these meagre victories indicate, action against individual foreign pornographers or larger distribution nodes could be achieved only if such action also benefited the co-operating state government, such as that of Germany or France.

More frequently, however, international negotiations had few if any tangible results. Communications between the Home Office and the Post Office Department of the United States regarding the Falstaff Press in 1934, for instance, met with the response that the enclosed specimens did not warrant investigation by the US government. Only three years later, after numerous additional incidents, did the US government pursue legal action against Falstaff Press, a prosecution that did not appear to result from British negotiations.[58] The Home Office kept lists of known Continental pornographers from 1900 on. While they sometimes sought information on the identities of some of these people, British officials rarely if ever succeeded in having them arrested by their respective governments and the same names remained on active lists for decades.[59]

All of these efforts represented paradoxical attempts to solve a simultaneously local and transnational problem through the use of tools available to the governing bodies of a nation-state. Unlike the anti-vice movement, which used transnational dialogue in order to form a set of heteronormative standards that transcended national borders, the international actions of the British state depended entirely on pressuring foreign governments to use the legal frameworks and legislative tools at their disposal. Negotiations depended on foreign governments asserting sovereignty over citizens within their own jurisdictions. Major actions occurred at the nation-state's points of entry and exit, checking bodies and goods as they crossed national borders. None of these approaches remotely conformed to the realities of the transnational trade, which depended on highly mobile people and goods flowing between local and small-scale production nodes.

PARLIAMENT

As the body with the highest public profile and the closest ties to civil society, Parliament serves as a crucial measure of how the British state viewed its own role in issues of obscenity regulation. Obscene publications appeared as a perennial issue in parliamentary debates. Debates and testimony typically involved the emergence of new technologies or forms of distribution, such as mutoscopes.[60] Other instances in which the pornography trade emerged as a concern usually focused on the question of foreign pornography. In 1938, for example, MP Richard Russell called attention to the increasing number of obscene publications imported from the US, inquiring as to whether or not the Customs Department had been instructed to take greater precautions.[61]

Despite this frequent attention to pornography, Members of Parliament displayed as much if not more concern about limiting regulatory efforts as they did with the obscenity issue itself. While legislators occasionally considered new legal measures with which to oppose the pornography trade, they enacted virtually nothing new during the first four decades of the twentieth century.[62] The only significant new legal measure enacted after 1900 was the 1908 Post Office Act, which included new prohibitions on mailing obscene matter among its lengthy provisions. Notably, however, this law simply built upon existing prohibitions on selling and transmitting obscene materials and was primarily used to intercept foreign pornography.[63] In addition, elected officials resisted any new regulations that would resemble censorship or excessive violations of privacy. In one 1929 debate, several MPs discussed whether Customs searches of publications had become too intrusive. A central question of the debate concerned "whether [the Financial Secretary of the Treasury] has any information as to the effect of this scrutiny on our tourist trade."[64]

Far more heated questioning arose from the 1929 actions of Home Secretary Joynson-Hicks (a.k.a. "Jix"), who instigated an investigation that Members of Parliament believed should have been under the purview of the police. As the notable women's suffrage supporter and Labour figure Mr Pethick-Lawrence stated after questioning Jix: "Does not the right hon. Gentleman see that, when he sets the law in motion, he is, in fact, exercising a censorship, whether he calls it by that name or not?"[65] As these debates indicate, parliamentary officials embraced the narrative of pornography as a largely foreign problem that would be best dealt with by a discreet and efficient Customs Office and the actions of local law enforcement. Moreover, they clearly feared accusations that they supported overt censorship or invasive policing of personal correspondence. In light of these concerns, Parliament generally resisted or equivocated when confronted with the possibility of increased policing of the pornography trade.

REBELS AND OUTLIERS

Despite this clear preferred approach to pornography, some officials within the British state did not always present a united front on the issue. Deviations from the general trend of minimizing publicity and deflecting attention from the role of domestic producers and consumers triggered frustration and condemnation. Samuel Smith, who served as a Liberal MP for Flintshire from the 1880s until his retirement in 1906, maintained his strident views about obscenity until the end of his tenure, even though public opinion had begun to shift as of 1901.[66] Despite his frequent attempts to bring greater attention to the issue of pornography during parliamentary debates, his colleagues displayed clear frustration and resentment. Following a lengthy speech by Smith on the need for action against obscene photographs and publications, Conservative Home Secretary Sir M. White Ridley began his counterargument with the following barb: "I do not doubt the sincerity of the hon. Gentleman who moved the reduction of my salary – for the very extraordinary reason that I am not able to control the morals of London."[67] Ridley's impatience with Smith appears notable for two reasons. First, it illustrates that obscenity had already lost much of its urgency as a political issue as early as 1900, with Ridley openly dismissing the possibility that his office would be able to exert control over the morality of British citizens. Second, as a Conservative baronet and eventual member of the peerage, Ridley would not seem to have much common ground with Labour figure Mr Pethick-Lawrence, the man who would echo many of his sentiments during his 1929 confrontation with Jix. As this example indicates, pornography did not emerge as a partisan issue in parliamentary politics, all parties adopting similar goals and positions and leaving outliers like Samuel Smith out in the cold on the issue of obscenity.

Tolerance for state officials who viewed the pornography trade as a major concern declined after 1900. The most striking example of this can be found again in the figure of Jix, Home Secretary from 1924 to 1929. Unlike many officials of the period, Jix openly and actively supported the efforts of organizations like the NVA and the PMC.[68] While he stopped short of demanding new legislation, he exercised his quasi-censorship powers far more rigorously than his predecessors had done. In addition, he made public statements regarding the dire threat posed by obscene and "borderline" publications.[69] While he maintained the general narrative of pornography as foreign in origin, his alarmist tone and tendency to speak publicly on the issue set him apart from most state officials of the period. While some have argued that Jix's tenure represented a retrenchment of British anti-pornography panic, this argument ignores the fact that Jix's efforts were reviled rather than widely supported. He may indeed have issued large numbers of warrants for seizing foreign packages of pornography, but these efforts focused almost entirely on foreign shipments, did nothing to address the domestic elements of the trade, and triggered a significant public backlash.[70] Jix's outspoken approach to pornography aligned with more general complaints about his personality and political style, perceived as bombastic and unseemly for the office.[71] Given Jix's general reputation as an out-of-touch buffoon, his treatment of obscenity provides a useful contrast with which to evaluate more acceptable approaches to the pornography threat.

These few individuals who deviated from the general goals of the state appeared all the more conspicuous given the concerted effort by different departments and officials to maintain a united front on the issue of obscenity even in the face of personal misgivings. The *Well of Loneliness* case offers a clear example of how an image of stability and unity was prioritized over genuine policy preferences. When deciding whether to go forward with the prosecution, various departments offered their input on the case. While some, like the Undersecretary of State, concluded that the book qualified as obscene, others disagreed.[72] One report from the Customs Office expressed agreement with the Undersecretary's office, but a subsequent memo to the Office of the Exchequer stated that the book did not in fact qualify as obscene under the law and that they would prefer that the prosecution did not go forward. Rather than make that official recommendation, however, they suggested that the prosecution was the only available course of action to avoid "flouting the publicly expressed opinion of the Home Secretary, and … [prejudicing] any proceedings he might take subsequently."[73]

As these examples illustrate, the individuals and larger subdivisions and ministries of the British state did not agree on the subject of obscenity, a category that necessarily includes pornography. Most significantly, the judiciary, police departments, and the Home Office differed on how to define the legal threshold for obscenity. In other situations, state entities concurred on the question of whether materials qualified as obscene, but diverged on the best course of action to address the issue. Jix's sin was not, therefore, that he disagreed with state inaction against pornography; the hostility he faced resulted from his decision to deviate publicly from broader trends rather than keep his concerns within official circles.

OBSCENITY AND PUBLIC OPINION

Although a united front on the subject of obscenity had to be maintained for the benefit of foreign states, it also served important domestic purposes. On this and other issues, the British state had a contradictory and combative relationship with public opinion. On the one hand, officials frequently cited vaguely defined public opinion as the best barometer of obscenity. On the other hand, they resisted members of the public whose opinion of obscenity ran toward the impractical or difficult to enforce. Explaining his decision not to investigate particular shops in 1923, Inspector Draper of the London Metropolitan Police stated: "I think it is also to the credit of these rubber goods shops that we seldom find them having anything to do with the sale of really obscene books or pictures. It is also a somewhat noticeable fact that, we have remarkably few complaints from the general public about them. Whatever complaint there is, generally comes from a Society specially formed to deal with such matters or adherents thereof."[74] Here, the majority public opinion outweighed the far more restrictive position of the nameless but vocal vice society members who lodged the complaint against the rubber goods shop.

State officials also explicitly rejected the authority of public opinion in numerous cases. In its negative assessment of the nautical adventure film *White Hands*, the British Board of Film Censors described it as "full flavoured, with an appeal to the public taste of rather brutal scenes."[75] In a similar rejection of public opinion, officials dismissed the positive reviews and lack of controversy that had initially greeted the release of *The Well of Loneliness*, instead deferring to the negative "expert" opinion of Rudyard Kipling.[76] The common defence among shopkeepers or publishers accused of distributing pornography that they had been in business for years without any member of the public complaining rarely if ever swayed legal authorities.[77]

In some cases, state officials openly framed public opinion as something to be manipulated rather than followed. A 1929 Home Office letter, after arguing that the actions the Home Office could take against pornography depended upon public support, went on to state: "Strangely enough the number of complaints in regard to books which reach the Home Office is very small in spite of the fact that the output of books of doubtful decency has certainly increased. The greatest hope for the future lies in a reassertion of a public belief in the ultimate decency of things."[78] Public standards on obscenity therefore mattered only when they bolstered existing state policy. The state's enforcement of heteronormativity depended heavily on appearing to reflect wider British cultural views while delegitimizing those public discourses judged to be either overly permissive or excessively zealous on issues of sexual deviance and enforcement of norms, leading to inconsistent relationships with the public.

Concern over public opinion often revolved around the issue of state censorship. Despite monitoring and prosecuting obscene publications, various state officials declared their unequivocal opposition to censorship. As defined by the Home Office, censorship meant a system by which written publications had to be approved prior to publication; it did not apply to the banning of materials after publication or distribution.[79] This idiosyncratic definition of censorship led to such policies as a stubborn refusal to provide a definitive list of banned texts, either to the British public or to foreign entities like the French government.[80] It also left the British state free to censor movies and later television, since their legal definition of censorship did not encompass film.[81] As other historians have argued, it also allowed them to engage in activities identical to censorship for all practical purposes but without using the term.[82]

While the British policed pornography far more strictly than many other countries, they issued smug criticisms of governments that practised their definition of censorship. The Irish Free State, for example, appointed a censor tasked with screening for obscene or blasphemous publications.[83] Press coverage critiquing the move raised the question of whether the "free" English press would be censored by the Irish authorities.[84] British self-image as reflected in the press and public discourse revolved around questions of a self-regulating and responsible society rather than one that required close monitoring. While the British state displayed constant concern with the nation's literature and popular entertainment, they policed these materials without creating new legislation or a state apparatus that would make official censorship a visible and undeniable reality.

FOREIGN COLLABORATION AND BRITISH SOVEREIGNTY

In 1925, the British government ratified the International Agreement for the Suppression of the Circulation of and Traffic in Obscene Publications.[85] Officially, this agreement obligated its participants to investigate and prosecute persons involved in the production or circulation of obscene publications.[86] In practice, however, the British state and other signatory governments made few changes to their existing policies. After the agreement was ratified, the Customs Office quickly informed the Home Office that they had no power to seize pornographic items exported from the country; this apparent loophole went unchecked and largely unremarked on for the next several decades.[87] Despite the formal ratification of an international agreement, the British state remained almost entirely focused on pornography of foreign origin and ignored the possibility that British pornographers could be contaminating the public morals of other nations. In one exception to this general rule, the state co-operated with foreign governments in the pursuit of expatriate British pornographers in the colonies or on the Continent. In these cases, British officials did not hesitate to work with governments capable of pursuing legal action. For example, in 1929 the Home Office learned of two British pornographers living in Italy and sent their information to the Italian government, declaring that "an interim reply which has been received from Rome indicates that the Fascist Government will take effective action."[88] This decision clearly indicates prioritization of British public image over the safety and well-being of its subjects, as Mussolini's treatment of dissenters, "pederasts," and various criminals had been thoroughly discussed in the British press by that point.[89]

A second significant exception to this indifference to pornography exported to other countries involved materials produced on British soil and sent to the colonies or Dominions. For example, a 1931 letter from S.W. Harris informed the commissioner of the South African Police that several London-based publishers had been convicted of publishing obscene books discovered in Cape Town shops.[90] Notably, the information in this letter did not come at the request of the South African police force, nor had their complaints prompted the prosecution of the publishers. Rather, British state officials acted on their own volition first to prosecute the offenders and then to disseminate information regarding their conviction. The contrast between these actions and their blunt refusal to pursue cases of British pornography exported to other nations demonstrates the significance of maintaining the appearance of British sexual morality not only in the metropole, but throughout the empire.

The importance of promoting a morally superior public image for the benefit of other nations appeared frequently in official correpondence and policy documents. British officials drew explicit comparisons between British and foreign morals, particularly regarding pornography. A 1906 New Scotland Yard memo claimed that pornography remained a problem in England despite having been "banished from London shops" because foreigners continued to import materials. This position placed the blame on other countries while erasing British involvement in pornography distribution.[91]

In response to reports that the French press had largely ignored a government circular about obscenity legislation, S.W. Harris noted that "in England it would have been made the subject of general comment."[92] In 1924, police dismissed rumours of pornographic films produced on British soil, pointing to Germany as the likely source even though they lacked any concrete evidence of the films' German origin.[93] This tendency to blame other countries by drawing comparisons to an allegedly insignificant domestic trade was not limited to Great Britain alone. For example, the 1930 League of Nations report on obscene publications contained several instances of member states blaming France for the circulation of pornography while minimizing their own country's participation.[94]

Like anti-vice organizations, the British state did not see all members of society as equally vulnerable to the risks of pornography consumption. As already discussed regarding the Falstaff Press case, they viewed involvement by people of colour as particularly troubling.[95] Even more alarming than the use of pornography by colonial subjects and other people of colour, however, was the visible consumption of pornography by white Britons in close proximity to those same colonial subjects. The incident in Port Said discussed in chapter 2 triggered such concerns due to the fact that the sale of pornography by Egyptians to British soldiers exposed less savoury elements of British sexuality in full view of people of colour.[96] Other incidents also centred upon pornography consumption among soldiers, particularly those stationed outside of the metropole. In 1940, for example, the London Metropolitan Police received reports that an unnamed distributor had sent three thousand indecent leaflets to members of His Majesty's Forces.[97] This focus on the sexual health and morality of soldiers was not uncommon. Much like the flurry of eugenic fervour triggered by sexually transmitted diseases during times of war, the consumption of pornography by enlisted soldiers caused far more concern than consumption by civilians, particularly if those soldiers were to be stationed outside the country.[98]

Concern over involvement of people of colour in pornography extended to the plots and characters in pornographic materials. As shown earlier in the chapter, the police and other state entities frequently declined to prosecute materials for fear of drawing attention or wasting resources even if they found them clearly pornographic. The materials that did warrant legal action can therefore provide insight into the concerns of state officials. Materials singled out for serious investigation often involved interracial encounters, with these elements highlighted in official reports. For example, reports produced by Detective Sidney Norman during a 1942 investigation into a pornographic novelist named D'Arcy Glinto emphasized that one of his books featured sex between a Caucasian woman, "a Japanese," and "a 'Dago.'"[99] In another story by the same author, the Caucasian female protagonist has sexual encounters with Jewish and Afro-Caribbean men.[100] While Norman described other obscene elements of the stories, including violence and various sexual acts, the ethnicity of the participants appeared most prominently in his account. Unlike numerous other cases of seized pornographic materials, the police actively pursued Glinto and sought to have him prosecuted rather than simply seizing his books from distributors, suggesting that the depictions of interracial sex may have struck a nerve.[101] It is also possible, however, that Glinto's depiction of a white woman having sex with Japanese and Italian men may have elicited an unusually strong response due to the wartime stress of 1942. One can only speculate about whether the same story would have elicited such a reaction prior to the 1940s.

The emphasis on pornography as a foreign phenomenon worked to erase British participation in the trade. As discussed in chapter 2, many of the pornographers operating out of France were British citizens.[102] In the British state's narrative, however, materials created and distributed by these British pornographers and in the English language became foreign by virtue of crossing national borders. This also concealed British participation by framing the conversation in such a way that it left no room for the British exporter. As invested as state officials were in pornography as a foreign contaminant, they simply did not allow for the possibility that Britain could be an equally contaminating factor for others. This ignorance cannot be attributed to the fact that British dealers sold pornography overseas; by 1912 the Home Office had addressed complaints from the US regarding indecent materials shipped from England, and in the next few years they learned of British suppliers selling to customers in countries around the world.[103] Despite these clear examples of British citizens actively contributing to the transnational trade, the British state never incorporated such cases into their broader policy efforts or public narratives.

QUESTIONS OF CLASS AND AGE

As discussed in chapter 4, the early twentieth-century press turned away from their Victorian practice of identifying pornography as a working-class vice, constructing it instead as material of invariably foreign origin. The British state largely followed this trend, identifying immigrants and overseas producers as far more responsible for the trade than Britons of any class. On the level of policymaking in particular, elected and appointed officials avoided overtly class-based assessments of the trade. Class did, however, affect the outcome of specific enforcement efforts. Street hawkers and small shopkeepers comprised the group most frequently investigated and prosecuted, with the result that more working- and lower-middle-class people faced arrest than the wealthy. For example, market hawker Arthur Sandford had already had numerous encounters with the police over a period of several years before his far more affluent supplier finally faced trial in 1930.[104] In several other cases, police arrested low-level hawkers but never located the publishers or producers of the materials.[105]

The official erasure of class from the rhetoric of pornography regulation had implications for the dynamics of pornography networks. While enforcement efforts targeting public hawkers disproportionately affected the working and lower-middle classes, this constituted only a small portion of the trade. Mail-order businesses and clandestine non-commercial circulation remained accessible to people of a broad range of class backgrounds. As a result, pornography networks in Britain formed and maintained a mixed-class dynamic that would have been far more difficult for a community that required physical encounters rather than long-distance interaction. The state's respect for the divide between public and private, while disproportionately affecting less affluent sellers, nevertheless nurtured queer spaces and networks that cut across class boundaries. The Benbow and Hyde network discussed in chapter 1 clearly illustrates this dynamic; in that context, the prostitute dominatrix Carmen Corti and an OBE both had the ability to interact and exchange pornography in a safe setting.[106]

While class was often ignored by policymakers, age remained a source of concern. The sale of pornography to underage youth triggered alarm at all levels of the British state, from the local police to the Home Office. Certain types of distribution to minors, however, proved more likely to catch the eye of state officials. While officials rarely if ever took note of mail-order pornography sent to working-class children or discovered in predominantly working-class schools, they reacted quickly to complaints of indecent materials sent to Eton or other elite institutions. In 1923, for example, the Home Office responded to the discovery of a graphically pornographic story sent from Chile to a boy at Eton by ordering the post office henceforth to open all mail sent from any Chilean address to any Eton student.[107] The Foreign Office also interceded in pornography cases involving Eton students, communicating with American authorities in an attempt to secure arrests.[108]

Paradoxically, British state officials displayed a complete lack of interest in the possibility of underage persons participating in the production or distribution of the trade. In 1952, an inquiry about the legal status of a sixteen-year-old nude model led the Office of the Undersecretary of State to conclude that the office had never studied the issue and had no information regarding underage nude models in its files.[109] In addition, even their concern for underage consumption had its limits. In 1909, the Home Office clashed with the anti-vice movement over a proposed bill that would increase penalties specifically for pornographers who sold to underage customers. The NVA and its allies supported the bill, while the Home Office considered it unnecessary. As they argued, British law enforcement already had the necessary legal tools to act on cases of pornography sold to minors.[110]

The British state's attempts to protect children from pornography consumption conformed to larger patterns relating to foreign products and public visibility. The highest levels of the British state proved most willing to act in cases involving elite children, which were also the cases that would be most likely to cause public scandal; pornography of foreign origin elicited even greater reactions in these cases. As in their other enforcement efforts, police actions against pornographers who sold to children focused almost entirely on shops and public streets. Moreover, the types of pornography accessible to young children tended to be available in highly visible public locations rather than catalogues.[111] The far more likely scenario of children being exposed to pornography through clandestine distribution networks remained largely ignored, and the more disturbing possibility of underage people participating as models or performers received no attention whatsoever. In other words, the state had no real desire or intention to pursue aspects of the trade that operated behind closed doors. Instead it sought to maintain a public facade of British moral superiority.

THE MAINSTREAM AND THE BORDERLINE

British state policy shared the anti-vice movement's concern with borderline indecency over unambiguously pornographic materials. Jix in particular promoted the idea that borderline indecency ultimately posed a greater threat than outright pornography. Nowhere did the fear of the borderline manifest itself more clearly than in the prosecution of the publishers of *The Well of Loneliness*. Few if any individual pornographic novels ever received direct attention from multiple government departments. The decision to prosecute typically rested with the police, and large stores of pornographic literature were discussed in official memoranda as an undifferentiated mass rather than as separate works with different authors and publishers.[112] Both *The Well of Loneliness* and its author Radclyffe Hall, in contrast, received direct attention from the Home Office and various other state bodies.

Fear of the borderline also dictated much of the British state's policy toward film. Truly pornographic films, while known to the authorities, almost never appeared in policy discussions or even in confidential state correspondence. Instead, the British Board of

Film Censors worked to eliminate sexual innuendo, implied miscegenation, and verbal vulgarity from all mainstream films.[113] Unlike pornographic novels and photographs, stag films had a very small potential audience and extremely limited possibilities for circulation due to the difficulties of transporting and screening films in secret. As a result, pornographic film had a minimal presence in public discourse and thus warranted far less state attention than the horrifying prospect of an interracial romance crossing the borderline to infect popular opinion.

The British state's concern over the borderline stemmed from the same fears found in the anti-vice movement. Like the NVA and PMC, the British state feared that overt sexuality, violence, and challenges to the social order could gradually become more acceptable throughout British society if allowed to exist in the mainstream. Unlike vice societies, however, there is no evidence that state entities were concerned with the actual "contamination" of British culture and sexuality either in private or public. Their focus remained strictly on making sure that the public sphere continued to appear pure and that unacceptable sexual practices like pornography remained confined to a manageable space. While this essentially resulted in the state and vice societies becoming allies on the issue of borderline entertainment, they did so with different motives and concerns. One of the unintended consequences of this policy was that more energy and attention went toward borderline or even mainstream works than overt pornography, thus directing anti-obscenity efforts away from the activities of British pornography networks and toward those of Hollywood and mainstream book publishers.

IDEOLOGIES OF PORNOGRAPHY AND POLICING

Given the patterns and conflicts discussed above, it is clear that the British state adopted an ideological view of pornography and its enforcement partially opposed to that of the anti-vice movement and the press, revealing a point of fracture between social groups often discussed as parts of the same hegemonic bloc. In some respects, the state's theorization of pornography aligned with that of civil groups. They framed pornography consumption as a general detriment to society, one possibly related to other forms of sexual immorality such as promiscuity and homosexuality.[114] They also viewed pornography as a problem intertwined with other issues such as drug use. For instance, a 1922 letter attributed the apparent rise in Continental pornography consumption to "the existence of drugging and doping, which apparently is gaining ground in all countries," adding, "There has even been a certain amount of it amongst the very phlegmatic Swiss."[115]

The state deviated from civil authorities, however, in its assessment of the nature of the threat and in its views on responsibility for enforcement. Vice societies pointed to the state as the actor ultimately responsible for dealing with issues of obscenity. State officials, however, adopted the position that much of the work against pornography should occur in the private sphere. In response to a demand from the PMC to take action against a periodical that advertised pornographic materials, the Home Office stated that the responsibility for protecting children against the threat of pornography lay with parents and teachers.[116] A minute note from a Home Office official broke with the anti-vice movement's views of state responsibility with the following analogy: "Pork chops are legal in Christian countries, but they are fatal to children under 9 months old. Nevertheless, we are never asked to ban pork chops. If we were, we would not ban them: and, if pressed, we would retort that the withholding of pork chops from children was the duty of mothers and nurses and not the duty of the S of S."[117]

Distaste for excessive regulation extended to materials that may have qualified as obscene under the law but had been produced for private or limited circulation rather than public display. While police dutifully investigated rumours of private pornographic film screenings in London, they concluded that a market for such products must be very small if the trade even existed.[118] In response to a series of disruptive complaints by a Mr O'Brien against Edward Carpenter's entirely non-pornographic yet legally obscene homophile manifesto *Homogenic Love,* the Undersecretary of State dryly described the work as "the pamphlet which roused the fury of Mr. O'Brien to the extent of a twenty-four page denunciatory reply, and to which my own retort would have consisted in the silence of the waste-paper basket."[119] He went on to observe that any readers of the pamphlet would almost certainly be homosexuals anyway, which meant that it could do little further harm.[120] In short, those members of the state or the public who failed to turn a blind eye to the more discreet circulation of obscene materials were viewed as bothersome and out of touch with reality.

Changing medical opinions on masturbation in general and pornography in particular also provide important context for the state's views on the issue. As discussed in chapter 5, during the first few decades of the twentieth century medical authorities and sexologists began to question the supposed physical horrors of masturbation. As seen in the race-hygiene hysteria following the discovery of poor health among Boer War recruits, individual health and sexuality often became matters of state concern during the early twentieth century.[121] The overall lack of urgency toward pornography and masturbation should not therefore be attributed to any broader trend toward less state attention to sexual deviance and its effect on bodily integrity. Instead it signifies that the threat of masturbation lost currency as a motivating factor for official pornography regulation just as it failed to galvanize the anti-vice movement. Unlike abortion and birth control, both of which had a direct relationship to larger eugenic concerns of race hygiene and military fitness, pornography became a sexual issue with far fewer implications for state policy and therefore warranted less attention and fewer resources.

Despite their public allegiance, tension often emerged between state officials and civil actors like the press and anti-vice campaigners regarding the issue of pornography. The Home Office and bodies like the London Metropolitan Police entertained delegations from the NVA and PMC, answering their inquiries and expressing gratitude for their contributions. Confidentially, however, they viewed vice societies as out of touch and unrealistic in their expectations. Upon receiving a draft of the PMC's proposed bill to prevent the "contamination" of children by pornography, S.W. Harris praised their intentions but found them "muddle-headed."[122] Another participant in the same correspondence bluntly referred to the bill as "absurd."[123] Civil organizations like the NVA still, however, had the ability to trigger an investigation. Between 1922 and 1932, several investigations of shops and publications began with complaints from H.M. Tyrer of the PMC.[124] Significantly, however, these investigations did not result in criminal charges, bolstering official views of vice societies as increasingly irrelevant.

Different entities within the British state sometimes had strained relationships with the newspaper industry. The London Metropolitan Police experienced far more criticism from the press than any other group. Members of the press called their dedication to fighting obscenity into question several times through the 1920s and 1930s, going so far as to claim high-level corruption.[125] Despite these occasional hostilities, however, neither the press nor the wider public ever pushed for extensive new campaigns against pornography. In fact, there is no evidence to suggest that the public viewed the state as negligent on the question of pornography, or that they fully understood the limits of state effort against the trade. Calls for stricter state involvement in anti-pornography efforts appear to have been limited to vice societies and a few middle-class commentators.

As in the case of civil actors like the press and the anti-vice movement, the state's contribution to the development of the early twentieth-century pornography trade can best be understood if we focus on the spaces where the state placed boundaries and where the trade operated. The British state apparatus adopted the position that they had three main responsibilities related to policing pornography. They guarded the purity of public space, thus facilitating clandestine circulation in private networks. They worked to prevent the "contamination" of British culture by foreign vice, leaving the domestic aspects of the trade largely ignored. Finally, they worked to protect specific "vulnerable" groups, primarily children and people of colour, leaving most adult British citizens in the metropole relatively free to participate in the trade as producers and consumers.

The formation and continuing activity of pornography networks should not, therefore, be viewed as a symptom of the state's weakened grip on heteronormativity. Instead, it signified the state's success. Enforcing normative standards need not and did not take the form of a panic or an enthusiastic enforcement effort.[126] The trade existed in relative safety and security, but voiceless and out of the public eye. Few outside of the anti-vice movement demanded greater action against pornography, but even fewer spoke in support of the right to consume or produce it. The interests of the British state did not require the destruction of the pornography trade. They needed only to convince the British public and foreign viewers that pornography had a negligible presence in British sexual culture, with a handful of foreigners and sexual deviants to blame for the few dirty books and pictures consumed behind closed doors. Why, the social problem was so minor that it did not even require censorship! Given these social goals, the British state's approach to the pornography trade can only be described as a resounding success. The fact that pornography networks and queer spaces with transnational connections flourished behind the scenes became, in this context, largely irrelevant.

WARTIME POLICY

Even the social and political cataclysm of the Second World War did not alter British policymakers' resistance to taking extreme measures against pornography. Despite the fact that living in a wartime context created social concerns and sexual panics, the reaction to pornography remained one of relative indifference. In fact, Members of Parliament expressed far greater concerns over unnecessary censorship than they did about pornography. In a 1940 parliamentary debate, for instance, MPs sought assurances that the Lord Chamberlain would not seek greater censorship powers relating to entertainment unless it proved absolutely necessary for the war effort.[127]

Continuity in pornography policy even extended to patently pointless exercises. Despite the fact that the demise of the League of Nations was clearly imminent and that it lacked substantive enforcement abilities in the early 1940s, the British government maintained its practice of submitting annual reports on the pornography trade throughout the war.[128] This lack of change in wartime policy was not due to any erroneous belief that the war had cut off the entirety of the pornography trade, as British authorities had claimed during the First World War. On the contrary, their own reports found that the loss of the Continental European trade had merely increased domestic production.[129] Instead, the British state continued to participate in the failed international anti-pornography efforts of the League of Nations due to a lack of acceptable alternatives. The British state's policies, which for so long had been geared toward promoting images of pornography as specifically foreign, could not easily change course and thus continued to facilitate the domestic British trade throughout the Second World War. Like so many other aspects of British anti-pornography policy in the early twentieth century, this was a gesture intended to reassure domestic and foreign observers that pornography would not be tolerated. It was, however, just that: a gesture.

CONCLUSION

When considering the social issue of pornography, the British state did not adopt as a goal the purification of British sexuality. Nor did it approach the regulation of pornography as a task necessary to protect those who might be sexually exploited or otherwise harmed in the production process. British state entities instead sought to fight pornography at those points where it threatened to shatter the image of Britain as a morally superior society. The imposition of heteronormativity in public spaces and at national boundaries served to bolster British superiority, but following pornography into the transnational and quasi-private networks of the pornography trade could only expose the limitations of the state's control over sexual morality. State authorities may have been able to dictate what could be shown on a public street, but they had little ability to follow the pornography trade into the private homes, back rooms, and post office boxes where pornography distribution and exchange practices thrived. The British state thus simultaneously limited and fostered the growth of the pornography trade, leading it to assume the specific shape of loose networks and queer spaces in the particular time and context of early twentieth-century Britain in a transnational world.

Conclusion

Let us now return to the anecdote featured at the beginning of this book. Despite the active and long-standing presence of networks of pornographers and consumers within Britain, intelligence operatives proved unwilling or incapable of interacting with this community. Special Operations Executive (SOE) agents seeking to design pornographic propaganda, rather than simply hiring one of many local nude photographers or obtaining pictures from abroad, instead fumbled through a comically lengthy and labour-intensive attempt to produce their own leaflet. In order to understand this distance between the SOE and Britain's community of local pornographers, one must understand the ways in which the pornography trade developed after 1900. As the evidence in the preceding chapters has shown, the British pornography trade organized as clusters of loose networks and clandestine groups, operating within spaces carved out by competing interests and conflicts between and within the state, the press, and civil authorities. Their social and sexual interactions, constructed as deviant and incompatible with normative sexuality, occurred outside the bounds of both the law and mainstream sexual culture. Given this context, the problems experienced by the SOE become far less baffling. For all its resources, the SOE lacked the understanding of the trade's specific practices and patterns of production, consumption, and interaction to access such spaces. The British state might have been able to police pornography to the extent of keeping it confined to limited spaces and hidden from public view, but it did so at the cost of encouraging the growth of networks that remained opaque and inaccessible to groups like the SOE.

The organization of the early twentieth-century British pornography trade and its relationship to other elements of society sets this specific pornography culture apart from other time periods and geographical locations.[1] Given the social and political environment and the technologies employed by the early twentieth-century British pornography trade, it appears unlikely that pornographers and consumers in earlier periods would have had the same level of organization and ability to remain active within networks over an extended period. Technological change also set the early twentieth-century trade apart from pornography in other contexts, as technologies like photography and typewriters allowed for the production of pornography affordable even to low-income members of the working class. For most of the nineteenth century, in contrast, pornography appeared mainly in published book form and remained prohibitively expensive for much of British society.[2] Until the development of the penny post and daily newspapers, the main forms of communication employed within British pornography networks, interactions remained dangerous and difficult. While shipments of pornographic books from France to England had occurred at least since the seventeenth century, pornographers' frequent relocation and movement around the British Empire and beyond required transportation technologies like railways and well-established shipping lanes. Only with these advances in communication and transportation could British pornographers and consumers participate in the complex transnational networks supplying so many of their materials.

In addition to technology, social changes also provide crucial context for understanding the specific conditions and practices of the trade during this time. Pornography remained far from socially or legally acceptable in early twentieth-century Britain, as can be seen in the numerous prosecutions discussed in this book. Legal penalties did, however, ease. While a Victorian pornographer could easily face years of hard labour if convicted, post-1900 producers and distributors rarely spent more than one month in prison and consumers typically escaped with a warning.[3] State authorities focused almost entirely on publicly visible or foreign imported pornography. Their counterparts in civil society, members of anti-vice organizations, sought to bring greater awareness to the issue of pornography but lacked the funds or public support to enact serious campaigns. In addition, they hung many of their hopes on precisely the type of comprehensive, binding international agreement that most in the British state sought to avoid. The press reinforced this relative inattention to pornography by focusing nearly all reporting on types of pornography distribution that deflected attention away from domestic networks and the multidirectional transnational flow of goods. As this book's last three chapters have discussed in detail, moral reformers and concerned government officials continued to fight against specific forms of pornography distribution, but post-1900 Britain lacked the kind of anti-obscenity panics that had raged in the nineteenth century.

In short, in early twentieth-century Britain multiple factors converged to produce spaces in which pornographers and their customers found it beneficial to engage in very different forms of interaction and economic activity. Their continuing marginalization prevented pornographers and consumers from being absorbed entirely into mainstream sexuality, but the reduced legal and social risks made quiet participation in a pornography network a more attractive option than in the past. Technological advancements meant that pornographers could produce photographs and stories without extensive training, while consumers could find pornography fitting their particular needs and interests. Finally, improved communications allowed members of pornography networks to cultivate ongoing business and personal relationships without sacrificing anonymity or even venturing outside of their homes in search of a pornography dealer. This ability to engage in a transaction without meeting face to face would have been particularly important for a woman, a member of the middle class, or someone else whose reputation could be seriously threatened by pornography consumption. Given the business practices, social context, and set of technologies employed within British networks and larger transnational systems, it appears unlikely that they would have organized along similar lines in earlier periods. This study therefore illuminates a specific moment in the history of pornography, one that deviates in many ways from the pornography cultures that preceded and followed it. Despite these unique qualities, however, the methodological framework employed in this book can still be applied to other contexts.

METHODS OF PORNOGRAPHY ANALYSIS

While mapping the early twentieth-century British pornography trade fills in a significant gap in the history of pornography, I would argue that this book's combination of porn studies and social history methods is its more significant contribution. As I have repeatedly insisted throughout this book, neither pornographic content nor its relation to mainstream sexuality can be understood without paying close attention to the surrounding material practices and social dynamics of production, consumption, and regulation. If we foreground the material details of how pornography was made, bought, sold, and used, both the content of pornographic materials and the relationships between different participants take on added dimensions. The gender dynamics of particular pornographic films or photographs, for example, acquire a completely different meaning when read in the context of networks that included both men and women as producers and consumers, a situation that challenges assumptions of exclusively male viewers. Exploring advertisements printed in various publications gives us glimpses not only into how individual people might have discovered pornography, but also into how networks were formed. Taking a close look at the technologies and physical spaces employed by a single pornographer like Richard Elias suggests larger patterns in the social and economic resources required to become active in the pornography trade. The importance of such questions has long been recognized by porn studies scholars, but has rarely been acknowledged in historical studies of pornography.

This book has also demonstrated the importance of contextualizing these material conditions with an eye toward the tensions between mainstream or heteronormative sexuality and categories constructed as deviant. For example, the racial stereotypes depicted in North African postcards, such as the strategic use of veils and head coverings, cannot be evaluated without close attention to imperialist narratives circulating in British society. Messages regarding race, class, and gender norms become dramatically different against the backdrop of mainstream entertainment that contained social messages approved by state and civil moral authorities. The practices and risks taken by pornographers cannot be fully understood without exploring the forces policing and constraining them. Studying pornography's social position and cultural significance thus requires a two-pronged approach: analyzing the conditions of production and consumption within the trade itself on the one hand and the surrounding social and cultural context on the other, remaining attentive to moments of contestation and interplay between the two.

This close examination of pornography's position in early twentieth-century British culture necessarily tells us much about normative sexuality in this period. The moments at which Britons chose to move against pornography or to tacitly ignore its circulation show us that normative sexual culture in this period can hardly be reduced to something as simple as liberated versus oppressed, pro-sex versus anti-sex. Rather, the specific moments in which pornography triggered anxiety and fear corresponded to larger social concerns. Pornography that threatened Britain's international reputation, undermined racial purity, or polluted public space warranted action, while other forms of pornography distribution did not. The language used to describe the threat of pornography also reflected specific concepts of good sexuality. Those who opposed pornography did not merely describe it as bad, but argued that it channelled sexuality into an inappropriate or unhealthy activity. This argument conversely shows us what early twentieth-century Britons considered an appropriate form of sexual expression. This study of pornography thus reveals not just the queer spaces and deviant sexualities of the pornography trade, but the shape of the normative culture surrounding it.

We should not, however, see this study as a mere exercise in methodology or a matter of abstract concepts. Those who lived and worked within the pornography trade had their lives profoundly marked by it. As so aptly observed by that nameless SOE operative, their path was indeed a thorny one. They may have had a path and the ability to move forward, but one step from that narrow path could mean pain and hardship. For Kitty Lichtenstein, deviating from the path meant fines that she could scarcely afford. For Harold Hall, it meant the less tangible but no less devastating public humiliation of a ruined reputation. For Richard Elias, stepping from the path quite possibly meant death; while Home Office records contain no record of what happened to him after his deportation to Poland, this occurred a scant eight years before a considerable portion of the country's population would be killed by the occupying forces of the Third Reich. These human stories are lost when pornography is discussed only in the abstract. Only by starting from the stories of people who produced, consumed, and regulated pornography can we arrive at its larger significance in the history of Britain and the world.

LINGERING QUESTIONS

This book is not an exhaustive account of the entirety of the transnational pornography trade between 1900 and 1945. On the contrary, my use of Britain as a lens through which to explore larger systems leaves the perspectives of many untouched. As I have shown throughout this book, the specific shape of the pornography trade depended on moments of encounter between local and transnational forces. While people from countries around the world participated in the same transnational system as the British networks described in this study, many of them existed in a very different local or national context. As a result, it is likely that pornography cultures that interacted with British networks and existed during the same period occupied a very different position in their own country or region of origin. João de Brito and his Portuguese collaborator Manuel de Sousa may have interacted and participated in the same transnational networks, but local conditions in Portugal meant that de Sousa occupied a very different context than the local British elements discussed here. Future research may work to illuminate these other localized nodes within the pornography trade's larger transnational systems.

There are also important questions of how the pornography trade and the culture of those involved changed in the postwar period. Historians studying other aspects of sexuality and culture generally agree that sexual restrictions and the enforcement of gender norms became more oppressive in the West during the Cold War.[4] If state and civil society became more hostile to homosexuality, ambiguous gender presentation, and extramarital sex, the same may very well be true of pornography use. Beyond social changes, technological innovations like television and lower-cost home filmmaking equipment suggest likely shifts in production and distribution during the 1950s and 1960s. Despite the important questions raised by the postwar context, the period between the end of this study's focus and the emergence of pornography as a public issue in 1972 remains virtually untouched by historians of either Britain or the United States. Research on this crucial period in the history of pornography would be a welcome addition to the literature on porn studies and the history of sexuality, and would benefit from adopting methods that dedicate close attention to conditions of production and consumption.

CONTEMPORARY THEORETICAL APPLICATIONS

Beyond contributing to our understanding of how the pornography trade developed and changed over time, this study also offers methodological and theoretical insights directly applicable to analysis of contemporary pornography. Recent events offer glimpses of how this analysis could be extended into later periods, particularly the contemporary British context. In December 2014, British lawmakers amended existing legislation to ban a variety of sexual acts from appearing in UK-produced porn.[5] Commentators in both the United States and the UK observed that several of the acts banned, such as face-sitting and roleplay, were those associated with femdom (female-dominant sex).[6] In addition, the inclusion of female ejaculation on the list of banned features seemed to be a transparent attempt to circumscribe depictions of female pleasure.

A subsequent face-sitting protest held at Parliament showcased sexually dominant women protesting perceived limitations on their sexual and artistic expression.[7] Even outside of the BDSM and pornographer communities, few observers took seriously the claim that all of the items on the new list of banned acts were forbidden on the grounds of safety (to my knowledge, the number of documented fatalities or serious injuries attributable to female ejaculation stands at zero). Instead, many public commentators suggested that the ban was based on the social meanings of the sex acts rather than any physical effects on the body.[8]

This incident stands out for the ways in which it illuminates the ongoing complexity of the interplay between heteronormativity and pornography in British society. While this instance of legal regulation and subsequent public protest bears little to no resemblance to the underground networks discussed throughout this project, it still offers a clear example of how pornography undermines rather than reinforces or reflects heteronormative sexuality. Despite pervasive narratives of "pornification" and constant anxiety surrounding the possibility that easy access to pornography warps sexual relationships, it would be an oversimplification to suggest that pornography has simply been subsumed into normative sexuality.[9] Rather, some forms of pornography now enjoy legality and general social acceptance, while others face legal stigmatization.

Applying the methods employed in this book, as well as in porn studies scholarship more broadly, to the recent bans and face-sitting protests has the potential to illuminate several important questions. For example, closely analyzing production and distribution patterns of pornography featuring these acts might reveal material differences between mainstream and femdom or feminist porn. Is British femdom porn produced by different social groups than those making mainstream, male-oriented pornography? Does this type of pornography circulate on specific websites or in queer and feminist shops? Do performers on these sets face different working experiences than performers operating within larger studios that produce male-oriented porn? While it is well beyond the scope of this project to address these questions, academic research and anecdotal accounts provide ample reason to suspect that conditions of production and distribution in queer and feminist porn differ significantly from those of mainstream porn studios.[10] If this is the case for British femdom producers, distributors, and consumers, both the state's choice to ban the acts and the pornographers' choice to publicly protest take on new dimensions. Without answers to these questions about the conditions surrounding femdom porn, the entire controversy appears decontextualized and unmoored from the specific histories and material realities of those involved.

The methods employed in this book could also provide deeper context for the actions of state and heteronormative civil society in deciding to ban these acts. Just as disparate reactions to interracial sex compared to sex between two Europeans helps us to map the contours of British heteronormativity between 1900 and 1945, the particular acts banned by the British government in 2014 provide us with crucial insights into sexual normativity and deviance in contemporary British society. While a much more comprehensive analysis would be needed to draw solid conclusions regarding the law, I speculate that bans on face-sitting and female ejaculation indicate ongoing discomfort with female sexual autonomy in contemporary Western societies. Pornography that reinforces male heterosexual dominance more easily fits within heteronormative sexual culture than queer or female-dominant pornography. This single quirk of British obscenity law thus serves as but one example of the ways in which attention to specific conditions of production, consumption, and regulation can continue to shed light on the particularities of heteronormativity and sexual culture. Many other readings can probably be drawn from the specific forms of pornography permitted and those banned by British law, and research into the changing parameters of permissible porn would be yet another welcome addition to our knowledge of sexuality and culture. As this book has shown, however, these are questions that must be explored using historically grounded methods and an eye toward the interplay between pornography and larger normative cultural forces.

Notes

INTRODUCTION

1 Memoranda on Japanese pornographic leaflets, 7 December 1943, and undated letter to B/B 210, HS 1/198.
2 This case is analyzed in greater detail in chapter 1.
3 The specific features of heteronormative sexuality during this period, as well as the mechanisms through which it was produced, will be discussed at length in future chapters.
4 For more on early modern historical porn cultures, see Hunt, *The Invention of Pornography.*
5 See for example Steinem, *Outrageous Acts and Everyday Rebellions*, 238.
6 See for example Williams, ed., *Porn Studies*, in which the vast majority of the volume's essays focus on video, comics, or other visual media rather than pornographic literature.
7 For a comprehensive analysis of the social purity movement and its use of the legal category of "obscenity," see Bristow, *Vice and Vigilance.*
8 Later chapters, particularly chapter 3, will delve into the slippery definitions of obscenity and its relationship to pornography in the specific context of early twentieth-century Britain.
9 Anais Nin, "Letter 085," 240.
10 See Marcus, *The Other Victorians.*
11 See Sigel, *Governing Pleasures*; Peakman, *Mighty Lewd Books*; McCalman, *Radical Underworld.*
12 Pornography as a global phenomenon has also received attention, but this has mainly taken the form of literary criticism or institutional

studies of imperial regulation. See Colligan, *The Traffic in Obscenity from Byron to Beardsley*, 2–5; Heath, *Purifying Empire*, 1–5.

13 See Colligan, *A Pornographer's Paradise.*

14 See Sigel, *Governing*, and Colligan, *Pornographer's Paradise*, for excellent examples of cultural history approaches. Heath, *Purifying Empire*, is a similarly well-done take on institutional and policy-related issues surrounding obscenity in the empire.

15 See Williams, *Hard Core*, 16, 23.

16 Dworkin, "Against the Male Flood," 30; Mackinnon, "Only Words," 101–2.

17 Philipson, "The Repression of History and Gender," 113.

18 Ferguson, "Sex War," 110.

19 See Williams, *Hard Core.*

20 See Attwood and Smith, "Anti/Pro/Critical Porn Studies," 7–23.

21 See Williams, ed., *Porn Studies.*

22 See Stardust, "'Fisting Is Not Permitted.'"

23 See Williams, *Hard Core.*

24 See Kaplan and Grewal, "Transnational Practices and Interdisciplinary Feminist Scholarship."

25 See chapter 2.

26 Ibid.

27 Ibid.

28 Hannerz, *Transnational Connections*, 19.

29 For an excellent analysis of the social processes and cultural norms through which heteronormativity is produced (albeit without employing the term itself) see Rubin, "Thinking Sex: Notes for a Radical Theory of the Politics of Sexuality."

30 See Thompson, *The Making of the English Working Class*, 11; See also Tabili, "Race Is a Relationship, and Not a Thing."

31 See Houlbrook, "Thinking Queer," 136.

32 For a thorough discussion of queerness and its relationship to the politics of sexuality, race, and class, see Cohen, "Punks, Bulldaggers, and Welfare Queens."

33 Eng, Halberstam, and Munoz, "Introduction: What's Queer about Queer Studies Now?," 7–8; see Smith, "Queer Theory and Native Studies."

34 See Shah, *Contagious Divides.*

35 For a discussion of controversies surrounding the term and its rejection by Teresa de Lauretis shortly after she coined it, see Jagose, *Queer Theory*, 127.

36 Warner, "Introduction: Fear of a Queer Planet," 16.
37 See Shah, *Contagious Divides.*
38 Somerville, "Queer," 203.
39 Houlbrook, *Queer London*, 5.
40 For example, see Cohen, "Punks, Bulldaggers, and Welfare Queens," for a discussion of racism and other issues in LGBT spaces.
41 Chapter 4 includes discussion of measures taken to destroy pornographic evidence after trials.
42 See minute notes, 28 March 1952, HO 354/162, in which the office says no legal information on underage nude modelling can be found due to its status as legal activity.

CHAPTER ONE

1 Deposition of William Brown and exhibit 3, 1923, CRIM 1/234.
2 See exhibit 40, letter from Carmen Corti to Mr Adams, 10 April 1923, CRIM 1/234.
3 Exhibit 3, 1923, CRIM 1/234; emphasis in original.
4 See Sigel, *Making Modern Love*, 125. See also Pine, "In Bizarre Fashion," 6.
5 Exhibit 69, letter from John Stewart, 26 September 1922, CRIM 1/234.
6 Exhibit 46, undated, CRIM 1/234.
7 See Sigel, *Governing Pleasures.*
8 For a similar and highly effective use of "networks" to describe fluid and shifting social groups without static membership, see Ross, "Survival Networks."
9 Mayhall, *The Militant Suffrage Movement*, 135–8.
10 See Weinbaum, ed., *The Modern Girl around the World.*
11 Gilbert, "Soldier's Heart," 199–205.
12 See Rose, *Which People's War?.*
13 Landy, *British Genres*, 248–9.
14 Weeks, *Sex, Politics, and Society*, 201.
15 Haste, *Rules of Desire*, 58–63.
16 See chapter 5 for more on changing medical views on masturbation.
17 See chapter 5.
18 Bland, "White Women and Men of Colour," 29–30.
19 Graves, *Labour Women*, 89–90.
20 See Weeks, *Sex, Politics, and Society*; McLaren, *Twentieth-Century Sexuality.*
21 See chapter 5 for a lengthy examination of this trend.

22 For discussion of the fears and anxieties surrounding perceived changes in masculinity and femininity during the interwar years, see Sigel, *Making Modern Love*, 11.
23 Colligan, *Publisher's Paradise*, 67–77.
24 Ibid., 20; chapter 6 will address these state policy changes more thoroughly.
25 See ibid.
26 See ibid., 20; For more on the Nichols case, see CRIM 1/60/4.
27 Letter from the Undersecretary of State, 2 August 1901, FO 83/2101; Imperial Ministry for Foreign Affairs, Austria, Report to the British Embassy, 20 November 1901, FO 83/2101.
28 BL, *Vigilance Record* #11, 1904, 7; *Vigilance Record* #3, 1906, 22; *Vigilance Record* #4, 1913, 32.
29 For example, see BNA, "Seizure of Obscene Literature," *Reynold's Newspaper*, 9 September 1900, 8; BNA, "Police Courts," *Leamington Spa-Courier*, 7 June 1907, 7.
30 BNA, "Picture Post-Card: Prosecution in Newcastle," *Sunderland Daily Echo*, 1 March 1904, 4.
31 BNA, "Picture Postcards Destroyed," *Manchester Courier*, 3 September 1904, 9.
32 BNA, "Pictorial Postcards: Seizures in Bath," *Bath Chronicle*, 15 December 1904, 2.
33 BNA, "Improper Postcards: Prosecution in Gloucester," *The Citizen*, 20 September 1907.
34 Letter from the General Post Office, October 1915, HO 144/1837.
35 See Colligan, *Publisher's Paradise*, 44.
36 KI, Supplement to English Special Photos List: Novelties 1913–1914, Photographic Erotica Producers (female) Great Britain.
37 Statement of Desmond William Gerald Lee, 6 May 1938, MEPO 3/939.
38 Statement of Sergeant Goult, 24 April 1930, MEPO 3/384, 1–2.
39 For an example related to rationing and black market violations, see Roodhouse, *Black Market Britain*, 161–2.
40 Letter to the Office of the Undersecretary of State, 3 March 1933, HO 45/24939.
41 See statement of Desmond William Gerald Lee, 6 May 1938, MEPO 3/939; see also statement of Sergeant Goult, 1930, MEPO 3/384.
42 Statement of Desmond William Gerald Lee, 6 May 1938, MEPO 3/939.
43 Statement of Sergeant Goult, 1930, MEPO 3/384, 2.
44 Deposition of Reginald McDonald, 14 February 1941, CRIM 1/1297, 2. While this example is from the Second World War rather than the

interwar years, the case file indicates that Haynes began his activities prior to the outbreak of war. In addition, his case is representative of broader trends dating from the 1920s and 1930s.

45 Letter from the Chief Constable's Office of the City of Manchester Re: Traffic in Obscene Publications, 25 October 1930, HO 144/22543. The Vagrancy Act prohibited certain public behaviours such as sleeping in the street and thus was often used in cases of pornography sales in a publicly visible location.

46 Report of the Liverpool City Police, 1929, HO 144/22543.

47 For examples of pornographers with multiple convictions, see indictment of Arthur Sandford, 21 October 1930, MEPO 3/935, 2.

48 Letter from detective inspector to acting superintendent, 20 February 1930, MEPO 3/384.

49 Statement of Trevor Evans, 26 July 1931, MEPO 3/935.

50 Albert Cooper, Central Officer's Special Report, 17 October 1931, MEPO 3/935, 5–6.

51 Statement of Albert Cooper, 31 July 1931, MEPO 3/935.

52 Statement of Harold Hawkyard, 18 September 1930, MEPO 3/935, 2.

53 For a particularly ludicrous example of Hollywood's interpretation of the mid-twentieth-century pornography trade, see Wood, dir., *The Sinister Urge*.

54 Reports by various police offices and constabularies, 1930, HO 144/22543; Chief Constables' Association (Cities and Boroughs of England and Wales), Appendix A: Information Regarding Obscene and Suggestive Publications, CUST 49/1638, 1.

55 Letter from the acting chief constable of the Central Police Office of Bolton to the undersecretary of state, 15 November 1930, HO 144/22543.

56 Pine, "In Bizarre Fashion," 10–12.

57 See chapter 2 for more on the example of Prussian photographer Wilhelm von Gloeden.

58 Statement of Detective Sidney Norman, 1942, CRIM 1/1409.

59 See Chief Constables' Association, Appendix A: Information Regarding Obscene and Suggestive Publications, CUST 49/1638, 7. Support for France's pornographic reputation can be found in Arthur Sandford's statement that "I get my cards from France so you know they'll be good."

60 Responses to League of Nations questionnaire, part II, HO 144/22543.

61 Deposition of Derrick Gresham, 7 November 1958, CRIM 1/3100.

62 Letter from Detective Inspector Gillard, 17 January 1920, MEPO 3/386.

63 Letter from Worcestershire Constabulary, 6 April 1923, MEPO 3/386.

64 For example, see BL, *Vigilance Record*, 1914–1918. Issues published during the war contain only scattered references to the issue of obscene publications, with far greater attention paid to other issues.

65 Report to the League of Nations, 1943, FO 371/39309, 2–3.

66 Ibid.

67 Ibid.

68 See letter from Sidney William Richards, undated, CRIM 1/1297.

69 Minute sheet, 27 March 1940, MEPO 2/4501.

70 MET, The Public Morality Council, Patrolling Officer's Report, 1940–41, A/PMC/040.

71 For an example of a study that shows the ways in which audience reception can complicate a pornographic film's original intended message, see Leap, "Language, Gay Pornography, and Audience Reception."

72 Report by Inspector Albert Cooper, 17 October 1931, MEPO 3/935, 2.

73 Letter from Graham Hawkins to Librairie Astra, 20 September 1936, CO 323/1591/4.

74 Letter from Cyril Benbow to T. Cockroft Esquire, 6 March 1923, CRIM 1/234.

75 See letter from Director of Public Prosecutions, 5 February 1930, MEPO 3/2459.

76 Mutoscopes were an early form of motion picture technology in which the customer looked through a stationary viewer in order to see pictures moving in sequence. Minute notes, 17 September 1901, HO 45/10267/X81934.

77 Letter from Reverend E.S. Roberts, 7 January 1903, FO 83/2101.

78 Letter from the Office of the Undersecretary of State, 12 January 1901, FO 83/2101; order form from K.S. Richards, 18 August 1939, CRIM 1/1297.

79 Statement of Leonard William Steer, 9 April 1937, MEPO 3/938.

80 Exhibit 6, order form from K.S. Richards, 18 August 1939, CRIM 1/1297.

81 Statement of Raphael Lee, 16 December 1950, MEPO 2/9132.

82 Untitled sketch, undated, FO 83/2101.

83 KI, undated letter from the Maorman Publishing Co. Youdelman Collection.

84 Index to ledger seized by Police, 15 October 1958, CRIM 1/3100.
85 Ibid.
86 See minute notes, 28 March 1952, HO 354/162, in which Home Office officials state that they have no information regarding nude modelling in their files.
87 For a thorough discussion of the complexities of the artists' model category in the slightly earlier context of the Victorian period, see Smith, *The Victorian Nude.*
88 BNA, "Untitled Advertisement," *Gloucester Echo,* 21 October 1941, 2.
89 Ibid. See also BNA, "Untitled Advertisement," *Nottingham Evening Post*, 27 March 1924, 2, and BNA, "Untitled Advertisement," *Nottingham Evening Post*, 26 March 1928, 2.
90 BNA, "A Public Danger: Photographer's Model Sent to Prison," *Derby Evening Telegraph*, 8 May 1940, 1.
91 BNA, "Girl Had Pepper Pot, Say Police," *Daily Mail*, 31 May 1948, 1.
92 BNA, "The Girl, the Hungarian, and the Baby," *Daily Mail*, 26 August 1936, 1.
93 "Trial of Gerardo Cappuccitto (17)," October 1903, *Old Bailey Online.*
94 "Trial of Frederick Luccioni, Joseph Luccioni," 21 October 1907, *Old Bailey Online.*
95 Report by Inspector Albert Cooper, 17 October 1931, MEPO 3/935, 4.
96 Ibid.
97 See Gay Paree Pictures, "A Free Ride," 1915–1923, *Grandpa Bucky Volume IV*.
98 See also KI, general catalogue #1, undated, Photozique Studios.
99 "One Out of Ten Americans Is Tattooed," *Life Magazine*, 21 December 1936, 30; Govenar, "The Changing Image of Tattooing in American Culture, 1846–1966," 213–14. While many of the images discussed here do not include information on the model's nationality, there is no evidence to suggest that British or Continental European tattooing practices would have differed significantly from that of Anglo-Americans.
100 Pine, "In Bizarre Fashion," 11.
101 Dupouy, *Yva Richard*, 124.
102 Faber, *Divas and Lovers*, 23–4.
103 Antecedent History of Charles Domec-Carre, undated, CRIM 1/3100.
104 Testimony of Maud Taylor, February 1900, CRIM 1/60/4.
105 Report by Detective Sergeant Skardon, 11 November 1936, MEPO 3/2459.
106 See Natter and Weiermair, eds, *Et in Arcadia Ego.*

107 Ibid, 109–11.

108 The early twentieth-century practice of making sexual contacts through classified ads and lonely hearts services has been analyzed at great length in Cocks, *Classified.*

109 Report to the League of Nations, 1943, FO 371/39309.

110 Ibid., 3.

111 Exhibit 1, letter from Harold Hall to Chief Inspector Stinton, 28 September 1949, CRIM 1/2030.

112 Exhibits 3 and 4, CRIM 1/2030.

113 BPCL, *Bedtime Stories*, December 1936.

114 Letter to the General Post Office, 31 October 1923, HO 45/24805.

115 Exhibit 11, 18 February 1937, CRIM 1/929; see also CRIM 1/891.

116 Statement of Anatole James, 30 September 1942, CRIM 1/463.

117 Letter to Divisional Detective Inspector, 17 July 1936, MEPO 3/935.

118 City of Manchester, Traffic in Obscene Publications – 1929, HO 144/22543.

119 See letter from Mervyn Hyde, 5 January 1923; advertisement placed by O.B. Clarence, 30 September 1923, CRIM 1/234.

120 KI, letters from Mr Packard to Goldenhind Press, 1935, folder The Miller Brothers, in which the term "action photo" is elaborated on as "sex action photo."

121 See for example Anonymous, *Private Anthropological Cabinet.*

122 See American Magazines in Respect of Which Orders for Destruction Have Been Made, 1933, CUST 49/1638.

123 Copy of exhibit 6, 18 August 1939, CRIM 1/1297.

124 KI, pamphlet for *Sadism and Masochism*, folder Esoterika Biblion Society.

125 Index, CRIM 1/3100.

126 Statement of Leonard Steer, 9 April 1937, MEPO 3/938, 2.

127 See BPCL, *Spicy Stories*, March 1938.

128 Undated Home Office Deputation, CUST 49/1638.

129 Report from the Director of Public Prosecutions, 6 December 1923, HO 45/24805.

130 Undated deputation, CUST 49/1638.

131 Deposition of Derrick Gresham, CRIM 1/3100, 3.

132 See KI, folder Esoterika Biblion Society.

133 Letter from the Scottish Office at Whitehall, 5 May 1902, and letter from E.S. Roberts, 7 January 1903, FO 83/2101.

134 Exhibit 3, 1923, CRIM 1/234.

135 See exhibit 17, 1923, CRIM 1/234; KI, untitled advertisement, Yva Richard.

136 Statement of Harold Hawkyard, 18 September 1930, MEPO 3/935, 1.

137 For comparison, a quart of milk cost 4 pence in 1914. Pember Reeves, *Round about a Pound a Week*, 99.

138 See statement of Leonard Steer, 9 April 1937, MEPO 3/938, in which Steer admitted to ordering materials from a female bookshop owner in Paris.

139 Statement of Detective Inspector Burmby, 1924, TS 27/208.

140 Identity book #329995, 7 April 1918, and statement of Carmen Corti, 14 September 1923, TS 27/208.

141 Statement of Inspector Burmby, 1923, TS 27/208.

142 Inventory of Furniture, Fixtures, and Effects at 4 Majestic Mansions Tottenham Court Road, 1924, TS 27/208.

143 Exhibit 40, 10 April 1923, CRIM 1/234.

144 Statement of claim, 25 March 1924, TS 27/208.

145 Sullivan, *A Critical Introduction to Queer Theory*, vi.

CHAPTER TWO

1 Indecent Films Private Shows in London, 1922, MEPO 3/386.

2 Ibid., minute notes, April 1922, MEPO 3/386; minute notes, 24 April 1922, HO 144/1837.

3 See Houlbrook, *Queer London*, 239; see also McClintock, *Imperial Leather.*

4 Walkowitz, *Nights Out*, 1–13.

5 Pennell, *A Kingdom United*, 108–10.

6 Bland, "White Women and Men of Colour," 29–30.

7 Linehan, *British Fascism and Anti-Semitism, 1918–1939*, 186–7.

8 See Davin, "Imperialism and Motherhood."

9 Cook, *London and the Culture of Homosexuality, 1885–1914,* 91.

10 Ibid.

11 For an in-depth analysis of this process and the community resulting from it, see Colligan, *Publisher's Paradise.*

12 Ibid.

13 Charles R. Wingfield, memorandum, 7 September 1903, FO 83/2101. This memo does not include estimates of the number of British customers in Paris, claiming only that the trade is substantial.

14 See KI, undated catalogue, Esoterika Biblion Society. This and other catalogues prominently advertised alleged Carrington reprints, indi-

cating that his name and press would have been well-known to pornography collectors.

15 List of American magazines with orders for destruction, undated, CUST 49/1638.

16 Chief Constables' Association, Information Regarding Indecent and Suggestive Publications, Appendix A, 4–5, CUST 49/1638.

17 Ibid, 10–11; Report by D.S. Skardon, 11 November 1936, MEPO 3/2459.

18 Imperial Ministry for Foreign Affairs, Austria, Report to the British Embassy, 20 November 1901, FO 83/2101.

19 Ibid.

20 KI, various catalogues, Yva Richard.

21 List of proscribed books, 27 August 1928, HO 45/15139; KI, folder, The Esoterika Biblion Society.

22 Home Office Warrants in Operation in Connexion with the Traffic in Indecent Wares, November 1912, HO 45/20912; Memorandum on Indecent and Obscene Articles from a Person Known to Be a Dealer in Obscene Wares, List of Known Dealers, 2 May 1900, CUST 46/199.

23 Memorandum on Legal Action by Charles Carrington, 7 October 1911, HO 45/10510/129433.

24 Replies to League of Nations questionnaire, 1930, HO 144/22543.

25 Ibid.

26 Ibid.

27 Exhibit 54, 1923, CRIM 1/234; emphasis in original.

28 Ibid.

29 Officer's Report on Trevor Evans and Charles Barnick, 2 September 1931, MEPO 3/935.

30 Letter from the Office of the Undersecretary of State, 9 October 1901, FO 83/2101.

31 Ibid., letter from the Undersecretary of State, 2 August 1901.

32 See minute notes, 24 September 1936, HO 45/20913, in which Home Office officials note that numerous attempts have been made to encourage American officials to take greater action to stem the tide of "numerous sex books" published in the United States, but without success.

33 The significant differences between late nineteenth- and early twentieth-century anti-pornography campaigns will be discussed at great length in chapters 5 and 6.

34 Exhibit 17, 1923, CRIM 1/234.

35 Officer's Report, 20 October 1923, and Officer's Report, 19 November 1923, MEPO 3/386.

36 BL, *Vigilance Record* #2, 1925, 11.

37 Letter from Division Detective Inspector, Criminal Investigative Department, 28 November 1911, MEPO 3/2459.

38 Minute notes, 21 October 1912, and United States Post Office to Chief Inspector of the Metropolitan Police, 11 July 1913, HO 144/10130.

39 LOC, box 3, volume 2, 240–1, 1909.

40 Home Office Warrants in Operation in Connexion with the Traffic in Indecent Wares, November 1912, HO 45/20912.

41 LOC, box 3, volume 2, 300–1, 1913.

42 LOC, box 3, volume 2, 312–13, 1914.

43 Statement of Charges, 24 March 1954, CRIM 1/2515.

44 Transport Department, letter from S.D. Chaplain Cuthbert, 17 June 1907, and British Consulate General of Port Said to the Director of Transports, 30 May 1907, MT 23/210.

45 Ibid.

46 Chief Constable to the Commissioner of New Scotland Yard, 9 November 1950, MEPO 2/9132. For more information on colonial policy discouraging sexual relations, see Tambe, "The Elusive Ingenue."

47 Letter from the Prime Minister's Department, 27 August 1928, Commonwealth of Australia, and reply letter from Home Office, Great Britain, 22 October 1928, HO 144/10130.

48 Geraci, "Lehnert and Landrock in North Africa," 294–8.

49 Lehnert and Landrock, eds, *Eastern Races and Beauty*, 5; see also KI, Anthropology (1001–1064), Image Collections.

50 KI, order form from Buchdruckerei Robert Peter, box Lehnert and Landruck ND, Image Collections.

51 Lehnert and Landrock, *Eastern Races and Beauty*.

52 Pohlmann, *Wilhelm von Gloeden,* 16–17.

53 KI, #248, Von Gloeden box 3, Image Collections.

54 Pohlmann, *Wilhelm,* 24.

55 See KI, box Female Figure Photographers Lehnert and Landruck ND, Image Collections.

56 Graham-Brown, *Images of Women: The Portrayal of Women in Photography of the Middle East*, 136.

57 KI, Von Gloeden box 3, Image Collections.

58 See, for example, *Private Anthropological Cabinet of 500 Authentic Racial-Esoteric Photographs and Illustrations.*

59 Leslie, *Wilhelm von Gloeden, Photographer*, 96.

60 The Dominion Division to the Chief Officer of Lagos and the Commissioner of Accra, 26 October 1923, HO 144/10130.

61 J.F. Henderson to the Solicitor of the Post Office, Washington, 17 October 1935, HO 45/20913.

62 BL: *Vigilance Record* #7, 1911, 54.

63 See Stoler, *Carnal Knowledge and Imperial Power.*

64 See BPCL, *Tattle Tales*, August 1935, 62; *Paris Gayety*, July 1934.

65 Leonard William Steer, statement, 9 April 1937, MEPO 3/938.

66 See Exhibit 18, 1923, CRIM 1/234.

67 See List of Books, Magazines, Novels, and Photographs, Seized at the Compton Bookstore, No. 4, Old Compton Street, 27 April 1938, MEPO 3/939; Sadie Blackeyes, *Miss*.

68 See for example BPCL, *Pictorial French Follies Fiction*, February 1930; *Spicy Stories*, January 1938, 36; *Spicy Stories*, February 1937, 17.

69 See Blackeyes, *Miss*; van Rod, *The Misfortunes of Collette.*

70 Anonymous, *Confessions of a Virtuous Wife.*

71 KI, Fort, Jean, 1935.

72 See Lehnert and Landrock, *Eastern Races and Beauty.*

73 KI, Catalogue Nude Art Studies from Life, 1905, Photographic Erotica Producers (Female) Federal Republic of Germany.

74 KI, Ad Just Out, 1930, Yva Richard.

75 See KI, Yva Richard; KI, box S and M, Female on Male 1890–1936, Image Collections. For arguments discussing flagellation as having particular cultural relevance in Britain, see Colligan, *The Traffic in Obscenity from Byron to Beardsley.*

76 Van Rod, *The Misfortunes of Collette;* Meusal, *Invitation to the Dance.*

77 Similar images available in Lehnert and Landrock, Image Collections, KI; figure 3 reproduced in BPCL, *Spicy Stories*, March 1938.

78 See KI Image Collections. Many photographs include educated guesses regarding national origin but no definitive proof. They are guesses made by the archivists and librarians, usually written on the back of photographs or in notations in the file.

79 Numerous other examples of this trend can be found reproduced in Dupouy, *Yva Richard: L'âge d'or du fetischisme*; Faber, *Divas and Lovers.*

80 See various undated catalogues in KI: Photography Erotica Producers (Female) Federal Republic of Germany.

81 UCLA, *Elysia: Valley of the Nude.*

82 UCLA, "Enchanting Beauties: A Cine Art Featurette."

83 See League of Nations Traffic in Women and Children Committee, Additional Replies from Governments to the Committee's Questionnaire, 15 July 1931, HO 144/22543.
84 Ibid., undated letter to S.W. Harris, HO 144/22543.
85 "Obscene Pictures and Books to Be Burned," *The Times*, 8 July 1936, 16.
86 Minute notes, 16 May 1930, HO 45/20913.
87 Ibid.

CHAPTER THREE

1 "Untitled Stag Film," *Grandpa Bucky*, vol. 4.
2 KI, unnamed photograph, 1922, box S and M, Female on Male: 1890–1936, Image Collections.
3 See Anonymous, "Flagellation at Clifton."
4 As stated in chapter 1, attempting to provide an all-encompassing description of early twentieth-century British heteronormativity would be a fruitless exercise. Chapters 4–6 will map the major concerns and priorities of heteronormative structures, but for the purposes of this chapter we will use the same broad set of characteristics identified in chapter 1.
5 Drawing a precise map of what constituted "mainstream" entertainment is as daunting as clearly outlining the precise boundaries of heteronormativity; see chapter 1 for my discussion of this issue and the importance of focusing on points of tension and contestation rather than creating isolated categories such as "heteronormative" and "queer" or "mainstream" and "subversive."
6 Burrows, *Legitimate Cinema*, 225.
7 Beaven, *Leisure, Citizenship, and Working-Class Men in Britain, 1850–1945*, 184–6.
8 Walkowitz, *Nights Out*, 236–7.
9 See McLaren, *Reproduction by Design*.
10 See Robertson, *The British Board of Film Censors*.
11 Sigel, "Censorship in Inter-War Britain," 68–9.
12 Zimring, "The Dangerous Art Where One Slip Means Death," 723–4.
13 For more on the relationship between the British state and mass media, see Chapman, *The British at War*.
14 See Williams, *Hard Core*; see also Attwood and Smith, "Anti/Pro/Critical Porn Studies."

15 See Tibbals, "Gonzo, Tranny, and Teens"; Petley, "The Regulation of Pornography on Video-on-Demand in the United Kingdom"; Mulholland, "'The Pathological Native' vs 'The Good White Girl.'"

16 See Williams, *Porn Studies.*

17 Such an approach has been used to great effect by queer theorists studying contemporary pornography sub-genres, such as lesbian BDSM. For example see Ross, "It's Merely Designed for Sexual Arousal," 280; See also Califia, "Identity Sedition and Pornography," 94.

18 For examples of articles that employ these types of categories (albeit while interrogating their boundaries and ambiguities), see Hines and Kerr eds, *Hard to Swallow: Hard-Core Pornography Onscreen.*

19 I use the term "literary pornography" to refer to written pornographic narratives. I use this term rather than synonyms like "written pornography" in order to distinguish it from pornographic comics, letters, or other media including a written component but relying primarily on visual elements or not relying on a fictional narrative. The term "literary" should not be construed as referring in any way to quality or distinctions between "literary" and "genre" narratives.

20 See Anonymous, *Sweet Seventeen*; van Rod, *The Misfortunes of Colette.*

21 See Anonymous, *Sweet Seventeen.*

22 See Cantab, *Two Flappers in Paris.*

23 KI, Edward Windsor, *The Hindu Art of Love.*

24 KI, undated order form, Falstaff Press.

25 Blackeyes, *Miss.*

26 Anonymous, *Lascivious Hypocrite.*

27 Blackeyes, *Miss*; van Rod, *Misfortunes.*

28 See Dworkin, "Pornography and Grief," 42.

29 See figure 3.3. For an example of work assuming a male viewer and female subject, see Mackinnon, "Not a Moral Issue."

30 Appel and Smith, *Lynching Photographs*, 16.

31 For example, see KI, Image Collections, box Fig Butt: 1880–1928, and box G Female Cloth Stand: 1890–1948, in which multiple models and series of photographs appear in the same setting, identifiable through features such as furniture and wallpaper.

32 See KI, Image Collections, box SDM and Sex 1901 to 1924; letter from Miss Joy Major, Youdelman Collection.

33 See UCLA, *Elysia: Valley of the Nude.*

34 For more on the definition and history of the stag film, see Sheaffer, "Smut, Novelty, and Indecency."

35 Thompson, *Black and White and Blue.*
36 KI, *A Reunited Foursome*, undated.
37 Ibid.
38 KI, *London Bridge*, 193?.
39 Weeks, *Sex, Politics, and Society*, 209–10.
40 The term "Tijuana bible" is of uncertain origin, although Art Spiegelman speculates that it may result from racist stereotypes or from the association between border cities and American vice. See Adelman and Spiegelman, eds, *Tijuana Bibles.*
41 See ibid.
42 See Eros Comix, ed., *The Tijuana Bibles*, vol. 9, 14, 31.
43 Adelman and Spiegelman, *Tijuana Bibles*, 129.
44 Ibid., 23.
45 See chapters 1 and 2 for a discussion of the most frequently seized pornographic items, which were more often photographs or postcards.
46 See BPCL, *French Follies*, August 1930.
47 BPCL, *French Follies*, May 1930, 17.
48 Ibid., 44–6.
49 Ibid.
50 See BPCL, *Gay Parisienne*, 1937.
51 For more on erotic correspondence and pulp fiction magazines, see Cocks, *Classified.*
52 See Trumbach, "Erotic Fantasy and Male Libertinism in Enlightenment England," 260, in which the author describes contemporary pornographic film as "almost never satirical or humorous."
53 See Adelman and Spiegelman, *Tijuana Bibles.*
54 See chapter 4.
55 See Steinem, "Erotica vs. Pornography," 238.
56 "Last Supper," in *Grandpa Bucky*, vol. 13.
57 See chapter 1.
58 For more on material culture and subversive reappropriation see Hebdige, *Subculture*, 2.
59 See Chapman, *British at War.*
60 See Scheid, *1000 Nudes: The Uwe Scheid Collection.*
61 UCLA, "Careful Investigation."
62 KI, *Lip Service*, undated.
63 KI, Anthropology Japan, Image Collections.
64 Anonymous, *The Way of a Man with a Maid*, part II, chapter II.
65 KI, Anonymous, *Sylvia.*
66 See Anonymous, *Sweet Seventeen*; Anonymous, *Painful Pleasures.*

67 For a vast quantity of examples, see KI, box SDM and Sex 1901–1924, box SDM Flag A 1920–1936, Image Collections.
68 See KI, unnamed 1921–1927 photo, box Sadomasochism-Flagellation, 1910–1947.
69 KI, Folder Photozique Studios.
70 KI, Image Collections, boxes H Male GRP, H Male GO.
71 Slade, "Bernard Natan," 76.
72 For more on the idea of compulsory heterosexuality and its relationship to other forms of sexual deviance, see Rubin, "Thinking Sex."
73 See Mackinnon, "Not a Moral Issue," 148.
74 See KI, *Three Pals* (1939).
75 For more on the importance of the male erection in contemporary theories of pornography, see Williams, *Hard Core.*
76 KI, *Reunited Foursome.*
77 See ibid.
78 "On the Beach," in *Grandpa Bucky*, vol. 4.
79 For more on late nineteenth- and early twentieth-century normative masculinity in Britain and western Europe, see Mosse, *Nationalism and Sexuality*, 31–6.
80 Deposition of William Brown, 1923, CRIM 1/234; ibid., exhibit 3.
81 See KI, box Anthropology
82 KI, box HO Male AN, box H Male Kneel.
83 Adelman, *Tijuana*, 73, 76.
84 Ibid., 76.
85 See chapter 1.
86 KI, AA 26 Album. J. Kinsey's notation seems to have relied on German statistics due to the fact that these were the only ones available on the topic.
87 See Bretschneider, ed., *Vincenzo Galdi*, *Wilhelm von Gloeden*, *Wilhelm von Pluschow*.
88 Faber, *Divas and Lovers*, 80.
89 KI, Supplement to English Special Photos List: Novelties 1913–1914, Photographic Erotica Producers (female) Great Britain.
90 The actual age of the models described as "young boys" is unclear from the catalogue. Pornographic photographs of underage children from this period are exceedingly rare and there appears to have been very little trade in such items, although this may be the result of court-ordered destruction of evidence after trials. While evidence is lacking, I speculate based on available evidence that any market for child pornography that existed during this period was of very small

and localized scale and that it employed different mechanisms of communication and exchange than those discussed in this book.

91 KI, art catalogue from Hugret, Livry-Gargan, France, 1925, Photographic Erotica Producers (female) France.

92 For example, see Epstein, dir., *The Celluloid Closet*. This film discusses numerous cases in which screenwriters and directors deliberately included covert references to homosexuality in mainstream films.

93 Judgment, CUST 49/1057, 5–6.

94 Hellman, *Six Plays by Lillian Hellman*.

95 See Richards, *Age of the Dream Palace*, 105–6.

96 Landy, *British Genres*, 248–9, 214–15.

97 Ibid., 192, 205.

98 Ibid., 196–7.

99 Ibid., 240–1.

100 Robertson, *The British Board of Film Censors*, 180–2.

101 Ibid., 65–6. For more on the general subject of morality and normativity in pre-1945 British cinema, see Richards, *The Unknown 1930s;* Gledhill and Swanson, eds, *Nationalising Femininity*.

102 Czinner, dir., *The Rise of Catherine the Great*.

103 Saville, dir., *First a Girl*.

104 Capra, dir., *The Bitter Tea of General Yen*.

CHAPTER FOUR

1 TDA, "Obscene Pictures and Books to Be Burned," *Times*, 8 July 1936, 16.

2 TDA, "Defiling the Post," *Times*, 4 January 1928, 9.

3 See Gorham, "'The Maiden Tribute of Modern Babylon' Revisited."

4 "The Suppression of Vice," *Old Jonathan, The District and Parish Helper* (1873), 60; see also Gertzman, *Bookleggers and Smuthounds*, 59, on the increasing size of the post-1930 American market.

5 See Seymoure-Ure, "Northcliffe's Legacy," 20–3.

6 For example, note differences in emphasis and content between social purity–oriented publications like the *Vigilance Record*, mainstream publications like the *Times*, and politically left-leaning magazines and papers such as the *New Statesman*.

7 See Chalaby, *The Invention of Journalism*, 192–3. Chalaby refers to journalistic control over the masses as the "magic mirror function of the media." For contrast, see Williams, *Marxism and Literature*, 112.

8 Conboy, *Press and Popular Culture*, 126–7.

9 Hampton, *Visions of the Press in Britain, 1850–1950*, 10.
10 Ibid., 142–3.
11 Williams, *Read All about It!*, 141–3.
12 Ibid., 140.
13 See also Catterall et al., *Northcliffe's Legacy*.
14 Bingham, *Family Newspapers?*, 1–3.
15 Bingham, *Gender, Modernity, and the Popular Press in Inter-War Britain*, 10–11.
16 See BNA, Emile de Laveleye, "How Bad Books May Destroy States," *Pall Mall Gazette*, 9 June 1888, 2; "The Nuisance of the Streets," *Pall Mall Gazette*, 15 January 1883, 12.
17 BNA, Laveleye, "Bad Books."
18 BNA, "Law and Police: Middlesex Sessions," *Pall Mall Gazette*, 18 March 1870, 5.
19 BNA, "Purity," *Northeastern Daily Gazette*, 12 May 1888; "London, Monday, January 15, 1883," *Morning Post*, 15 January 1883, 4.
20 See BNA, "The Sale of Obscene Photographs," *Dundee Courier*, 6 October 1884.
21 BNA, "Law and Police: Middlesex Sessions," *Pall Mall Gazette*, 18 March 1870, 5.
22 TDA, "Police," *Times*, 16 February 1889, 5.
23 BNA, Laveleye, "Bad Books."
24 BNA, "Sale of Obscene," *Dundee Courier*.
25 BNA, "Impure Literature in the Streets," *Leeds Mercury*, 10 September 1885, 7; "The Nuisance of the Streets," *Pall Mall Gazette*, 15 January 1883, 12.
26 Forgacs, *The Gramsci Reader: Selected Writings, 1916–1935*, 380–1.
27 See Timeline of Indecent Publications Policy, undated, CUST 49/1638.
28 See Sigel, *Governing Pleasures*. See also Colligan, *Publisher's Paradise*.
29 BNA, "Nudist Photos Sent through the Post," *Western Daily Mail and Bristol Mirror*, 21 September 1934, 7.
30 BNA, "The Camorra Trial," *Devon and Exeter Gazette*, 18 March 1911, 6.
31 See BNA, "A Jap's Smuggling Trick," *Dover Express and East Kent News*, 2 September 1923, 11.
32 BNA, "Magazines to Be Destroyed," *Daily Mail*, 30 June 1938, 13.
33 BNA, "Improper Postcards," *Citizen*, 20 September 1907.
34 See BNA, "Complaint over Pictures," *Daily Mail*, 4 January 1932, 1.
35 BNA, "Alleged Obscene Literature," *Reynolds's Newspaper*, 22 April 1900, 8.

36 BNA, "Bookseller Sentenced," *Western Morning News and Daily Gazette*, 16 April 1935.

37 BNA, "Napoleon Hayard," *Dundee Courier*, 25 October 1900, 7.

38 See BNA, "Keeping Our Post Clean," *Nottingham Evening Post*, 6 December 1923, 7; "White Slave Traffic," *Sheffield Daily Telegraph*, 27 May 1910, 7.

39 BNA, "Keeping Our Post Clean," *Nottingham Evening Post*, 6 December 1923, 7.

40 TDA, "Traffic in Obscene Publications," *Times*, 31 August 1923, 7.

41 See TDA, "Parisian Filth" in "Obscene Pictures Prosecution," *Times*, 4 August 1932, 7; BNA, "French Pictures through the Post," *Western Gazette*, 29 February 1924.

42 TDA, "Indecent Photographs from Spain," *Times*, 6 December 1923, 4; BNA, "Periodicals Found in Bristol Shop," *Western Daily Press and Bristol Mirror*, 30 April 1936, 8.

43 BNA, "A Drunken Wife," *Shields Daily Gazette and Shipping Telegraph*, 29 October 1904.

44 BNA, "Police and Peep Show," *Western Daily Press*, 4 December 1917, 7.

45 BNA, "P.C. Wanted 'Something Exciting to Read,'" *Western Morning News and Daily Gazette*, 13 May 1938, 11.

46 See BNA, "Improper Postcards," *Citizen*, 20 September 1907.

47 BNA, "Deaf and Dumb Photographer Heavily Fined," *North Devon Journal*, 29 August 1935, 7.

48 See BNA, "Glasgow Print-Seller's Appeal," *Evening Telegraph*, 19 December 1930, 10.

49 BNA, "Alleged Obscene Publications," *Leamington Spa Courier*, 7 June 1907, 7.

50 TDA, "The Assizes: Midland Circuit," *Times*, 21 February 1902, 8.

51 BNA, "Boy Shopkeeper Fined," *Daily Mail*, 12 May 1937, 11.

52 Ibid.

53 LSE, *Report of the Seventh International Conference for the Suppression of Traffic in Women and Children* (1927) 4NVA/4/22/23, 78.

54 See Bourke, *Working-Class Cultures in Britain, 1890–1960*, 34–6.

55 See Stengers and van Neck, *Masturbation*, 154–5.

56 BNA, "The Guardian of Morals," *Dundee Courier and Advertiser*, 1 March 1929, 6.

57 Ibid.

58 For one example of many letters to the editor criticizing Joynson-Hicks, see BNA, Geoffrey Faber, "A Literary Censorship?," *Times*, 18

October 1928, 16; see also PRO, Metropolitan Police Office, Gadfly, "Jix, or Novel by Novel," in Metropolitan Police Office, MEPO 3/384.

59 Examples of censorship-related disputes between Jix and his parliamentary colleagues can be seen in 225 *Parliamentary Debates*, 28 February 1929, 2157–63. For more on censorship efforts by the Home Office such as issuing postal warrants, see Colligan, *Publisher's Paradise*.

60 BNA, "White Slavery," *Nottingham Evening Post*, 10 March 1927, 1.

61 See League of Nations Traffic in Women and Children Committee, "Obscene Publications: Replies from the Governments to the Committee's Questionnaire" (Geneva, 1931).

62 TDA, "Cocaine Debauchery," *Times*, 2 May 1922, 17.

63 Greenaway, *Drink and British Politics since 1830*, 95.

64 Valverde, "Racial Poison: Drink, Male Vice, and Degeneration in First-Wave Feminism," 43–4. It should be noted that female temperance supporters targeted alcohol consumption among both men and women in the name of racial hygiene.

65 Untitled clipping, *Times*, 19 November 1906, HO 45/10930/149778.

66 "Rex v. de Marney," *Magisterial Cases Volume XII*, 20–3

67 For example, see TDA, "House of Commons: Divorce Cases," *Times*, 23 April 1887, 8.

68 See ad in BNA, *Illustrated Police News*, 1 December 1900, 11; "For Sale and Wanted," *Essex Chronicle*, 23 January 1920.

69 Exhibit 82, 1923, CRIM 1/234.

70 BNA, "Dealers in Filth," *Nottingham Evening Post*, 2 October 1923, 5.

71 Letter to the undersecretary of state, 27 February 1901, HO 45/10267/X81934; See also MEPO 3/942. Mutoscopes were an early form of motion picture technology in which the viewer watched a short scene through an eyepiece in the machine.

72 Letter from the Mitre Press to the Daily Mail, 11 August 1933, HO 45/24939.

73 KI, "Undated Catalogue." Esoterika Biblion Society.

74 Letter from the Superintendent of Police, 14 December 1929, MEPO 3/383.

75 Newspaper clipping, "Noblemen and Horrible Films: Why Are the Culprits Protected?," publication unspecified, 10 March 1923, MEPO 3/386.

76 "Secret Films: Amazing Revelations," *John Bull*, 29 March 1924, MEPO 3/386.

77 Report by Inspector Draper, 12 June 1924, MEPO 3/386.

78 PRO, Memo to Mr Harris, Home Office Papers, HO 144/22543.

79 BNA, "Vicar's Letter to a Lady," *Courier*, 10 July 1913, 4.

80 BNA, "Officer in the Dock," *Derby Daily Telegraph*, 28 May 1918.

81 For more on this topic, see Weeks, *Sex, Politics, and Society*, 151–2.

82 For example, Harold Hall was a respected Methodist lay minister prior to being charged with the exchange of obscene letters. See Exhibit 1, letter from Harold Hall to Chief Inspector Stinton, 28 September 1949, CRIM 1/2030.

83 Potter, "Webs, Networks, and Systems," 628.

84 See Anderson, *Imagined Communities.*

85 This will be discussed at length in chapter 5.

86 This aspect of state attitudes toward pornography will be addressed in chapter 6.

CHAPTER FIVE

1 While not all of these groups necessarily described themselves as "vice societies," the term will be used here for the sake of clarity. It should be understood to include all private organizations or charities whose stated goals included opposition to sexual immorality, including pornography.

2 LSE, *Report of the Seventh International Conference for the Suppression of Traffic in Women and Children* (1927) 4NVA/4/22/23, 63.

3 BL, *Vigilance Record* #3, 1927, 39.

4 Resistance to severe legal penalties for pornographers and other factors related to the British state will be discussed more fully in chapter 6.

5 For a similar analysis of the NVA's distance from public opinion and the state applied to the specific issue of prostitution, see Bartley, *Prostitution*, 193–4.

6 LSE, draft minutes of the 5th Annual Conference, 1928, 4BNC/B/1.

7 See S.W. Harris, minute notes, 19 June 1929, HO 45/13296.

8 See White, *The First Sexual Revolution.*

9 Hall, *Sex, Gender, and Social Change in Britain since 1880*, 85.

10 Ibid., 104, 107–8.

11 See LSE, 4NVA/4/22/23.

12 See BL, *Vigilance Record* #1, 1916.

13 For reports of three separate delegations of this type, see BL, *Vigilance Record* #2, 1904; *Vigilance Record* #3, 1912; *Vigilance Record* #3–4, 1929.

14 LSE, Enclosure 1: Notice on the Origin of the International Conference, 4NVA/4/22/09, 3.

15 MET, Annual Report, 1933, A/PMC/098, 17; See also Bristow, *Vice and Vigilance*, 165.

16 See MET, A/PMC/207/001-062, 1930s–1960s.

17 MET, Letter to Mr Mackenzie, 26 August 1941, A/PMC/40.

18 Ibid., Summary of Patrol Work.

19 Hall, *Sex, Gender, Social Change*, 86.

20 See LSE, Annual Report, 1918, box 094 3, AMS/C/04/01–02.

21 See LSE, Executive Committee Minutes, 10 November 1936, 3AMS/A/01/17; LSE, Rangoon: Summary of Correspondence Recd. from Mr Conyers Baker, sec. YMCA at Rangoon, 25 June 1916, 3AMS/D/37/02.

22 LSE, Minutes of the International Bureau Committee, 21 June 1899, 4IBS/1/1.

23 See various papers in LSE, Obscene Literature, 1933, 4IBS/5/2/09.

24 For similarities in jargon at the local and national levels, see MET, Association for Preventative and Rescue Work, Hammersmith, Annual Report, 1933, A/LWC/140; BL, *Vigilance Record* #1, 1920, 5.

25 MET, Committee Minutes, 1935–1941, A/LWC/23.

26 MET, Stepney Association, Annual Report, 1929, A/LOC/590; See also MET, London Diocesan Council for Wel-Care, Executive Committee Minutes, 1927–1929, A/LWC/009.

27 Hall, *Sex, Gender, and Social Change*, 102.

28 See also MET, Association for Rescue Work in the Deanery of Hammersmith (including Chiswick), Twenty-Second Report, 1930, A/LWC/137; MET, Hammersmith, 1933, A/LWC/140; MET, St Anne's Training Home for Girls, Report, List of Subscribers, and Statement of Accounts, 1938, A/LWC/310.

29 LSE, Seventh International, 1927, 4NVA/4/22.

30 MET, Suggestions for Possible Action against Pornographic Literature, undated, A/PMC/79.

31 LSE, Board of Education Juvenile Organizing Committee, Social Hygiene Questionnaire: Draft Replies as from the White Cross League, undated, 4/NVA/4/01.

32 MET, *The Shield*, 1942, A/PMC/192, 76.

33 See DNB, Laite, "Neilans, Alison Roberta Noble (1884–1942)."

34 See MET, *The Shield*, A/PMC/192.

35 BL, *Vigilance Record* #1, 1920, 3–4; *Vigilance Record* #2, 1920, 15.

36 BL, *Vigilance Record* #1, 1915, 2.

37 See LSE, Correspondence regarding the Eugenics Publishing Company, 1934, 4NVA/4/22/04.

38 BNA, "Refuse to Settle Down: Northern Girls Strongly Criticized," *Sunderland Daily Echo*, 27 May 1932, 6.

39 LSE, National Vigilance Association, A Brief Record of 50 Years' Work, 1935, 4NVA/2/1, 12.

40 LSE, Tracts for Rangoon, Number 9: Into the Deeps, 3AMS/D/37/02; LSE, Letter regarding Port Said, 1905, 4NVA/4/26.

41 BL, *Vigilance Record* #1, 1920, 6–7.

42 For a pamphlet employing language of race renewal, see MET, "Great Issues," 1928, A/PMC/199/1. See also Hall, *Sex, Gender, and Social Change*, 95.

43 See Bland and Doan, eds, *Sexology in Culture*.

44 As in previous chapters, "transnational" should be understood as a term for cultural flows that transcend national and imperial borders rather than necessarily referring to the physical movement of bodies. While some aspects of the anti-vice movement involved physically crossing borders, the majority of their interaction involved long-distance dialogue.

45 See LSE, *Report*, 4NVA/4/22/23.

46 BL, *Vigilance Record* #2, 1912, 15.

47 LSE, Letter from Bascom Johnson to F.A.R. Sempkins, 19 January 1934, 4NVA/4/22/01.

48 BL, *Vigilance Record* #6, 1915, 47.

49 LSE, Letter from F.A.R. Sempkins to Sr Sangro, 25 July 1927, 4NVA/4/01.

50 LSE, 50th Annual Report of the Executive Committee, 1935, 4NVA/2/1; BL, *Vigilance Record* #8–9, 1914, 61.

51 MET, Report and Statement of Accounts, 1903, A/PMC/097.

52 See ibid., 6–9.

53 See LSE, *Report*, 4NVA/4/22/23, viii–xvi.

54 LSE, Preparatory Conference, Holland: Delegates, 1935, 4IBS/5/2/27.

55 LSE, Letter to Sir Ewart Greaves, 8 March 1935, 4/IBS/5/2/26.

56 See ibid.

57 LSE, *Report*, 4NVA/4/22/23, 63.

58 MET, *Facts about Prostitution: With Some Notes about "Affairs,"* 1940, A/PMC/195, 1.

59 MET, *The Shield*, A/PMC/192, 63.

60 BL, *Vigilance Record* #7, 1910, 55.

61 Ibid.

62 MET, Public Morality Council, Annual Report, 1932, A/PMC/098, 29.

63 BL, "Obscene Pictures and the 'Black Peril' in South Africa," *Vigilance Record* #7, 1911, 54.

64 BL, "Native Demoralisation: A Vile Traffic," *Vigilance Record* #7, 1911, 54.

65 LSE, Letter to F.A.R. Sempkins, 23 August 1933, 4NVA/4/22/04; see also Calcutta Vigilance Association, Annual Report, 1927–28, 8.

66 BL, "Backward Peoples and Film Censorship," *Vigilance Record* #11, 1926, 89.

67 LSE, Letter to Miss Baker, 23 October 1925, 4NVA/4/22/12.

68 See chapter 3.

69 See Hall, "Forbidden by God, Despised by Men."

70 See ibid., 377–8; Ellis, *Studies in the Psychology of Sex*, 250.

71 LSE, *Report*, 4/NVA/4/22/23, 78.

72 LSE, "Representative Opinions on 'The Sex Side of Life' by Mary Ware Dennett," 1929–1930, 4NVA/4/04/3.

73 Dennett, *The Sex Side of Life*, 8; emphasis in original.

74 See also MET, *Facts*, A/PMC/195, 5.

75 Letter from Wedlake, Letts, and Birds, Solicitors, 26 May 1928, HO 45/23588.

76 BL, *Vigilance Record* #3, 1912, 24.

77 BL, *Vigilance Record* #3–4, 1929, 20.

78 BL, *Vigilance Record* #1, 1912, 5.

79 LSE, Bristol and Southwestern Counties Branch of the NVA, Annual Report, 1915, 4/NVA/21, 7.

80 MET, Letter, A/PMC/40.

81 For a similar case see ibid., Letter from Church-Woman, in which an anonymous informer submitted a complaint and sample of obscene "specimen glass" displayed in a shop window.

82 MET, Suggestions, A/PMC/79.

83 LSE, Rules of the British Committee for the Suppression of Traffic in Women and Children, 2 November 1931, 4BNC/B/1.

84 LSE, Resolution, undated, 4IBS/5/2.

85 LSE, Report of Preparatory Conference, Brussels, 1939, 4IBS/5/2/39.

86 See LSE, 4NVA/4/22/23–27.

87 LSE, Letter to Mr Hymans, 23 September 1929, 4NVA/4229.

88 BL, *Vigilance Record* #7, 1910, 55.

89 LSE, Letter to F.A.R. Sempkins, 4NVA/4/22/04.

90 For more on the links between imperialism and the late nineteenth- to early twentieth-century women's movement, see Burton, *Burdens of History*.

91 BL, *Vigilance Record* #2, 1928, 13.

92 See BL, *Vigilance Record* #3–4, 1929, 13.

93 LSE, *Report*, 4NVA/4/22/23, 65.

94 BL, *Vigilance Record* #3–4, 1929, 22.

95 See BL, "Obscene," *Vigilance Record* #7, 1911, 54.

96 LSE, Bristol and Southwestern Counties Branch of the National Vigilance Association, Annual Report, 1915, 4NVA/2/1, 10

97 Ibid., Annual Report, 1930.

98 BL, *Vigilance Record* #5, 1904, 3.

99 LSE, Bristol, Annual Report, 1915, 4NVA/2/1, 6; BL, "Undesirable Women and the Army," *Vigilance Record* #12, 1914, 88.

100 See LSE, National Vigilance Association, Annual Report, 1935, 4NVA/2/1, 6–7.

101 See Tambe, "The Elusive Ingenue."

102 MET, Annual Reports, 1901–1912, A/PMC/097.

103 LSE, NVA, Annual Report, 1935, 14.

104 BL, *Vigilance Record* #8–9, 1914, 61; LSE, NVA, Brief Account, 4NVA/2/1, 15.

105 LSE, Appeal by Edward Greaves, 25 August 1936, 4NVA/4/23/13.

106 LSE, 7th Appeal, 1933, 4NVA/4/23/10.

107 LSE, Reminder, 1934, 4NVA/4/23/11.

108 For comparison, see BL, *Vigilance Record* #1–12, 1904, and #1–12, 1915.

109 BL, *Vigilance Record* #1–12, 1904.

110 BL, *Vigilance Record* #1–12, 1910.

111 BL, *Vigilance Record* #1–12, 1927 and 1928.

112 MET, Patrolling Officer's Report, June 1941, A/PMC/189. This report lists only one indecent publication case compared to fourteen disorderly houses.

113 See LSE, Correspondence from G. Tomlinson, box FL350, 1942, 4/IBS2/A/7/17.

114 MET, Bulletin: Glimpses at the Work of the Public Morality Council, 1945, A/PMC/202, 6.

115 See Memorandum on the So-Called White Slave Traffic, 6 February 1936, MEPO 3/988.

116 Ibid.

117 LSE, Executive Committee Memo, 12 January 1937, 3AMS/A/01/17, 3.

118 See BL, *Vigilance Record* #4, 1920, 32.

119 LSE, Seventh Appeal, 1933, 4NVA/4/23/10.

120 See LSE, Brief Record, 4/NVA/2/1, which insists that improvement began after the 1885 formation of the Association.

121 See ibid.; BL, *Vigilance Record* #9, 1920, 67; MET, Annual Report, 1913, A/PMC/097.

122 See Bland, "The Trials and Tribulations of Edith Thompson."

123 See "Modern Society's Sins," *Western Daily Press*, 10 October 1928.

124 LSE, Letter from Alison Neilans to F.A.R. Sempkins, 18 January 1932, 4NVA/4/22.

125 LSE, Letter from Cohen, 7 March 1930, and Letter from F.A.R. Sempkins, 6 March 1930, 4NVA/4/22.

126 LSE, Letter from Cohen to F.A.R. Sempkins, 10 October 1928, 4NVA/4/22/09.

127 Ibid., 2.

128 Ibid.

129 LSE, Notice on the Origins of the International Conference, undated, 4NVA/4/22/09, 3.

130 Ibid. See also BL, *Vigilance Record* #9, 1908, 68.

131 LSE, Notice, 4NVA/4/22/09.

132 Ibid.

CHAPTER SIX

1 Letter from the Office of the Undersecretary of State, 25 February 1910, HO 45/10510/129433.

2 See Colligan, *Publisher's Paradise.*

3 Williams, *Marxism and Literature*, 112.

4 See chapter 5.

5 See Tambe, "The Elusive Ingenue."

6 For a similar dynamic involving uneven enforcement and associations between foreignness and queer contagion, see Houlbrook, *Queer London*, 238–40.

7 Hattersley, *The Edwardians*, 1–3.

8 See Sigel, *Making Modern Love*, 89; Beers, "Punting on the Thames," 309.

9 Graves and Hodge, *The Long Week-End*, 17, 141.

10 See Hopkinson, *The Irish War of Independence.*

11 Reynolds, *British Foreign Policy in the Inter-War Years*, 4–11.

12 See Gramsci, *Selections from the Prison Notebooks*, 526.

13 See Weeks, *Sex, Politics, and Society*, 220.
14 Ibid., 114.
15 Ibid., 220; see also Isherwood, *Christopher and His Kind.*
16 For an overview of the different uses of "transnationalism" as a category, see Vertovec, *Transnationalism.* See also Glick-Schiller et al., "Transnationalism: A New Analytic Framework for Understanding Migration," 9–10.
17 See Waltz, *Theory of International Politics*, 93–7.
18 Statement of Sergeant Goult, 24 April 1930, MEPO 3/384, 1–2.
19 See Statement of Harold Hawkyard, 18 September 1930, MEPO 3/935.
20 Officer's Report, 4 May 1938, MEPO 3/939.
21 See minute notes, April 1922, MEPO 3/386; letter from the Office of the Undersecretary of State, 9 October 1901, FO 83/2101; see also MEPO 3/935.
22 See Responses from Borough Police, October–November 1930, HO 144/22543.
23 Letter from Inspector Draper, 31 January 1923, HO 45/11446.
24 Minute notes, undated, MEPO 3/385.
25 Minute note, 15 July 1908, MEPO 3/385.
26 Chief Constables' Association, Appendix A, 1929, CUST 49/1638.
27 Letter from Chief Constable's Office, Preston, 18 October 1930, HO 144/22543.
28 Ibid.; City of Glasgow Police List, HO 144/22543.
29 Ibid.
30 Petition from the People of Guernsey, April 1924, HO 45/11709.
31 League of Nations Traffic in Women and Children Committee, Additional Replies from Governments to the Committee's Questionnaire, 15 July 1931, HO 144/22543, 25.
32 Minute sheet, 1890, HO 144/178.
33 BL, *Vigilance Record* #2, 1919, 23–4.
34 BL, *Vigilance Record* #5, 1911, 40.
35 Sherman and Hopkins, *Imprisonment in America*, 65.
36 Sigel, *Governing Pleasures*, 84.
37 BNA, "Futility of Short Prison Sentences," *Evening Telegraph*, 24 November 1927, 4. It should be noted that the title refers to short prison sentences rather than fines for most offenders and includes demands that prison be restricted to crimes that warranted lengthy sentences.
38 See Letter to Undersecretary of State, 27 February 1901, HO 45/10267/X81934.
39 Memo to D.A.C.C, 21 October 1930, MEPO 3/935.

40 MET, Annual Report, 1932, A/PMC/098.

41 Letter from Director of Public Prosecutions, 13 December 1932, HO 45/24939.

42 Letter from S.W. Harris to A. Crapper, 15 February 1928, HO 45/23588.

43 Harris, *My Life and Loves.*

44 KI, 1930 circular, and undated circular, folder Jack Brussell.

45 Ibid.

46 Letter from John Anderson to Reverend Kerr, 24 February 1928, HO 45/23588.

47 Letter from the Home Office, 29 December 1938, CO 323/1656/6.

48 Minute Notes, Undated, and Letters from the Dominion Division to the Commissioner of Accra and the Chief Officer of Lagos, 26 October 1923, HO 144/10130.

49 Letter to A.N. Galsworthy, 1949, CO 859/224/5.

50 See chapter 5.

51 J.F. Henderson to the Solicitor of the Post Office, Washington, 17 October 1935, HO 45/20913.

52 BL, *Vigilance Record* #9, 1911, 72.

53 See chapter 2.

54 Letter to the Undersecretary of State, 9 October 1901, FO 83/2101.

55 Order of Expulsion, 20 February 1901, FO 83/2101.

56 Letter to the Marquess of Lansdowne, 13 September 1901, FO 83/2101.

57 Minute notes, 16 May 1930, HO 45/20913.

58 Letter from the Post Office Department Office of the Solicitor to G.F. Porter, 30 June 1939, HO 45/20913.

59 List of Known Dealers, 2 May 1900, CUST 46/199; list of Le Sourire and Le Journal Amusant Advertisers, 12 March 1924, HO 45/24805.

60 Mutoscopes were an early form of motion picture technology that required the viewer to peer into an eyepiece. See Great Britain, Papers by Command, vol. 9, 21 May 1908, 44.

61 337 *Parliamentary Debates*, Commons, 14 June 1938, 36–7.

62 Timeline of Indecent Publications Policy, 1930, CUST 49/1638.

63 Post Office Act, 1908 (8 Edw 7 c 48); see Colligan, *Publisher's Paradise*, 49.

64 227 *Parliamentary Debates*, 29 April 1929, 1294–5.

65 225 *Parliamentary Debates*, 28 February 1929, 2157–63; DNB, Harrison, "Lawrence, Frederick William Pethick-, Baron Pethick-Lawrence (1871–1961)."

66 85 *Parliamentary Debates*, 13 July 1900, 1539–50; DNB, Norgate, "Smith, Samuel (1836–1906)."

67 Ibid., 1552; DNB, Lucas, "Ridley, Matthew White, first Viscount Ridley (1842–1904)."

68 BL, *Vigilance Record* #3–4, 1929, 20.

69 Ibid., 22.

70 Colligan, *Publisher's Paradise*, 49.

71 DNB, Thompson, "Hicks, William Joynson-, first Viscount Brentford (1865–1932)."

72 Memorandum to the Chancellor of the Exchequer, 1928, CUST 49/1057.

73 Ibid.

74 Report by Inspector Draper, 11 January 1923, MEPO 3/2459.

75 British Board of Film Censors, Report on *White Hands*, undated, HO 45/22906.

76 Rudyard Kipling, Statement on the Well of Loneliness, 26 October 1928, DPP 1/88.

77 Statement of Sergeant Goult, 9 April 1930, MEPO 3/386.

78 Memo on the Position of the Home Office, 1935, HO 45/20913.

79 Timeline, CUST 49/1638; letter from the Associated Booksellers of Great Britain and Ireland, 16 November 1928, HO 45/15139; see also Sigel, *Making Modern Love*, 21.

80 Ibid.

81 For extensive discussion of the formal censorship of film, see HO 45/22906.

82 See Colligan, *Publisher's Paradise*, 49.

83 "The Free State Censorship," *New Statesman*, 1 September 1928, HO 45/20912.

84 Ibid.

85 Timeline, CUST 49/1638.

86 Ibid.

87 Ibid.

88 3 May 1929, letter to S.W. Harris, HO 144/22543.

89 Despite the fact that Mussolini received glowing praise from such leaders as Winston Churchill and Austen Chamberlain, newspaper coverage of his actions against organized labour demonstrate that he was sufficiently unpopular among the British public that trade unions threatened a strike should he come to England to participate in 1925 treaty negotiations. Lamb, *Mussolini and the British*, 74–7.

90 Letter from S.W. Harris to the Commissioner of the South African Police, 24 October 1931, HO 144/22543.

91 Letter from the Commissioner of the Police, 11 April 1906, HO 45/10930/149778.
92 Letter from S.W. Harris to the British Embassy in France, 26 September 1930, HO 45/20913.
93 Letter from Inspector Draper, 29 March 1924, MEPO 3/386.
94 League of Nations, Traffic in Women and Children Committee, Obscene Publications, Additional Replies from Governments to the Committee's Questionnaire, 15 July 1931, HO 144/22543.
95 J.F. Henderson to the Solicitor of the Post Office, Washington, 17 October 1935, HO 45/20913.
96 See chapter 2.
97 Untitled, 27 March 1940, MEPO 2/4501.
98 Robb, "The Way of All Flesh," 589.
99 Testimony of Sidney Norman, March 1942, CRIM 1/1408.
100 Ibid.
101 Ibid.
102 See chapter 2.
103 Letter from Division Detective Inspector, Criminal Investigative Department, 28 November 1911, and letter from Colombo Office of the Deputy Inspector-General of Police to Commissioner of Scotland Yard, 11 December 1925, MEPO 3/2459.
104 Detective Inspector's Report, 17 July 1936, MEPO 3/935.
105 Report of the Liverpool City Police, 1929, HO 144/22543.
106 See chapter 1.
107 Letter to the General Post Office, 31 October 1923, HO 45/24805.
108 Letter from the Marquis of Lansdowne, 13 March 1902, FO 83/2101.
109 Minute Notes, 28 March 1952, HO 354/162.
110 Letter from the Undersecretary of State to the Public Morality Council, 24 September 1929, HO 45/13296.
111 For examples related to mutoscopes, see HO 45/10267/X81934.
112 For examples of official documents employing loose categories such as "nude" and "flagellation" and lists of book titles with no authors named, see Central CID Office, List of Books, Magazines, Novels, and Photographs Seized at the Compton Bookstore, 27 April 1938, MEPO 3/939.
113 See Robertson, *The British Board of Film Censors*.
114 See various documents throughout MEPO 3/758, in which police list possession of pornographic cards as one of numerous interconnected sexual vices practised at the Caravan Club.
115 Report to the Marquess Curzon, 19 May 1922, HO 45/20912.

116 Minute notes, 1932, HO 45/24939.

117 Ibid.

118 Letter from Inspector Draper, 29 March 1924, MEPO 3/386.

119 Memo by the Undersecretary of State, 4 August 1909, HO 144 1043/183473.

120 Ibid.

121 Weeks, *Sex, Politics, and Society*, 162; see also Davin, "Imperialism and Motherhood."

122 Minute note, 19 June 1929, HO 45/13296.

123 Ibid.

124 Complaint from H.M. Tyrer, 27 July 1932, HO 45/24939; Report by Inspector Draper, 11 December 1922, MEPO 3/2459.

125 Letter from Mr Bicknell to Mr Howgrave-Graham, 4 December 1929, MEPO 3/383.

126 For a similar take on the complexities of policing queer sexualities, see Houlbrook, *Queer London*, 36–7.

127 Extracts from Parliamentary Debates, vol. 360, columns 708–9, 1 May 1940, MEPO 2/8407.

128 See Report to the League of Nations for 1943, FO 371/39309.

129 Ibid.

CONCLUSION

1 As discussed in the introduction, many historians have analyzed pornography production and distribution for earlier time periods, but their conclusions do not point to similar forms of organization. See Sigel, *Governing Pleasures*.

2 See ibid., 120.

3 See "Trial of Duncan Cameron (61)," 21 November 1886, "Trial of Henry Ireton (42)," 10 January 1876, and "Trial of William Lazenby (42)," 18 September 1876, all available in *The Proceedings of the Old Bailey*, all of which include sentences of one to two years' imprisonment. For comparison, see Obscene Publications, Question 1: Offenses Discovered, 1931, HO 144/22543, in which the maximum term of imprisonment listed was six months and the majority of penalties consisted of fines with no term in prison.

4 See Emmons, ed., *Cold War and McCarthy Era*.

5 Christopher Hooton, "A Long List of Sex Acts Just Got Banned in UK Porn," *Independent*, 2 December 2014.

6 Laura Smith-Spark, "'Face-Sitting' Protest Held over UK Porn Censorship Law," *CNN*, 12 December 2014.

7 Ibid.

8 Ibid.

9 See Paul, *Pornified*.

10 See Royalle, "Porn in the USA."

Bibliography

ARCHIVAL COLLECTIONS

PRO: Public Record Office, London

CO: Colonial Office Papers
CRIM: Central Criminal Court
CUST: Customs Office
DO: Dominions Office
DPP: Director of Public Prosecutions
FO: Foreign Office Papers
HO: Home Office Papers
HS: Records of the Special Operations Executive
MEPO: Metropolitan Police Office
TS: Treasury Solicitor

LSE: London School of Economics

AMS: Records of the Association for Moral and Social Hygiene
BNC: Records of the British National Committee
NVA: Records of the National Vigilance Association

MET: London Metropolitan Archives

LWC: Records of the London Diocesan Council for Wel-Care
PMC: Records of the Public Morality Council

BPCL: Browne Popular Culture Library, Bowling Green, Ohio

Pulp Magazine Collection

UCLA: Film and Television Archive, University of California, Los Angeles
Motion Picture Collection

KI: Kinsey Institute, Bloomington, Indiana
Image Collections
Manuscript Collection
Youdelman Collection

LOC: Library of Congress
NYSSV: Records of the New York Society for the Suppression of Vice

NEWSPAPERS AND PERIODICALS

TDA: Times Digital Archive
The Times

BL: British Library
Vigilance Record

BNA: British Library Newspaper Archive (Digital)
The Citizen
Courier
Daily Mail
Derby Daily Telegraph
Devon and Exeter Gazette
Dover Express
Dundee Courier
Essex Chronicle
Evening Telegraph
Illustrated Police News
Leamington Spa Courier
Leeds Mercury
Morning Post
North Devon Journal
Northeastern Daily Gazette
Nottingham Evening News
Pall Mall Gazette
Reynolds's Newspaper

Shields Daily Gazette
Western Daily Mirror and Bristol Mercury
Western Gazette
Western Morning News

Other Periodicals

CNN
Guardian
The Independent
John Bull
Life Magazine
The New Statesman
Old Jonathan: The District and Parish Helper

ONLINE DATABASES, BLOGS, AND PUBLICATIONS

Hansard's Parliamentary Debates
Old Bailey Trials Online
DNB: *Oxford Dictionary of National Biography*

SECONDARY LITERATURE AND COMMERCIALLY PRODUCED PRIMARY SOURCES

Adelman, Bob, and Art Spiegelman, eds. *Tijuana Bibles: Art and Wit in America's Forbidden Funnies, 1930s–1950s*. New York: Simon and Schuster, 2004.

Allan, C.E., ed. *Magisterial Cases Volume XII*. London: Law Publishers and Printers, 1907.

Anderson, Benedict. *Imagined Communities: Reflections on the Origins and Spread of Nationalism*, rev. ed. New York: Verso, 2006.

Anonymous. *Confessions of a Virtuous Wife*. Venice: 193?.

Anonymous. *Lascivious Hypocrite; or, the Triumphs of Vice*. New York: Erotica Biblion Society, undated.

Anonymous. *Painful Pleasures*. Gargoyle Press, 1931.

Anonymous. *Private Anthropological Cabinet of 500 Authentic Racial-Esoteric Photographs and Illustrations*. New York: Falstaff Press, 1934.

Anonymous. *Sweet Seventeen: The True Story of a Daughter's Awful Whipping and Its Delightful and Direful Consequence*. Paris, 1910.

Anonymous. *The Way of a Man with a Maid*. Erotika Biblion Society, 1935.

Appel, Dora, and Shawn Michael Smith. *Lynching Photographs*. Berkeley: University of California Press, 2008.

Attwood, Feona, and Clarissa Smith. "Anti/Pro/Critical Porn Studies." *Porn Studies* 1, nos. 1–2 (2014): 7–23.

Bartley, Paula. *Prostitution: Prevention and Reform in England, 1860–1914*. London: Routledge, 1999.

Beaven, Bread. *Leisure, Citizenship, and Working-Class Men in Britain, 1850–1945*. Manchester: Manchester University Press, 2005.

Beers, Laura. "Punting on the Thames: Electoral Betting in Interwar Britain." *Journal of Contemporary History* 45, no. 2 (2010): 282–314.

Bingham, Adrian. *Family Newspapers? Sex, Private Life, and the British Popular Press, 1918–1978*. Oxford: Oxford University Press, 2009.

– *Gender, Modernity, and the Popular Press in Inter-War Britain*. Oxford: Oxford University Press, 2004.

Blackeyes, Sadie. *Miss*. Paris: Librairie Drouin, 192?.

Bland, Lucy. *Banishing the Beast: Feminism, Sex, and Morality*. London: Tauris Park, 2002.

– *Modern Women on Trial: Sexual Transgression in the Age of the Flapper*. Manchester: Manchester University Press, 2013.

– "The Trials and Tribulations of Edith Thompson: The Capital Crime of Sexual Incitement in 1920s England." *Journal of British Studies* 47, no. 3 (July 2008): 624–48.

– "White Women and Men of Colour: Miscegenation Fears in Britain after the Great War." *Gender and History* 17, no. 1 (April 2005): 29–61.

Bland, Lucy, and Laura Doan, eds. *Sexology in Culture: Labeling Bodies and Desires*. Chicago: University of Chicago Press, 1998.

Bourke, Joanna. *Working-Class Cultures in Britain, 1890–1960: Gender, Class, and Ethnicity*. New York: Routledge, 1994.

Bretschneider, Anette, ed. *Vincenzo Galdi, Wilhelm von Gloeden, Wilhelm von Pluschow: Aktaufnahmen aus der Uwe Scheid*. Aachen: Rimbaud, 1993.

Bristow, Edward. *Vice and Vigilance: Purity Movements in Britain since 1700*. Dublin: Gill and Macmillan, 1977.

Burrows, Jon. *Legitimate Cinema: Theatre Stars in Silent British Films, 1908–1918*. Exeter: University of Exeter Press, 2003.

Burton, Antoinette. *Burdens of History: British Feminists, Indian Women, and Imperial Culture, 1865–1915*. Charlotte: University of North Carolina Press, 1994.

Califia, Pat. "Identity Sedition and Pornography." In *PoMoSexuals: Challenging Assumptions About Gender and Sexuality*. Edited by Carol Queen and Lawrence Schimel, 87–106. San Francisco: Cleis Press, 1997.

Cantab, A. *Two Flappers in Paris*. New York: Erotica Biblion Society, 19?.
Capra, Frank, dir. *The Bitter Tea of General Yen*. Columbia Pictures, 1933.
Catterall, Peter et al., eds. *Northcliffe's Legacy: Aspects of the British Popular Press, 1896–1996*. New York: St Martin's Press, 2000.
Chalaby, Jean. *The Invention of Journalism*. New York: St Martin's Press, 1998.
Chapman, James. *The British at War: Cinema, State, and Propaganda, 1939–1945*. London: I.B. Tauris, 1998.
Cocks, Harry. *Classified: The Secret History of the Personal Column*. New York: Random House, 2009.
Cohen, Cathy. "Punks, Bulldaggers, and Welfare Queens: The Radical Potential of Queer Politics?" *GLQ* 3 (1997): 437–65.
Colligan, Colette. *Publisher's Paradise: Expatriate Literary Culture in Paris, 1890–1960*. Amherst: University of Massachusetts Press, 2014.
– *The Traffic in Obscenity from Byron to Beardsley: Sexuality and Exoticism in Nineteenth-Century Print Culture*. Basingstoke: Palgrave Macmillan, 2006.
Conboy, Martin. *The Press and Popular Culture*. London: Sage, 2002.
Cook, Matt et al. *A Gay History of Britain: Love and Sex between Men since the Middle Ages*. Oxford: Greenwood World, 2007.
– *London and the Culture of Homosexuality, 1885–1914*. Cambridge: Cambridge University Press, 2003.
Czinner, Paul, dir. *The Rise of Catherine the Great*. Janus Films, 1934.
Davin, Anna. "Imperialism and Motherhood." *History Workshop* 5 (Spring 1978): 9–65.
Dennett, Mary Ware. *The Sex Side of Life: An Explanation for Young People*. Printed by author, 1919.
Dupouy, Alexandre. *Yva Richard: L'âge d'or du fétichisme*. Paris: Éditions Astarte, 1994.
Dworkin, Andrea. "Against the Male Flood: Censorship, Pornography, and Equality." In *Feminism and Pornography*. Edited by Drucilla Cornell, 19–38. Oxford: Oxford University Press, 2000.
– "Pornography and Grief." In *Feminism and Pornography*. Edited by Drucilla Cornell, 39–44. Oxford: Oxford University Press, 2000.
Ellis, Havelock. *Studies in the Psychology of Sex*, vol. 1. London: University Press, 1900.
Emmons, Caroline S., ed. *Cold War and McCarthy Era: People and Perspectives*. Santa Barbara: ABC-Clio, 2010.
Eng, David L., Judith Halberstam, and Jose Esteban Munoz. "Introduction: What's Queer about Queer Studies Now?" *Social Text* 23, nos. 3–4 (Fall–Winter 2005): 1–17.

Epstein, Rob. dir. *The Celluloid Closet*. Tristar Pictures, 1995.
Eros Comix, ed. *The Tijuana Bibles*, vol. 9. Eros Comix, 2008.
Faber, Monika, ed. *Divas and Lovers: Photographic Fantasies from Vienna between the Wars*. London: Thames and Hudson, 1998.
Ferguson, Ann. "Sex War: The Debate between Radical and Libertarian Feminists." *Signs* 10, no. 1 (Autumn 1984): 106–12.
Forgacs, David, ed. *The Gramsci Reader: Selected Writings, 1916–1935*. New York: New York University Press, 2000.
Geraci, J. "Lehnert and Landrock in North Africa." *History of Photography* 27 (2003): 294–8.
Gertzman, Jay. *Bookleggers and Smuthounds: The Trade in Erotica, 1920–1940*. Philadelphia: University of Pennsylvania Press, 1999.
Gilbert, Sandra. "Soldier's Heart: Literary Men, Literary Women, and the Great War." In *Behind the Lines: Gender and the Two World Wars*. Edited by Margaret Higonnet et al., 199–205. New Haven: Yale University Press, 1987.
Gledhill, Christine, and Gillian Swanson, eds. *Nationalising Femininity: Culture, Sexuality, and British Cinema in the Second World War*. Manchester: Manchester University Press, 1996.
Glick-Schiller, Nina et al. "Transnationalism: A New Analytic Framework for Understanding Migration." *Annals of the New York Academy of Sciences* 645 (1992): 1–24.
Gorham, Deborah. "'The Maiden Tribute of Modern Babylon' Revisited: Child Prostitution and the Idea of Childhood in Late-Victorian England." *Victorian Studies* 21, no. 3 (1978): 353–79.
Govenar, Alan. "The Changing Image of Tattooing in American Culture, 1846–1966." In *Written on the Body: The Tattoo in American and European History*. Edited by Jane Caplan, 212–33. Princeton: Princeton University Press, 2000.
Graham-Brown, Sarah. *Images of Women: The Portrayal of Women in Photography of the Middle East, 1860–1950*. New York: Columbia University Press, 1988.
Gramsci, Antonio. *Selections from the Prison Notebooks*. Edited by Quentin Hoare and Geoffrey Nowell Smith. London: Elec Book, 1999.
Grandpa Bucky's "Naughty" Triple XXX Rated Stags, Loops, and Peeps, vol. 4. Seattle: Something Weird Video, 2006. DVD.
Grandpa Bucky's "Naughty" Triple XXX Rated Stags, Loops, and Peeps, vol. 13. Seattle: Something Weird Video, 2006. DVD.
Graves, Pamela M. *Labour Women: Women in British Working-Class Politics, 1918–1939*. Cambridge: Cambridge University Press, 1994.

Graves, Robert, and Alan Hodge. *The Long Week-End: A Social History of Great Britain, 1918–1939*. Reissue Edition. New York: W.W. Norton, 1994.

Great Britain. House of Commons. Papers by Command. Volume 9.

Greenaway, John. *Drink and British Politics since 1830: A Study in Policy-Making*. New York: Palgrave Macmillan, 2003.

Hall, Lesley A. "Forbidden by God, Despised by Men: Masturbation, Medical Warnings, Moral Panic, and Manhood in Great Britain, 1850–1950." *Journal of the History of Sexuality* 2, no. 3 (January 1992): 365–87.

– *Hidden Anxieties: Male Sexuality, 1900–1950*. Oxford: Blackwell, 1991.

– *Sex, Gender, and Social Change in Britain since 1880*. 2nd ed. New York: Palgrave Macmillan, 2013.

Hampton, Mark. *Visions of the Press in Britain, 1850–1950*. Urbana: University of Illinois Press, 2004.

Hannerz, Ulf. *Transnational Connections: People, Culture, Places*. New York: Routledge, 1996.

Harris, Frank. *My Life and Loves*. Paris: Privately printed, 1922.

Haste, Cate. *Rules of Desire: Sex in Britain, World War I to the Present*. London: Chatto and Windus, 1992.

Hattersley. Roy. *The Edwardians*. London: Little, Brown, 2004.

Heath, Deanna. *Purifying Empire: Obscenity and the Politics of Moral Regulation in Britain, India, and Australia*. New York: Cambridge University Press, 2010.

Hebdige, Dick. *Subculture: The Meaning of Style*. London: Methuen, 1979.

Hellman, Lillian. *Six Plays by Lillian Hellman*. Vintage, 1979.

Hines, Claire, and Darren Kerr, eds. *Hard to Swallow: Hard-Core Pornography Onscreen*. New York: Wallflower Press, 2012.

Hopkinson, Michael. *The Irish War of Independence: The Definitive Account of the Anglo-Irish War of 1919–1921*. Dublin: Gill and Macmillan, 2014.

Houlbrook, Matt. *Queer London: Perils and Pleasures in the Sexual Metropolis, 1918–1957*. Chicago: University of Chicago Press, 2005.

– "Thinking Queer: The Social and the Sexual in Interwar Britain." In *British Queer History: New Approaches and Perspectives*. Edited by Brian Lewis, 134–64. Manchester: Manchester University Press, 2013.

Hunt, Lynn, ed. *The Invention of Pornography: Obscenity and the Origins of Modernity, 1500–1800*. Cambridge: Zone, 1996.

Isherwood, Christopher. *Christopher and His Kind, 1929–1939*. New York: Farrar, Straus and Giroux, 1976.

Jagose, Annamarie. *Queer Theory: An Introduction*. Melbourne: Melbourne University Press, 1996.

– ed. *The Routledge Queer Studies Reader*. New York: Routledge, 2012.

Kaplan, Caren, and Inderpal Grewal. "Transnational Practices and Interdisciplinary Feminist Scholarship: Refiguring Women's and Gender Studies." In *Women's Studies on Its Own: A Next Wave Reader in Institutional Change*. Edited by Robyn Wiegman, 66–81. Durham: Duke University Press, 2002.

Lamb, Richard. *Mussolini and the British*. London: John Murray, 1997.

Landy, Marcia. *British Genres: Cinema and Society, 1930–1960*. Princeton: Princeton University Press, 1991.

Leap, William. "Language, Gay Pornography, and Audience Reception." *Journal of Homosexuality* 58, nos. 6–7 (2011): 932–52.

Leslie, Charles. *Wilhelm von Gloeden, Photographer: A Brief Introduction to His Life and Work*. New York: Soho Photographic Publishers, 1977.

Linehan, Thomas. *British Fascism and Anti-Semitism, 1918–1939: Parties, Ideology, and Culture*. Manchester: Manchester University Press, 2000.

Mackinnon, Catharine. *Feminism Unmodified: Discourses on Life and Law*. Cambridge, MA: Harvard University Press, 1987.

– "Only Words." In *Feminism and Pornography*. Edited by Drucilla Cornell, 94–120. Oxford: Oxford University Press, 2000.

Marcus, Steven. *The Other Victorians: A Study of Sexuality and Pornography in Mid-Nineteenth-Century England*. New York: Basic, 1966.

Matthew, H.C.G., and Brian Harrison, eds. *Oxford Dictionary of National Biography*. Oxford: Oxford University Press, 2004.

Mayhall, Laura E. Nym. *The Militant Suffrage Movement: Citizenship and Resistance in Britain, 1860–1930*. Oxford: Oxford University Press, 2003.

McCalman, Iain. *Radical Underworld: Prophets, Revolutionaries, and Pornographers in London, 1795–1840*. Cambridge: Cambridge University Press, 1988.

McClintock, Anne. *Imperial Leather: Race, Gender, and Sexuality in the Colonial Contest*. London: Routledge, 1995.

McLaren, Angus. *Reproduction by Design: Sex, Robots, Trees, and Test-Tube Babies in Interwar Britain*. Chicago: University of Chicago Press, 2012.

– *Twentieth-Century Sexuality: A History*. Oxford: Blackwell, 1999.

Meusal, Walter. *Invitation to the Dance*. New York: Gargoyle Press, 1935.

Mosse, George. *Nationalism and Sexuality: Respectability and Abnormal Sexuality in Modern Europe*. New York: Howard Fertig, 1985.

Mulholland, Monique. "'The Pathological Native' vs 'The Good White Girl': An Analysis of Race and Colonialism in Two Australian Porn Panics." *Porn Studies* 3, no. 1 (2016): 34–49.

Natter, Tobias, and Peter Weiermair, eds. *Et in Arcadia Ego: Turn of the Century Photography*. Zurich: Edition Oehrli, 2000.

Nin, Anaïs. "Letter 085." In *Letters of Note: An Eclectic Collection of Correspondence Deserving of a Wider Audience*, vol. 1. Edited by Shaun Usher. San Francisco: Chronicle Books, 2013.

Paul, Pamela. *Pornified: How Porn Is Damaging Our Lives, Our Relationships, Our Families*. New York: St Martin's Press, 2006.

Peakman, Julie. *Mighty Lewd Books: The Development of Pornography in Eighteenth-Century England*. New York: Palgrave Macmillan, 2003.

Pember Reeves, Maude. *Round about a Pound a Week*. 2nd ed. London: G. Bell and Sons, 1914.

Pennell, Catriona. *A Kingdom United: Popular Responses to the Outbreak of the First World War in Britain and Ireland*. Oxford: Oxford University Press, 2012.

Petley, Julian. "The Regulation of Pornography on Video-on-Demand in the United Kingdom." *Porn Studies* 1, no. 3 (2014): 260–84.

Philipson, Ilene. "The Repression of History and Gender: A Critical Perspective on the Feminist Sexuality Debate." *Signs* 10, no. 1 (Autumn 1984): 113–18.

Pine, Julia. "In Bizarre Fashion: The Double-Voiced Discourse of John Willie's Fetish Fantasia." *Journal of the History of Sexuality* 22, no. 1 (January 2013): 1–33.

Pohlmann, Ulrich. *Wilhelm von Gloeden: Taormina*. Munich: Schirmer/Mosel, 1998.

Potter, Simon. "Webs, Networks, and Systems: Globalization and Mass Media in the Nineteenth- and Early Twentieth-Century British Empire," *Journal of British Studies* 46, no. 3 (July 2007): 621–46.

Reynolds, P.A. *British Foreign Policy in the Inter-War Years*. Westport: Greenwood Press, 1974.

Richards, Jeffrey. *Age of the Dream Palace: Cinema and Society in Britain, 1930–1939*. London: Routledge, 1984.

– *The Unknown 1930s: An Alternative History of the British Cinema, 1929–1939*. London: I.B. Tauris, 1998.

Robb, George. "The Way of All Flesh: Degeneration, Eugenics, and the Gospel of Free Love." *Journal of the History of Sexuality* 6, no. 4 (April 1996): 589–603.

Robertson, James C. *The British Board of Film Censors: Film Censorship in Britain, 1896–1950*. London: Croom Helm, 1985.

Roodhouse, Mark. *Black Market Britain: 1939–1955*. Oxford: Oxford University Press, 2013.

Rose, Sonya O. *Which People's War? National Identity and Citizenship in Wartime Britain, 1939–1945*. Reprint edition. New York: Oxford University Press, 2006.

Ross, Becki. "'It's Merely Designed for Sexual Arousal.'" In *Feminism and Pornography*. Edited by Drucilla Cornell, 264–317. Oxford: Oxford University Press, 2000.

Ross, Ellen. "Survival Networks: Women's Neighbourhood Sharing in London before World War I." *History Workshop* 15 (Spring 1983): 4–27.

Royalle, Candida. "Porn in the USA." In *Feminism and Pornography*. Edited by Drucilla Cornell, 540–50. Oxford: Oxford University Press, 2000.

Rubin, Gayle. "Thinking Sex: Notes for a Radical Theory of the Politics of Sexuality." *The Lesbian and Gay Studies Reader*. Edited by Henry Abelove et al., 3–44. New York: Routledge, 1993.

Saville, Victor, dir. *First a Girl*. Gaumont British Picture Corporation, 1933.

Scheid, Uwe. *1000 Nudes: The Uwe Scheid Collection*. Cologne: Benedikt Taschen, 1994.

Seymoure-Ure, Colin. "Northcliffe's Legacy." In *Northcliffe's Legacy: Aspects of the British Popular Press, 1896–1996*. Edited by Peter Catterall et al., 9–26. New York: St Martin's Press, 2000.

Shah, Nayan. *Contagious Divides: Epidemics and Race in San Francisco's Chinatown*. Berkeley: University of California Press, 2001.

Sheaffer, Russell. "Smut, Novelty, and Indecency: Reworking a History of the Early-Twentieth-Century American 'Stag Film.'" *Porn Studies* 1, no. 4 (2014): 346–59.

Sherman, Michael, and Gordon Hopkins. *Imprisonment in America: Choosing the Future*. Chicago: University of Chicago Press, 1983.

Sigel, Lisa Z. "Censorship in Inter-War Britain: Obscenity, Spectacle, and the Workings of the Liberal State." *Journal of Social History* 45, no. 1 (Fall 2011): 61–83.

– *Governing Pleasures: Pornography and Social Change in England, 1815–1914*. New Brunswick, NJ: Rutgers University Press, 2002.

– *Making Modern Love: Sexual Narratives and Identities in Interwar Britain*. Philadelphia: Temple University Press, 2012.

Slade, Joseph W. "Bernard Natan: France's Legendary Pornographer." *Journal of Film and Video* 45, nos. 2–3 (Summer–Fall 1993): 72–90.

Smith, Alison. *The Victorian Nude: Sexuality, Morality, and Art*. Manchester: Manchester University Press, 1996.

Smith, Andrea. "Queer Theory and Native Studies: The Heteronormativity of Settler Colonialism." *GLQ: A Journal of Gay and Lesbian Studies* 16, nos. 1–2 (2010): 42–68.

Somerville, Siobhan. "Queer." In *Keywords for American Cultural Studies*, 2nd ed. Edited by Bruce Burgett and Glenn Hendler, 203. New York: New York University Press, 2014.

Stardust, Zahra. "'Fisting Is Not Permitted': Criminal Intimacies, Queer Sexualities, and Feminist Porn in the Australian Legal Context." *Porn Studies* 1, no. 3 (2014): 242–59.

Steinem, Gloria. *Outrageous Acts and Everyday Rebellions*. New York: H. Holt, 1995.

Stengers, Jean, and Anne van Neck. *Masturbation: The History of a Great Terror.* New York: Palgrave, 2001.

Stoler, Ann Laura. *Carnal Knowledge and Imperial Power: Race and the Intimate in Colonial Rule.* Berkeley: University of California Press, 2002.

Sullivan, Nikki. *A Critical Introduction to Queer Theory*. New York: New York University Press, 2003.

Tabili, Laura. "Race Is a Relationship, and Not a Thing." *Journal of Social History* 37, no. 1 (2003): 125–30.

Tambe, Ashwini. "The Elusive Ingenue: A Transnational Feminist Analysis of European Prostitution in Colonial Bombay." *Gender and Society* 19, no. 2 (April 2005): 160–79.

Thompson, Dave. *Black and White and Blue: Adult Cinema from the Victorian Age to the VCR*. Toronto: ECW Press, 2007.

Thompson, E.P. *The Making of the English Working Class*. New York: Vintage, 1966.

Tibbals, Chauntelle Anne. "Gonzo, Tranny, and Teens: Current Trends in US Adult Content Production, Distribution, and Consumption." *Porn Studies* 1, nos. 1–2 (2014): 127–35.

Trumbach, Randolph. "Erotic Fantasy and Male Libertinism in Enlightenment England." In *The Invention of Pornography: Obscenity and the Origins of Modernity, 1500–1800*. Edited by Lynn Hunt, 253–82. Cambridge: Zone, 1996.

Valverde, Mariana. "Racial Poison: Drink, Male Vice, and Degeneration in First-Wave Feminism." In *Women's Suffrage in the British Empire: Citizenship, Nation, and Race*. Edited by Ian Christopher Fletcher et al., 33–50. New York: Routledge, 2000.

van Rod, Aime. *The Misfortunes of Colette*. Gargoyle Press, 192?.

Vertovec, Steven. *Transnationalism*. New York: Routledge, 2009.

Walkowitz, Judith. *Nights Out: Life in Cosmopolitan London*. New Haven: Yale University Press, 2012.

– *Prostitution in Victorian Society: Women, Class, and the State*. Cambridge: Cambridge University Press, 1982.

Waltz, Kenneth N. *Theory of International Politics*. Boston: Addison-Wesley, 1979.

Warner, Michael. "Introduction: Fear of a Queer Planet." *Social Text* 29 (1991): 3–17.

Weeks, Jeffrey. *Sex, Politics, and Society: The Regulation of Sexuality since 1800*. 2nd ed. London: Longman, 1989.

Weinbaum, Alyce Eve, ed. *The Modern Girl around the World: Consumption, Modernity, and Globalization*. Durham, NC: Duke University Press, 2008.

White, Kevin. *The First Sexual Revolution: The Emergence of Male Heterosexuality in Modern America*. New York: New York University Press, 1993.

Williams, Kevin. *Read All about It! A History of the British Newspaper*. New York: Routledge, 2010.

Williams, Linda. *Hard Core: Power, Pleasure, and the "Frenzy of the Visible."* Berkeley: University of California Press, 1989.

– ed. *Porn Studies*. Durham, NC: Duke University Press, 2004.

Williams, Raymond. *Marxism and Literature*. Oxford: Oxford University Press, 1977.

Windsor, Edward. *The Hindu Art of Love*. New York: Falstaff Press, 1937.

Wood, Ed, dir. *The Sinister Urge*. Headliner Productions, 1960.

Zimring, Rishona. "'The Dangerous Art Where One Slip Means Death': Dance and the Literary Imagination in Interwar Britain." *Modernism/Modernity* 14, no. 4 (November 2007): 707–27.

Index